The Making of Contemporary Europe

The Making of
Contemporary Europe

R. Ben Jones

HOLMES & MEIER PUBLISHERS, INC.
NEW YORK

First published in the United States of America 1980 by
HOLMES & MEIER PUBLISHERS, INC.
30 Irving Place, New York, N.Y. 10003

Library of Congress Cataloging in Publication Data

Jones, R Ben.
  The Making of Contemporary Europe.
  Bibliography: P.
  Includes index.
  1. Europe – Politics and Government – 1945–
  2. European Economic Community. 3. World Politics –
  1945–
  I. Title.
  D1058.J63   1981   940.55   80–21063

ISBN 0–8419–0668–8 Hardback
ISBN 0–8419–0669–6 Paperback

PRINTED IN GREAT BRITAIN

Contents

List of Maps, Tables and Diagrams

Acknowledgments

The author and publishers wish to thank the following for permission to reproduce copyright material in this book: *NATO Review*, Brussels (p. 33); The Economist Newspaper Ltd, London (pp. 36 and 82); Hugo Radice, University of Leeds (p. 131); *Problems of Communism*, US International Communication Agency, Washington, D.C. (p. 147); Macmillan, London and Basingstoke, and Free Press, Inc., New York (pp. 147 and 162) Reprinted with permission of Macmillan Publishing Co., Inc. from *The Soviet Union Since the Fall of Khrushchev*; by Archie Brown and Michael Kaser. Copyright © 1975 by Archie Brown and Michael Kaser. Times Newspapers Ltd, London (p. 164); and Edward Arnold (Publishers) Ltd, London (p. 174). The diagrams on pages 148 and 150 are reprinted by permission of Penguin Books Ltd from Mary McAuley, *Politics and the Soviet Union*, Penguin Books, 1977, pp. 199 and 273, copyright © Mary McAuley, 1977.

1

The Background to Contemporary Europe

The French Revolution and the wars of Napoleon unleashed social and political forces that dominated the thought and experience of Europe for at least a century and a half. Unprecedented economic and industrial expansion in the nineteenth century carried Europe to a peak of dominance throughout the world; and on the eve of the First World War, the political leaders of the Great Powers of Europe confidently and assertively imagined only a world in which they were unquestioned masters. After the horrors of that war, few realised what changes had overtaken their world. The Versailles Settlement, aiming to produce a world within which another such war would be an impossibility, was couched in very nineteenth-century terms. Twenty years later, the Second World War starkly revealed how much of that world had disappeared. The settlement after the war was reached by men whose whole experience had been moulded by an age that was slipping away. It would be harsh to judge their settlement a bad one, but some would say it looked back too much and was ill-suited to the needs of the latter half of the century. They would go on to argue that instead of re-establishing the national states that existed between the wars, it should have asserted a new political reality. In the 1980s, those national states survive – but in a very different relationship. Some would argue that the continued existence of these national states is essential to maintain an identity of interests: others would argue that the days are for combinations of countries and not for little states.

The aggressive assertion of the national state had been among the most powerful of those forces released by the French Revolution. It was an assertion that weighed heavily on the nineteenth century. Italy and Germany were 'made'; Latin America broke free of Portugal and Spain; and, in a different way, the United States was forged into the great power we know today. But nationalism was more than a political force. Its impact was writ large on the culture of nineteenth-century Europe, in art, music, literature and even language. By the end of the century, political leaders could readily appeal to nationalist sentiment to gain the support of growing electorates and to claim a mandate for aggressive policies. It was to be one of the causes of the First World War – indeed, the hatred of the French for the Germans reached a new intensity in the slaughter of that war. France lost a million and a half men: Germany a million and three-quarters – Russia lost as many. It was common to talk of the loss of a generation, and the memorials in every village testify to the war being a people's war, as none had been before. It was not a matter of small armies fighting limited engagements, but of the entire population mobilised for total war. Every family was affected, both by the loss of life and by the privations and social policies of modern war. In hopes of escaping from a repetition of so destructive a war, idealists looked to the League of Nations, formed in 1919. It failed. A Second World War, of even greater destructive power over a far greater area, changed the whole political balance of the world in the 1940s.

The experience of total war brings permanent social changes. For all its hectic efforts in the twenties to recover the zest of pre-war days, the social world in Western Europe had been shrewdly altered. Abroad, the European empires stretching across Africa and much of Asia remained, but in far less certain hands. Within Europe, the Austro-Hungarian Empire was replaced by a series of small new states, and the old frontiers of Tsarist Russia were thrust back behind new Baltic States and a recreated Poland. Political uncertainty characterised this new Europe, augmented by a growing economic crisis. Old markets had been lost during the war; reparations and protective policies confined trade, and inflation compounded the economic problems. The German mark collapsed, and in 1929 began a world slump of such proportions as to raise fears that the capitalist world was plunging to destruction. Britain responded by establishing that Commonwealth Preference (1932) that Joseph Chamberlain had urged thirty years before; USA with the New Deal; Germany with rearmament under Hitler – indeed, the slow economic recovery did not quicken until Europe began to rearm in the mid-thirties.

The experience of those inter-war years left a powerful memory among the survivors of the Second World War: there had been mass unemployment, wasted resources, and the state had been obliged to extend social welfare provision on a scale never before conceived. Even before the certainty of victory, men were planning for a new and ideal world after the war that would avoid the economic nationalism and protective policies that had contributed to the distress and failure of those inter-war years. A new economic system based on international cooperation was envisaged. In 1944, the Bretton Woods Conference established the International Monetary Fund (IMF) and the International Bank for Reconstruction and Development (the 'World Bank') as international financial organisations to assist nations with their balance of payments problems, and so to help towards a smoother-running international economy. Nineteenth-century Free Traders had argued that the removal of national protective tariffs would help remove differences between nations and contribute to world peace: protective tariffs had interrupted world trade and contributed to national hostility both before and after the First World War. The hope now was to move towards much freer trade between nations throughout the world. An International Trade Organisation was proposed, but this failed to gain sufficient support; however, in 1947 a more limited General Agreement on Tariffs and Trade (GATT) was signed, which was to have an impact on trading policies in the fifties and sixties. The stage was set, after the Second World War, for a greater degree of international cooperation than ever before.

But a new factor had appeared during the century to divide nations. In 1914, national hatreds divided the people of Europe: but there was little ideological division among them. That came with the war. By 1917 the war had reached deadlock: faced with the likelihood of the USA sending troops to help Britain and France, the German High Command hit on a desperate stratagem. Taking advantage of a spontaneous revolution that had broken out in Russia, they arranged for Lenin to leave Switzerland and reach Petrograd (as St Petersburg was then called).

Lenin was the leader of the Bolsheviks who sought a fundamental social and economic revolution – the Communist Revolution. He envisaged that this would come in the advanced industrial states – in Germany, since it had not yet come in Britain. He anticipated that workers and revolutionary leaders would seize control of the country and spread their revolution abroad so that the capitalist world would be overthrown, as was predicted by Marxist theory. The German High Command had no interest in promoting the Communist Cause. They gambled on Lenin provoking such a revolution in Russia that they could happily withdraw their troops to fight in the West and achieve victory before the Americans arrived. In the unlikely event of his being successful (the Bolsheviks were a very small group) it was expected that he would take Russia out of the war, and thus release the troops so vitally needed. In the event, the Bolsheviks seized power and created the first successful Communist state. After much strife, civil war and famine, a much reduced Russia emerged as the Union of Soviet Socialist Republics (USSR). This introduced a new ideological division in Europe, for the Communists were committed to the overthrow of the capitalist world. Consequently, the West was anxious to build a line of non-communist states (at the expense of former Tsarist territory) as a *cordon sanitaire* across Eastern Europe. Communist and Capitalist, East and West, viewed each other in a mutually hostile and distrustful light: here lay at least a part of the origin of the 'Cold War' of the forties and fifties.

Lenin's successor, Stalin, cut Soviet Russia off from the West, speaking of 'Socialism in one country'; but the West feared a 'Red Peril' directed from the Moscow Kremlin through its agents in other countries, the national communist parties, to overthrow liberalism and the capitalist system. There was evidence of Stalinist interference through the medium of obedient national communist parties. The most obvious case was the Spanish Civil War, in which the political left wing was so distraught with internal strife that it contributed to Franco's victory and the outlawing of the Communist Party in Spain.

Communism was not the only new ideology that disturbed Europe. There was Fascism, which lay as far to the right of the political spectrum as Communism was to the left. Fascism did not have the clear ideological statement that was a part of the strength of the Communists. It arose from many factors – from extreme nationalism, from a moral purpose as sincere as the Liberal and Communist ideologies to achieve as perfect a state as possible (Fascism and Nazism are not entirely synonymous), from the bitterness of defeat after the First World War particularly among demobilised officers in Italy and Germany, from the experience of economic hardship and mass unemployment in the twenties, and from the dynamism of charismatic leaders like Mussolini and Hitler.

The Fascists are the antithesis of the Communists (although their organisation and their methods are sometimes curiously similar). At least a part of their appeal in the West between the wars was their evident determination to destroy the left wing in politics, and particularly the Communists – which meant opposing Russia. This was a feature common to fascist movements throughout Europe – in France it reached almost civil war proportions in the thirties. Riots and violence were commonplace. In Germany anti-Communist violence appeared long before Hitler came to power; afterwards, in Nazi Germany it was very dangerous to be a communist. (An interesting contemporary portrayal of this conflict in the Berlin of the early thirties is given in Christopher Isherwood's novel, *Mr Norris Changes Trains*.)

The Nazis clearly regarded themselves as the protectors of Europe against the Slavs and Communists (the 1939 Nazi-Soviet Pact is explicable in terms of Stalin seeking to postpone a likely invasion). Some historians have asserted that Hitler's aim was less the defeat of France (to wipe away the shame of 1918) than the destruction of Soviet Russia. For this reason, it is argued, the West was more inclined to tolerate the evident revival of German militarism under him because it would be hurled against Stalin. This same idea was advocated by senior German officers in 1944 when they sought an accommodation with the West in order to avoid total defeat – they would surrender in the West and turn against the advancing Soviet armies. Their suggestion was not taken up.

The Second World War did more than destroy Nazi Germany. Much of what survived from nineteenth-century Europe went as well. Temporarily, the European economy was in ruins, but, although Fascism had been eliminated for the moment, the ideological split between East and West survived. During the war, the old national states were widely condemned as morally bankrupt – they had brought Europe to the horrors of two world wars, and in the hour of greatest need they had failed their people (France, in the *dégringolade* of 1940, suffered an emotional as well as a military defeat). There was a widespread desire to launch an international organisation that would produce a better and more equitable peace than that of 1918 – the United Nations Organisation was altogether larger and more significant than the League of Nations. There was also a desire to seek more genuine cooperation between countries, to continue that close collaboration forged by the needs of fighting a common enemy into the years of peace. The rôle of government had grown immeasurably during the war, directing the war economy, controlling employment and the movement of people, extending to the rationing of food and necessities. Social welfare policies of a very extensive kind (like the British Welfare State) were seen as a necessity for post-war Europe. The field of government would remain extensive after the war, both as an administrative machine for maintaining social policy and as a major factor in the management and conduct of the economy. The idea of a planned economy – anathema to nineteenth-century liberals – seemed generally acceptable in the forties ('indicative planning' was the new term). And there was widespread acceptance of the idea of economic cooperation, both on a bilateral plane and through international organisations, for national economies had proved so ill-equipped to handle economic problems and the recovery between the wars.

Abroad, the old European empires were partly recovered – but a new atmosphere was apparent, an atmosphere that dated from the twenties if not earlier, and colonial leaders now claimed for their countries that national independence in which European states had gloried. Within twenty years the empires were to go. Some went peacefully by constitutional de-colonisation, some in bitter civil war, at least one (French Indo-China) in a war that dragged on for thirty years, drawing in the USA and at times coming close to provoking a further world war. Within Europe there was a new realisation, only partly concealed by the idealist enthusiasm for the United Nations Organisation, that diplomatically the world had changed. The balance of power, which for at least two hundred years had been determined by the relationship of a few European powers, was now clearly and unassailably held by the two Super-Powers, the USA and the USSR – later to be joined by the Republic of China. The Second World War was indeed a watershed.

It is not to be wondered at that in the euphoria of victory Western Europe should have looked beyond the discredited nation state. The United Nations Organisation had its headquarters in the USA and seemed (in the forties) to be capable of handling world diplomacy with its Security Council, and of relieving major world problems through its specialist agencies. It was a natural desire to supplement this with a federal union of European States, both for economic recovery and the maintenance of peace.

Proposals for different forms of international association have a long history – they can be easily identified in the writing of Sully, of Penn, of St Pierre, perhaps even in the ideas for a Congress System proposed by Castlereagh. But these were idealist schemes that tended to be leagues of rulers. They were conceived in worlds very different from the mid-twentieth century; worlds that had no conception of twentieth-century democracy, of governments responding and being responsible to public opinion – worlds, indeed, which still looked to international relations as to matters of family arrangements over landed property. They were worlds in which the dynamic power of a modern state administrative machine would have been utterly foreign. They were not suited to the modern world, especially one in the conditions of 1945.

If the French Revolution and the Napoleonic Wars had brought totalitarian warfare into Europe, the First World War had democratised the whole process of war and politics. In the twenties, and especially as the League was seen visibly to be failing, and economic conditions grew worse, a European Idea of unity in politics and trade emerged. It had the support of a wide spectrum of political opinion – which was to be the feature of the European movement in the forties, for its leaders were drawn from left-wing, centre and right-of-centre parties. And it was not merely the concern of political cranks or simple idealists. At the Trades Union Congress in 1927, Ernest Bevin, labour leader and later to become British Foreign Secretary (1945), made a famous appeal for European unity to meet economic perils. In 1929 Aristide Briand, a politician with a European reputation, published a widely acknowledged Plan for a 'federal bond'. More specifically, there were customs unions. In 1922 the Belgian-Luxembourg economic union was established – to be enlarged under the impact of economic depression by its extension at the Geneva international economic conference in 1927 to include the Netherlands. (This was the embryo of the Benelux union of 1944, to be tied the more closely by a common tariff in 1948.) The Oslo

Convention (1930) to peg tariffs, and the Ouchy Agreement (1932) on lowering tariffs, were not successful, partly because Britain opposed them.

In addition there were a series of projects associated with private individuals, like the Pan-European Movement (1923) founded by Count Coudenhove-Kalargi as an anti-Soviet organisation – a movement that was to influence Winston Churchill, although the British Foreign Office regarded its author as a crank. During the thirties, particularly in response to Hitler's Germany with its growing potential for aggression, a mass of writings was published urging (without being at all clear as to details) closer unity among European nations. Even Clement Attlee (leader of the British Labour Party and Prime Minister after the war and not a man given to emotional outbursts) was to write in *Labour's Peace Aims* (1939), 'Europe must federate or perish'. Much of these thirties' writings were ephemeral, pragmatic or emotional responses to circumstances: it was the experience of the Second World War that concentrated opinion into a search for an alternative to the nation state.

The influence of the Resistance

The very speed of the German victory in the West in 1940 had a shattering effect on morale. This itself was enough to call in question the vitality and effectiveness of liberalism and traditional nationalism. That there was not wanting a group of leading politicians, normally on the right wing of politics, to cooperate with the German occupying forces added a further dimension. It was not long before the finger of suspicion was pointed at them as men who were prepared to sacrifice their country in order to destroy the political left wing – a charge that took on a new meaning after the German invasion of Russia (1941) released the Communists from the inhibiting effects of the Nazi-Soviet Pact of 1939. But rationalisations about the motives behind men's actions come after the events.

At the outset, the Resistance was an individual choice, a spontaneous response to defeat and the chaos and disillusionment that followed. Only later was a formal organisation built up and links forged between the men and women who risked their lives and those of their families, while their political leaders, gathered in London, sought to give cohesion and greater effectiveness to the movement in their country, and to link it with similar movements in other countries. The political leaders in London were not out of touch with their followers, but they had greater opportunity to formulate policy and to look to the future, particularly as the tide of fortune turned against the Nazis, and to reveal the common elements in the idealism of the Resistance that appeared throughout Nazi Europe.

Within the Resistance, there was a wide spectrum of political beliefs and of those uncommitted in politics, simple patriots, some of whom had been members of right-wing groups, some full members of the Communist Party; and there were necessarily great differences between the small and very security-minded urban groups and the larger, more open groups in rural areas. Many were the bonds that formed their unity, but at first it was not political belief. After 1941 the Communists became important because of their close party cell organisation – although their losses were heavy, too – but it would be wrong to suggest they came to dominate the Resistance, for there was evidence of freemason groups and of liberal Roman Catholic groups strengthening the organisation of the Resistance. Those active in the field had little time for dreaming of the future, but they were not indifferent to it, and the desire to escape from the burden of the political past that had led Europe to a second war of even greater destructive power was very strong. If there was any political alignment of consequence, in France for instance, it was between the right-wing patriots and communists who wanted immediate action, and the socialists, with their Jacobin tradition, who preferred to await the *insurrection nationale*. But the overwhelming purpose was the defeat of Nazi Germany, a purpose that made it possible to link together underground groups throughout Europe, the more so as they showed a surprising agreement in their ideals for the future. As Hitler developed a New Order for Europe under the dominance of the Third Reich, the Resistance developed in theory the framework for a New Order of a different sort, that was to be boldly proclaimed later in the war by the European Resistance Declaration (1944):

> Federal Union alone can ensure the preservation of liberty and civilisation on the continent of Europe, bring about economic recovery, and enable the German people to play a peaceful rôle in European affairs.

Widespread support for a future federal Europe appeared early in the war, whether among the various governments in exile, or among those working in occupied Europe, or among those in prison. Documents were produced quite independently by the French, German, Italian, Czech, Dutch, Yugoslav and Polish Resistance, and it is not certain which produced the first formalised call for a Federal Europe. It would seem to be the Italians who first stepped clearly beyond the bounds of local patriotism by printing clandestinely the Ventolene Manifesto (1941), a plan for a European federation, and then launching (in Milan, 1943) the European Federalist Movement. Others were thinking on the same lines, and it is worth quoting from the declaration of the Committee of National Liberation in Algiers, August 1943:

> There will be no peace in Europe if states re-establish themselves on the basis of national sovereignty, with all that this implies by way of prestige policies and economic protectionism. . . . The countries of Europe are too small to give their people the prosperity that is now attainable and therefore necessary. They need wider markets. . . . To enjoy the prosperity and social progress that are essential, the States of Europe must form a federation or a 'European entity' which will make them a single economic unit.

The thinking behind what was to emerge as the European Common Market was becoming clear. After the Liberation, the French Committee for European Federation called the first European Federalist Conference in Paris (March 1945 – the formal ending of the war in Europe, V. E. Day, was in May) and the road to a European Union seemed open. Only in a federal union, it was argued with some validity, could the German nation achieve acceptance once more into a European family, or frontiers be fairly settled in disputed areas of mixed populations.

Churchill's influence

Whatever doubts have been cast over his later career, Winston Churchill's reputation at the end of the war was of great significance and that he should be associated with the European Movement was viewed as a great triumph. It was a little while before differences between his views and those of the federalists became clear. Britain stood apart from much of the debate over unity in Europe. For example, there was a profound difference between Britain – which had stood alone and self-confident against Nazi Germany – and Occupied Europe in which guilt feelings over early failures were added to the actual sufferings of occupation. Yet Churchill, at the moment of defeat, in June 1940, had offered a union with France based on common citizenship. This was more radical than a war-time alliance, and many have regarded it as a momentous departure from Britain's insular traditions, the more so as Churchill was associated with the idea of European unity.

But it would be wrong to make too much of his association with this idea, or of his common citizenship offer. Churchill was a war leader and a pragmatist. He was concerned with the present, not the distant future. The common citizenship offer (which may have been suggested to Churchill by Jean Monnet) was aimed at keeping France in the war – and it failed of its immediate purpose for the Vichy régime was collaborationist. In 1940, also, Anthony Eden, the British Foreign Secretary, proposed two generalised war aims – the destruction of Nazism and the provision 'of some form of European Federation' which might promise a European defence system, customs union and common currency; but when Stalin called for a specific statement of war aims (November 1941) none was made.

It is not unlikely that Churchill had no clearly defined European vision, and his embracing of European unity did not extend to Britain joining in. John Colville (his Assistant Private Secretary 1940–1) recalls:

> He never for one moment during or after the war contemplated Britain submerging her sovereignty in that of a United States of Europe or losing her national identity. . . . In January, 1941, at Ditchley, he went so far as to say that there must be a United States of Europe and that it should be built by the English: if the Russians built it there would be Communism and squalor; if the Germans built it there would be tyranny and brute force. On the other hand, I knew he felt that while Britain might be the builder and Britain might live in the house, she would always preserve her liberty of choice and would be the natural, undisputed link with the Americas and the Commonwealth.

Realism, however, was tempered by sentiment in Churchill's attitude to Europe. Behind the need to destroy Nazism lay the fear of Bolshevism and Soviet dominance of Eastern Europe. He viewed the proposed Four Power Plan (1942) for a post-war world run by four great powers in terms of Britain playing umpire between the United States and the Soviet Union, with Europe as a series of groups of federated states (Balkan, Danubian, Scandinavian, etc.) much on the lines of Count Coudenhove-Kalargi's anti-Bolshevik schemes for a Pan-European Union. The Foreign Office thought the whole idea impracticable, nevertheless Churchill lent his prestige to the Pan-European movement.

At the Dumbarton Oaks Conference (September 1944), at which the foundations for the United Nations Organisation were established, Churchill advocated a Council of Europe – but wanted the US included; his calls for a united Europe were never translated into a coherent plan of action, and did not include Britain. His famous Zurich speech (1946) was promoting a Franco-German partnership (against Russia), not British leadership of Europe, for her way lay with the 'Atlantic Alliance'. Fear of Soviet aggression increased as final victory approached, and he was doubly anxious to maintain the US presence in Europe – and to prevent Stalin seizing Eastern Europe by default. Stalin, for his purposes, had every reason to seek to establish a *cordon sanitaire* against the West, and equally every reason to fear any future German war of revenge. Indeed, Soviet policy was concerned lest Britain were to organise a Western European bloc against them – Eden was anxious to quieten their fears in this respect.

After Roosevelt, Stalin and Churchill met at Yalta in the Crimea early in February 1945 (see page 17), Churchill repeatedly warned the United States against Soviet advance, seeking aid to prevent it in a curious reversal of Canning's famous theory – the 'Iron Curtain' telegram to Truman (12 May 1945) was only the most direct of several. But the United States was anxious to withdraw substantially from Europe once the war was over – hence Churchill's return to the theme of European unity (the advocacy of the Resistance had been too radical for him). When he suffered electoral defeat in 1945, he left office with no effective European policy. Nor had the new Labour administration. Ernest Bevin, the new Foreign Secretary, for all that he had advocated European unity in his famous TUC speech of 1927, rejected the ideology of the federalists. His preoccupation was the developing rift between the Super-Powers and his European policy was concerned with securing a continuance of the US military and economic presence in Europe; thereafter, Britain might dominate an inter-governmental European union, linked to members' overseas territories, to serve as a Third Force independent of either the US or the Soviet Union, but only with the added security of US forces on the continent. In all this, the idealist declarations of the Resistance – Europe of the federalists, as it were – had little place. The future unity of Europe was to grow, not out of diplomacy and foreign policy, but out of the organisation and administrative machinery of more limited economic policies – the Europe of the functionalists, as it were. In political realities and the administration through which a complex modern state is governed, lay the answer to the problem of how to unite Europe: throughout the generation following the war there was to be persistent rivalry between these two views as to the means to achieve a common end.

Idealism was in full flood as allied armies advanced on Germany (and stayed the Japanese advance in the Far East). It was most obvious in the formation of

Europe's changing frontiers

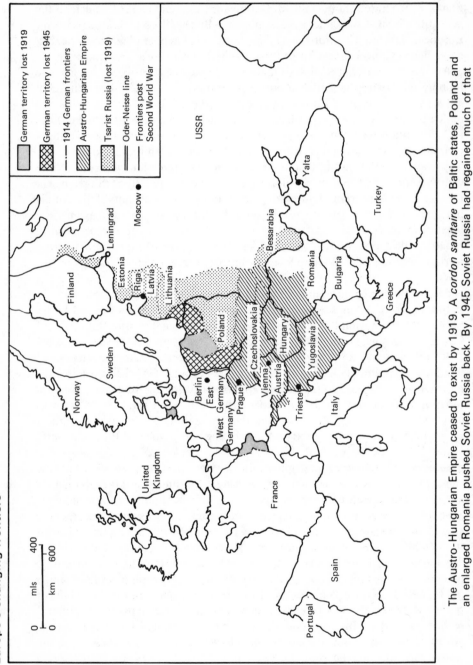

The Austro-Hungarian Empire ceased to exist by 1919. A *cordon sanitaire* of Baltic states, Poland and an enlarged Romania pushed Soviet Russia back. By 1945 Soviet Russia had regained much of that lost territory, and Poland had been shifted westwards at German expense.

the United Nations Organisation, begun at Dumbarton Oaks in 1944 and completed at San Francisco in June 1945. It was launched with the determination that it should not suffer the same sad fate as the League of Nations after the First World War. As a gauge of popular emotion of the time, it demonstrated the widespread acceptance of the need for international cooperation. Its diplomatic and political influence was to have an impact on the fifties and sixties, but in particular, its specialist organisations did much to save Europe (and other areas in the world) after the war from complete collapse.

Meanwhile, Europe's affairs emerged: there was no formal settlement. A series of conferences between the leaders of the Great Powers was held – conferences that revealed the rifts developing between them and which were to dominate the post-war world. The idealists did not determine the shape of post-war Europe. The first of the important conferences was at Teheran in November 1943, at which Churchill's hopes for a British ascendancy in Greece were dashed by the decision to concentrate upon a second front in France. Of even greater importance was the decision to allow Soviet Russia to advance her frontiers westwards, to what she had gained by the Nazi-Soviet Pact and, indeed, towards the 1914 frontiers of Tsarist Russia. Poland was to be compensated with German territory; Romania would simply lose Bessarabia because she had joined the Axis Powers. The failure to reach precise details over frontiers caused Churchill grave concern, but served to maintain the appearance of allied unity. At Yalta, in February 1945, Stalin's suggestion of the Oder-Neisse Line as the frontier between Germany and Poland was deferred – it was never settled. But Germany was to be occupied and divided into four zones of occupation, with Berlin under direct Joint Four Power control. This was confirmed at Potsdam, in August 1945, but again no firm decisions were taken on German frontiers with Poland, although it was agreed to take what reparations were necessary from occupied territories.

Post-war Europe

The experience of war promoted a strong desire to construct a world of greater social justice. This was characterised in Britain by the Beveridge Report, 1942 (Britain's Resistance Charter, as it has been called). In Europe the common experiences of occupation provided a bond of unity between classes and encouraged the adoption of an all-embracing social programme in each country. Big electoral gains were secured in the West by the centre, socialists and communists (all prominent in the Resistance). But it was not long before the old party politicians had established themselves: the unity of the Resistance would not survive the peace. Nor did the Resistance effectively purge collaborators from public life. In 1945 there was little rational basis for the overflowing of vengeance, and summary justice was meted out before allied army units could establish control. A significant number were killed and executed, especially where old political and personal scores were to be settled. Yet, after all the suffering and hatred, the surprising thing was the small number of those purged – even in Germany, where ambitious schemes of de-nazification had been prepared.

The ideal of a new Federal Union of Europe faded quickly, as much from the return of old political attitudes as from the overwhelming economic difficulties immediately in the wake of the war. The ideal of a 'united Europe' was passed on to private associations and a division soon developed between those promoting federalism and those preferring functionalism (setting up only that minimum of political institutions that was indispensable to common action – things could grow organically thereafter).

The Resistance failed to exert a moral authority over practical politics: the hopes of idealists were crushed by the political manipulators. Its influence lay strongly with the federalists and it may have played a significant part in the development of some institutions. It may well have helped forward the already half-formed Benelux (1944-Belgium, Netherlands, Luxembourg); the three small countries hoped to hold their own economically in the post-war world against major powers. (Although it was not realised at the time, Benelux was something of a precursor of the EEC.) The influence of the Resistance was present too in the formation of the Council of Europe (1949) and the Nordic Council (1953), and partly also the EEC itself. What in 1939 was still thought of as the ideas of cranks, had become respectable by 1949, for Article 1 of the Council of Europe states the aim:

> to achieve a greater unity between its Members for the purpose of safe-guarding and realising the ideals and principles which are their common heritage and facilitating their economic and social progress.

That 'social progress' was apparent in the legislation of Western European countries in the late forties, and the 1946 Constitution of the Fourth French Republic actually stated 'on conditions of reciprocity France shall accept the limitations of sovereignty necessary to the organisation and defence of peace'. The Italian Constitution (1947) and the West German *Grundgesetz* (1949) carried similar provisions, and the Danish Constitution (1953) carried a less specific clause.

The failure of European integration, 1945–57

Many people felt that some form of European integration made sense, not only in terms of the idealism at the end of the war, but also because of a common culture and the need to survive economically and avoid a return to the pre-war protection that had damaged trade and economic development. There was also a rising fear of Soviet Russia: cooperation, if not integration, seemed a sensible guarantee of defence policy. Yet in both these fields, the cause of European integration failed. As regards the former, it has been suggested that part of the cause was Churchill's electoral defeat – yet his 'United States of Europe' did not include Britain: 'We are with Europe, but not of it', he said. Britain would help and support a European unity movement, but would remain aloof; she would welcome and be a member of a Council of Europe, provided, in Ernest Bevin's words, its structure were 'as little embarrassing as possible'.

In 1947 the *Union Européenne des Fédéralistes* called a conference at Montreux which adopted the idea of summoning, as it were, an 'estates general' of Europe to the Hague in 1948 uner the magic name of Churchill. The Hague Congress launched a European Movement with a National Council in each member country, and presided over by the veterans, Churchill, Léon Blum, Alcide de Gaspari and Paul-Henri Spaak (a wide political spectrum). Article 3 of its Resolutions stated:

> . . . the European nations must transfer and merge some portion of their sovereign rights so as to secure common political and economic action for the integration and proper development of their common resources.

Bidault, then French Prime Minister, enthusiastically called for a customs and economic union and for a European Assembly to draft a federal constitution for Europe. But the Council of Europe that emerged in 1949 was without powers and was endowed with a purely consultative assembly chosen from member nations' parliaments. As the first post-war political organisation covering much of western Europe, it was a considerable achievement for the federalists, but it was an empty one. National sovereignty was in no danger, and defence policy was specifically excluded. For all the enthusiasm it engendered, its evident lack of power condemned it and Paul-Henri Spaak resigned as President in 1951, making a particularly bitter speech: 'If a quarter of the energy spent here in saying "No", were used to say "Yes" to something positive, we should not be in the state we are today.'

Clearly, as an agent of political unification, the Council of Europe was a failure: but it continues to do useful work as a forum for ideas and a sounding board for policies, as well as consultative and advisory work in a wide number of fields, for example Human Rights, social and educational policy, transport, civil aviation and agriculture.

Defence policy, the most obvious area for close cooperation at the very least, also proved unable to establish European unity. Britain, indeed, dealt with Europe almost in the way of pre-war diplomacy, through mutual aid pacts. The first was the Treaty of Dunkirk (1947) between Britain and France, directed primarily against the possibility of any future German aggression. The German Question was a crucial one for post-war diplomacy – some even viewed a European Federation as a means of permanently dismembering Germany, since it was clear the Soviet Zone would not be allowed to join. The Treaty of Dunkirk was extended in 1948 to form the Treaty of Brussels, a fifty-year treaty for collective defence including Benelux. Britain saw it as the prototype of an expanding series of similar pacts (though this policy was overtaken by the creation of NATO).

When the pressures of the Korean War (see pages 26–7) made a rearming of West Germany a necessity, the West German Chancellor, Adenauer, was happy to agree since it would be a step towards his country being once more accepted within the pale of western nations. France proposed the European Defence Community, less to promote European integration (placing national forces under a supra-national authority would be a major step towards integration) than to prevent an independent West German military force appearing (see page 54). In any case, the proposal failed because the French Assembly refused to accept it in 1954. This was the low water mark for European unity and a sad moment for the federalists who had looked forward to creating a New Europe by some great leap forward. Jean Monnet announced he would not seek re-election as President of the High Authority of the European Coal and Steel Community (see page 59), but would pursue his schemes for integration through a new pressure group, (the Action Committee for the United States of Europe). But the Brussels Treaty was expanded into the Western European Union (October 1954) to include Italy and West Germany, all with close cooperation with NATO, still, however, as cooperation between governments, not as integration of policy or administration. So the Western European Union proved a disappointment to the federalists. They had hoped to settle the problem of the Saarland through it, by placing the Saarland under a European Commissioner under the auspices of WEU as the first 'federal state' of Europe. France, for her part, had hoped to detach the province from Germany and unite it with herself, in the name of old-style nationalism. But a referendum in the territory gave a firm two to one majority in favour of incorporation into West Germany (from 1 January 1957).

2

The Cold War and the Defence of the West

Fearing a German attack, and without a western alliance, Stalin had agreed to the Nazi-Soviet Pact of August 1939. It was a strange alliance between sworn enemies and it proved an embarrassment to Communist Parties in the West, who, obedient to directives from the Kremlin, were obliged to reverse their open hostility to Nazis. The Pact made the invasion of Poland easier for Hitler and guaranteed him against a war on two fronts whilst he dealt with the West. For Stalin, it meant avoiding the attack he anticipated, and it gave him the Baltic States and half of Poland. It was an added cause for the West to hate Stalin. But the launching of Barbarossa, the German invasion of Russia, in 1941 produced a reversal of attitude in the West and the Russians became popular allies; by 1942 a Grand Alliance linked the USA, Soviet Russia, Britain and the West. It was, however, founded on the negative aim of defeating Hitler; what should happen after the war was a different matter – and in the circumstances it was not an unwise decision to defer the matter by leaving it to the United Nations, as was agreed at Dumbarton Oaks in 1944.

The Grand Alliance outlasted the war, but it was under strain. For example, his incipient distrust of Bolshevism led Churchill to favour a federal grouping of European states as a bastion against Soviet Russia, along the lines of Count Coudenhove-Kalargi; and General Smutts, the veteran South African leader, supported the anti-Russian view in a speech in November 1943, calling attention to the fear of a new Soviet dominance in Eastern Europe. The West's tardy progress towards opening a new front (the Normandy landings) Stalin interpreted as a British move to allow Russia to bleed a little more. He suspected the secret negotiations over surrender between the German generals in Italy and the Western Allies as being an anti-Russian move, and he was not mollified when the Allies rejected the German High Command's suggestion of surrender to them so that the remaining German Army might be used against Russia. It was already clear that Churchill favoured taking Berlin and Prague before the Russians, and Stalin interpreted this as the opening of a new struggle for control of Central Europe.

Roosevelt, the US President, made it clear that US troops would be withdrawn after the victory as soon as was possible. Some argued from this that Europe would be open to the Russian steamroller and urged close cooperation in self defence. Already the division of Europe was beginning. In 1943 a Russian suggestion that each country of the Nazi empire, as it 'fell away from Germany', should be placed under a joint military and political commission was ignored, and Italy was placed under an Anglo-American Control Commission. US policy favoured spheres of influence. Britain was clearly intended to control the Mediterranean, and Churchill pushed this home on his visit to Moscow in 1944, where he proposed a division of the Balkans between Britain and Russia in the proportions 90:10 for Greece, 25:75 for Bulgaria, 50:50 for Yugoslavia and Hungary and 10:90 for Romania. The proposal was accepted: there was much *realpolitik* in the division of Europe. In the context it is not surprising that de Gaulle, representing France, having failed to commit Britain to a positive line of action for the future security of Western Europe, should sign a twenty-year Treaty of Alliance and Mutual Assistance with the Soviet Union (December 1944).

By 1945 it was clear that Stalin was pushing his frontiers into Eastern Europe. He was later to be castigated as a latter-day Tsar, restoring, if not extending the frontiers of 1914 – but with a difference, for there was a crusading fervour about the Russian advance. As the troops penetrated into Eastern Europe disquieting fears about atrocities against aristocrats and bourgeois 'enemies of the people', prompted by the mystery of the Katyn massacre, were heightened by the surprising failure of the Red Army to help the Warsaw Rising (August 1944).

At the Yalta conference (February 1945) Russia was effectively allowed *de facto* control over Eastern Europe. One sign of the possible consequences was given in Romania – one of the Axis powers, for which she lost Bessarabia and Bukovina. Shortly after the signing of the Declaration on Liberated Europe, allowing liberated countries to establish democratic institutions of their choice, Soviet pressure for a communist government culminated in the celebrated visit of Andrei Vyshinsky to King Michael requiring him to accept the communist leader Petrie Groza, and slamming the door so hard that he cracked the plaster round the door frame.

The Polish Question provoked considerable Western pressure. Poland was not taken over – a point missed by some western historians when outlining the westward advance of communism. Disputes over the composition of the new government and the holding of free elections soon broke out and the acrimonious correspondence reached a peak when Stalin, in March 1945, accused the West of negotiating with Germany behind his back. In this context, Eisenhower's refusal to accept the idea of a race for the major capitals meant that the Russians took Vienna in April 1945 and Berlin on 2 May. But there was no united stand by the West – despite repeated urgings from Churchill to Truman, the new US President, including the famous telegram of 12 May: 'An iron curtain is drawn down upon their [Russian] front. We do not know what is going on behind . . . .'. Division was openly admitted by the time of the Potsdam conference (August 1945) and no agreement was reached over the new Poland or the Oder-Neisse Line (its western frontier with Germany), nor over Trieste, disputed between Italy and Yugoslavia.

Eastern Europe was left to Russia, and by 1947 communist régimes controlled all but Greece and Czechoslovakia. Germany and Austria were divided into four zones of occupation, and although the allies were as yet determined to punish Germany through reparations and occupation and prevent her once again threatening the peace of the world, nevertheless fear of Soviet Russia was beginning to replace fear of a revived Germany – and the big gains of communists in the elections in France and Italy added to these fears. It was clear that Russia was not exhausted by the war. Pressed by the USA she declared war on Japan – it was one way of shortening the war in the Pacific, and it could give political advantage to the Soviet Union as well as control, at least for the moment, of Port Arthur. The Soviet forces mounted a *Blitzkrieg* of considerable proportions that was very successful indeed. It was perhaps less surprising when the condition of the Japanese troops is taken into account – Manchuria was a training area, the high command had just been changed and morale among the troops was low, indeed they seemed to be awaiting an armistice. The two atomic bombs that brought the war to a dramatic end may well not have been a military necessity since Japanese food supplies had been cut and surrender could only have been a matter of a few months away. They served, however, as an object lesson to the Soviet Union, and some have argued that that was their principal point. But this argument seems too simple: US sources seem to show a considerable confidence that they could handle the Soviet Union, and in terms of public opinion it was not until the summer of 1946 (a full year after the bombs) that a poll showed that the US public thought Soviet imperialism was a greater threat to world peace than British – this partly explains Truman's reticence to respond to Churchill's anti-Russian warnings. As to the Soviet Union, she was well aware that the US would not share an occupation of Japan with her, nor allow an occupation of extensive areas of the Chinese mainland which would increase Soviet presence in the Pacific. As it was, she secured control over Port Arthur until 1954, when she withdrew in agreement with China, whose volunteers were secure in North Korea. The Soviet Union in 1944 had the capacity to move forward into Europe further than the Elbe, an advance France could not have stopped and Britain would have been unable to contain; but there was little likelihood of this in 1945 – Stalin was no fool, he could not take on the United States. A direct military threat was not a likely thing, but Stalin could well support with finance and agents a possible *coup* by communists in Italy.

In fact, what Stalin did was to create a *cordon sanitaire* of dependent satellites; his suspicions of western attitudes were deep rooted and had some foundation. The West, meanwhile, abided by the Yalta agreement and took the necessary steps to return prisoners of war and refugees to their countries of origin. Some of these had been active collaborators; some had seized on the German invasion as an opportunity to escape from Soviet control; some were simple prisoners of war: all were in danger of execution or imprisonment on their return. There was violent resistance to forcible repatriation, a resistance that was carefully concealed at the time from public opinion in the West – but it was a sign that official opinion read as confirming the stories of terror and arbitrary government that were beginning to seep through about Stalin's dictatorship.

In terms of power politics, Britain particularly, secure in the basic support of the USA, failed to appreciate that the world was in 1945 divided into two Super-Power groupings – and for the moment, the West held the ace in the atomic bomb. It is easy to forget that Soviet Russia had as much cause to fear the West as the West evidently feared her: it was not only the western resistance to a régime committed to the historical inevitability of the destruction of capitalism, there was also more than a suspicion that the West might have combined with Hitler or at least the German army to destroy Bolshevism. It was a genuine fear and it continued after the war. The failure of the Western Powers to exact a full total of reparations from their respective occupation zones seemed to add support to the fear that the West sought a re-unification and restoration of their former enemy to use against Soviet power. Mutual suspicion between East and West dominated the problem of Germany and neither side was prepared to accept as genuine the solutions put forward by the other to settle the German problem. To the Russian proposal that a disarmed Germany be reunited on the basis of the new frontiers without an army of occupation and without disturbing the existing balance and security of Europe, the West replied with loud demands for free elections. As late as 1949 much useful propaganda was being derived by the West from the apparent refusal of Russia to agree to a reunited Germany (on their terms).

In Central Europe, Soviet Russia was as obsessed with security as the West was with the communist threat. That both attitudes were exaggerated reactions to what was unlikely to be a genuine threat does not invalidate the reality of the fear at the time. But it is rare in history to find two opposed forces as clearly distinct as some historians would seek to present the powers of East and West. The stereotype of a loyal and united West may be as inadequate an interpretation of the diplomacy and politics within Europe and America as is the stereotype of a subject East totally dominated by Soviet Russia.

The diplomats of the late forties were men whose experience was formed in two world wars and by the failures of the inter-war period. It would have been remarkable indeed had they interpreted their world in terms of the later fifties. As it was, the hope for a 'return to normalcy' (quite as much as the advice of what has been called the Riga School of US diplomats who had observed the Soviet Union between the wars from the comparative safety of the Latvian capital) may be an adequate explanation of the speedy ending after the war of Lend Lease arrangements. There was much idealism, with eyes focused on the United Nations Organisation, but there was realism too. That neither France nor Britain could assume the defence of Europe was rapidly understood, and it became Ernest Bevin's prime concern to maintain a significant US presence in Europe.

The opportunity came with the Greek civil war, when Bevin played a clever hand, virtually blackmailing the USA into a commitment to European defence far beyond the immediate needs of Greece and the Eastern Mediterranean. Greece had been delineated as within the British sphere of interests, as much to preserve the British route through Suez, as to keep the Soviet Union out of the Mediterranean. In the confused situation within Greece, Britain, in 1944, had prevented a communist *coup* and supported the monarchy, although that institution had been collaboratist. There was no positive intervention or aid from Stalin – perhaps in confirmation of the agreement over spheres of influence in the Balkans which he and Churchill had made in 1944. (This itself might be an argument that Western fears of Stalin's aggression were exaggerated.) By 1946 civil war had begun and the communists, with no great help from Russia, were at first successful. Britain could not well stand the strain of further war and Bevin successfully committed the USA to European defence by withdrawing from Greece and obliging the US to step into the vacuum in support of 'free peoples who are resisting attempted subjugation by armed minorities or by outside pressures'. In effect this was a guarantee to the West against communist *coups* and it has been graced with the title of the Truman Doctrine (1947), a specific check to Soviet expansion. The Grand Alliance was giving way to a hostile military balance.

The Truman Doctrine, in effect, showed that the USA would assume Britain's former rôle of 'world policeman'. It was couched in simple crude terms, contrasting the ideal of American democracy with the repression associated with communism. It secured the use of US troops first in Greece (and Turkey), then in Europe and subsequently throughout the world. However, the desire to contain communism led the USA to support régimes that were as far from democratic ideals as they were from freedom.

On the economic front, US efforts to sustain western Europe took the form of Marshall Aid (see page 51), open to all European countries. Stalin rejected it on the grounds that it was economic imperialism with possible political and military overtones. In order to strengthen communist party unity, he formed Cominform (September 1947) of which all communist parties were members and which served to tie them to Moscow policies. It had an immediate effect in France where serious industrial unrest threatened the future of the young Fourth Republic, and in Italy where there was an unusually violent general election campaign (1948) in which both the Vatican and President Truman intervened, and which the Christian Democrats won. Defeated, the communist parties of Western Europe retired into a defensive position, maintained by rigid discipline – from which the next generation was to break away (see page 187). But a successful communist *coup* in Czechoslovakia (February 1948) revealed the limitations of US policy. The Treaties of Dunkirk (1947) and of Brussels (1948) might link Britain, France and Benelux for defence (see page 19) but East and Central Europe was clearly under Russian dominance. The division of the post-war world into two hostile camps was revealed: the Cold War, with each side prepared for aggression from the other but deterred from open war by fear of the consequences, had begun in earnest. Not even the rift in communist unity caused by President Tito of Yugoslavia pursuing an independent line, and his subsequent 'excommunication' by Stalin in 1948 (a shrewd comment on the judgment of those who interpret Soviet policy at this time as one of complete control of its satellites), altered the balance.

If a further test of the resolve of either side was needed, it was provided by the German problem. Disagreements over the future of Germany, whether arising from French fears of a revival of German militarism or Soviet concern lest a reunited Germany might be instrumental in anti-Soviet policies of the West, or Western fears of creating a political vacuum in Central Europe which a communist régime might then fill, had prevented a peace treaty being signed. The country, its eastern territories now Polish, remained divided into four occupation zones under an Allied Control Authority, with Berlin, the old capital and symbol of German reunification, firmly within the Russian Zone but divided into four sectors. By 1948, the three western zones (France being pressurised) were united to become the new Federal Republic of West Germany with a new currency aimed at cutting inflation and laying a sound basis for economic growth. The Russians responded by sealing off Berlin from the West (June 1948). It was a deliberate and calculated move: if the West surrendered Berlin, they would suffer a diplomatic rebuff comparable with a military disaster and any hope thereafter of reuniting a Germany of their own choice (with or without the 'Oder-Neisse lands') would be gone. Stalin must have calculated (correctly) that the West, even with the advantage of the atomic bomb, would not advance on Berlin. General Clay, the US commander, suggested it, but Truman over-ruled him. There was to be no war over Berlin, nor would there be in future, for the West refused to play a positive rôle in the serious 1953 East Berlin workers' riots, or even over the construction in 1961 of the Berlin Wall dividing the city. What saved the West was the Berlin Air Lift, maintained at great cost until May 1949. They would not surrender their hold on Berlin. Stalin recognised defeat and communications were restored. The Berlin Air-Lift was a major victory for 'containment' and close links were forged between the US, her allies and West Germany. Europe was divided.

A communist East German Democratic Republic, with its capital in East Berlin, was established in 1949 to rival West Germany. Neither officially recognised the other. Within two years of the Nazi defeat, when the Allies were agreed on punishing Germany in a way that would prevent her threatening European and world peace again, both East and West (though both in principle favoured reunification) had changed their policy to a defensive partnership with their half of Germany in opposition to their former allies.

The North Atlantic Treaty Organisation (NATO)

In April 1949 the Brussels Treaty Organisation was enlarged into the North Atlantic Treaty Organisation (NATO) by the Treaty of Washington (its twelve members were joined by Greece and Turkey (1952) and West Germany (1955). It was an Atlantic Alliance for the defence of West Europe, assuming (as NATO has continued to assume) that Russia would be the aggressor, and founded on the principle of unity of action: 'an armed attack against one or more of them in Europe or North America shall be considered an attack against them all' (Article 5). The Tropic of Cancer was to be the southern boundary. Bevin's policy had come to fruition: if the treaty merely guaranteed that the USA would supply military forces in case of need, in effect it firmly linked both the USA and Canada to the defence of West Europe, whose member nations now felt a new sense of security – for which the USA paid most of the bill. For them it was a revolutionary step – it was that very 'entangling alliance' against which George Washington had warned some 160 years before: it would mean a large standing army in peace time and it would involve the US in World War Three from the outset, were it to begin in Europe.

This did not bring stability to Europe, the more so as the Cold War took another turn in June 1950, when the Korean War began. The Cold War had become global, and the USA was soon involved in a full-scale complex war in

Korea on behalf of the United Nations, which lasted until 1953. That a conflict between North and South Korea was likely had been obvious for some time. What was less obvious was whether it was deliberately promoted by Russia. The evidence is not at all clear, but would seem to point to a North Korean invasion of the South to forestall and check an invasion about to be launched by the South. It is possible that Russia did not intend so soon to risk a further major involvement, but that she was drawn into it as much to support North Korea as to support the new communist Republic of China.

The structure of NATO

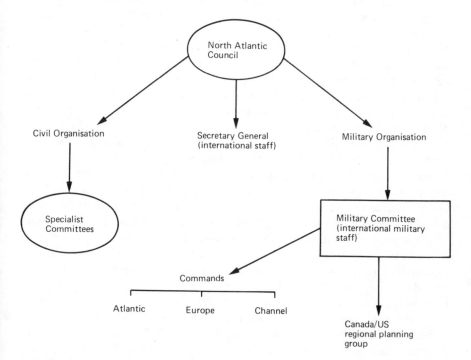

The North Atlantic Council comprises the Foreign Ministers of all member states and meets twice a year in a member's capital. When in permanent session, composed of members' ambassadors, it meets weekly. Its chairman is the Secretary General, and decisions are taken by common consent (it is possible for a member to apply a veto). When discussing military policy it meets as the Defence Planning Committee (excluding France).

A wide range of Specialist Committees, composed of representatives from member states, assist the Council. Since 1966 nuclear defence policy has been handled by the Nuclear Defence Affairs Committee and the Nuclear Planning Group. Since 1969 a Committee on the Challenges of Modern Society has advised on environmental problems.

The Secretary General is Chairman of the Council and the Defence Planning Committee and has right of initiative. He may intervene informally in cases of dispute between members.

The Military Committee comprises the Chiefs-of-Staff of all members except France and Ireland. It meets three times a year and as required, but has Permanent Military Representatives for permanent session. Liaison exists with the French High Command.

It is significant that Russian control over a satellite appears to have been so slight in 1950 as to allow it to precipitate a major war. Deliberately to provoke an outright conflict with the USA, when the USA had overwhelming atomic capability, was not a reasonable course of action. Russia had atomic bombs probably in 1949, but neither the quantity nor the means to deliver them against US targets. As it was, the use of the atomic bomb was ruled out by the personal decision of President Truman (who, indeed, dismissed General MacArthur, the victor of the Pacific war against Japan, for advocating its use). For the moment, warfare would remain 'conventional'.

The Korean War was 'limited', but its influence was immense. Direct television reporting carried battle scenes into US homes (nearly twenty years later the same effect on a grander scale was to help swing public opinion heavily against the Vietnam War). The war cost twenty-two million dollars and 35 000 US lives. China lost a million men, while North and South Korea lost between five and six per cent of their population and their territories were devastated. This was no side issue, no mere separation of contestants. It tied Japan the more securely to US policy, and the scene was set for Vietnam. It led to the strengthening of NATO, the rearmament of West Germany and a crash H-bomb development programme by the USA. What was ostensibly a UN police action had become in effect a US war fought primarily by US soldiers for US reasons.

The economic consequences of the war were considerable (see page 56) and in Europe it had immense political impact. American forces were affected and NATO partners were called upon to make a greater contribution to mutual defence in the West. None of the member states was well placed to do so, and the obvious answer, notwithstanding the decisions of less than six years before, was to rearm West Germany, the more so as she had been launched upon a period of rapidly increasing prosperity. So complete a change of front provoked widespread opposition – and not only in France. The Pleven Plan and the proposed European Defence Community (see page 57) were both attempts to raise an acceptable West German force under 'European' control. Their failure led to the creation of the Western European Union (October 1954) within NATO and the creation of a distinct West German national army – precisely what the French had struggled to avoid. That same month, the Soviet Union formed the Warsaw Treaty Organisation (Warsaw Pact) in retaliation.

Warsaw Pact (Warsaw Treaty Organisation, WTO)

If Stalin had imposed a strong control from the Kremlin upon the activities of communist parties throughout the world, a far more open policy, especially towards Eastern Europe, has been pursued since his death (1953). They have been treated more as colleagues, with an increasing degree of latitude in running their own affairs. The old western stereotype of a monolithic organisation controlled in minute detail by Moscow bureaucrats no longer applies in the Communist bloc, and of this the Warsaw Pact is an admirable illustration.

It resembles NATO (without the formalised institutions), providing for consultation on international problems, exchange of views on political matters and a joint command for the armed forces; but, unlike NATO it is backed by a

complex series of bilateral treaties of friendship and mutual assistance between
member nations and the Soviet Union. Thus the joint defence of Eastern Europe
is only partly dependent on the Pact and the Soviet Union has concluded separate
agreements for stationing troops on member nations' territory, following the
serious Polish riots and the Hungarian rising of 1956. The agreements with
Romania lapsed in 1958 (though it appears Russian troops were back in
Romanian territory in 1979) and with Albania in 1961. In these cases, Soviet

The structure of the Warsaw Treaty Organisation

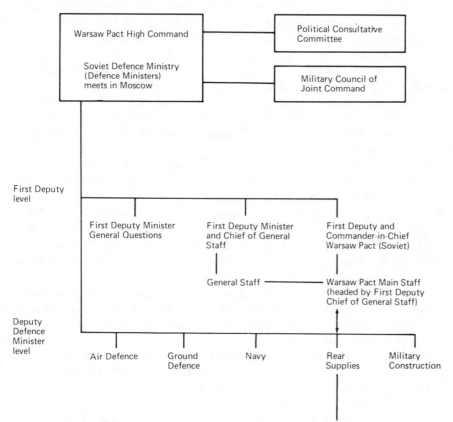

The Warsaw Pact, reorganised in 1969,
is a highly integrated military organisation with standardised modern
equipment, a unified (Soviet) command and closely integrated forces.

The principal power centre is the Soviet
Defence Ministry, and the Soviet military command is clearly in control of
Pact forces. The Political Consultative
Committee acts as a forum for the
discussion of differences between Pact
members, and is important for coordinating members' foreign policies.

The Joint High Command, with permanent military representatives from
each allied force, is the main channel of
communication in peacetime 'to strengthen defensive capability, prepare
military plans in case of war and decide
on the deployment of troops'.

troops were withdrawn – evidence of flexibility and a degree of independence of action.

Within the organisational structure, the Political Consultative Committee is composed of First Secretaries of member nations' Communist Parties, Heads of State and Foreign and Defence Ministers. A Permanent Commission, which makes recommendations on matters of general foreign policy, and a Joint Secretariat, under a Soviet official with a representative from each member state, meet in Moscow. In 1969 there was a reorganisation that made the Council of Defence Ministers the highest military body, no longer subordinate to the Commander-in-Chief. The military staff includes senior officers from member countries. In the event of war, the forces of member nations would be operationally subordinate to the Soviet Union High Command. Air defence throughout the Pact countries is centralised in Moscow with separate group headquarters – the Northern Group at Legnica (Poland), Central at Melovica (north of Prague), Southern at Budapest and the Soviet forces in East Germany at Zossen-Wünsdorf near East Berlin. The cohesion of the Pact was strengthened by the Soviet intervention in Hungary in 1956, and the executions that followed, since the possiblity of Hungary quitting the Pact had been one of the determining factors in launching the invasion.

The 1960s saw a critical change in relations with the West. The triumph of Sputnik (1957) – the fortieth anniversary of the Communist Revolution – and Yuri Gagarin's first manned orbit in extra-terrestrial space (1961) may have led Khrushchev to challenge the US in terms of nuclear missile strategy. There were several indications of a switch in Soviet policy, for example the U2 spy plane incident which led to the collapse of the Paris Summit (1960) and the Berlin crisis (1961) involving the building of the Berlin Wall. A climax was reached in the Cuban Missile Crisis (1962) when nuclear war was risked over supplying missiles to Cuba. That Khrushchev stood down and recalled the missiles, at whatever cost in personal prestige (it was assumed to have played a part in his fall), was indicative of the Soviet Union's realisation that they had not yet achieved nuclear parity with the United States.

Allowing for the technological gap, it was predicted that it would take thirteen years to reach parity and a huge Soviet armaments programme was launched for this purpose, at the expense of other areas of the Soviet economy – including consumer goods and the standard of living. Meanwhile, closer attention was paid to the effectiveness of conventional forces in Central Europe, with important manoeuvres beginning in 1961 after the appointment of Marshal Grechko as Commander-in-Chief of the Warsaw Pact Forces (he was succeeded in 1967 by Marshal Yakubovsky). In 1966 the 'Vlatava' manoeuvres were used to simulate nuclear weapons strategy: Russia was developing for the Central (European) Area the use of tanks with surface-to-surface missiles, so that small-scale nuclear warheads (called tactical, or theatre weapons, having a limited destructive power) would be likely to be used at an early stage in any conflict, and possibly at the initial stage of a *Blitzkrieg*. Great progress was made during the sixties on the integration of conventional forces (standardisation of weapons, a tremendous advantage in warfare, was already far advanced), especially of air forces of member countries, and logistics were centrally managed. The 1968 invasion of

Czechoslovakia clearly demonstrated Soviet facility in handling large ground forces and airforces over a considerable distance with impressive speed of movement and logistic support. It was a large-scale *Blitzkrieg* managed by General Maryakhin, Deputy Minister of Defence for the Rear Section. In comparison, the landing of US Marines in the Dominican Republic (1965) was very unimpressive. Following the Czech invasion, links between the Permanent Commission for Coordination of Military Industries of COMECON (Council for Mutual Economic Assistance) and the Warsaw Pact developed – clearly the Warsaw Treaty Organisation was well ahead of NATO on the use of conventional forces and their integration in operational conditions.

There have been disagreements over the political rôle of the Warsaw Pact – which argues for a flexibility of approach by the Soviet Union. Albania, for example, took her opposition to what she regarded as interference in her internal affairs so far that she seized the Soviet submarine base at Valona (1961) and in 1968 denounced the Warsaw Pact after the Czech invasion. (Albania currently regards herself as the most pure of the communist states in her adherence to Marxist-Leninism.) So small a country could be ignored, however embarrassing to the Soviet Union (Albania's close relations with China came to a diplomatic end in 1979, but they had proved an annoyance for ten years). More seriously, Romania challenged the plans for integration and the increased share of the cost borne by COMECON and the WTO. More than Warsaw Pact affairs were involved. For example, there was considerable resentment at Soviet attempts to influence foreign policy, following moves to coordinate East European support for Soviet Foreign Policy. Despite personal visits by Marshal Grechko and Brezhnev himself, an actual breach occurred, leading in 1966 to Romania calling for the withdrawal of Russian troops (a parallel was drawn with the French withdrawal from NATO) and an official visit by Chou-en-lai at a time when Sino-Soviet relations were at a very delicate point. In January 1967 Romania also opened diplomatic relations with West Germany. There were less significant murmurings in other member countries, although East Germany was anxious to strengthen the Pact under Soviet direction.

The Czech crisis broke when none of the points of stress within the WTO had been resolved. Initially, the handling of the crisis suggested a determination to settle differences by discussion (no formal WTO meeting was called, since this would have involved Romania). The possibility of Czechoslovakia quitting the Pact, as Hungary had tried to do in 1956, seems to have strongly influenced the decision to intervene. The way was prepared throughout May and June, with troop movements associated with manoeuvres, followed by a large-scale Rear Services exercise (to secure logistics). Pressure was put on Romania by manoeuvres taking place on her Bessarabian frontier, and this proved sufficient. The invasion, using troops also from East Germany, Bulgaria, Poland and Hungary, was an object lesson to both East and West as to the efficiency and quality of Warsaw Pact forces, and the coordination of national forces was impressive. Husak replaced Dubcek as the leader of Czechoslovakia, but there were few repressive actions in comparison with those following the Hungarian invasion of twelve years before. Romania's unreliability was one of the reasons for the increased attention paid to the railway ferry from Odessa to Varna in

Bulgaria, for the transport of troops. By 1979, Romania had again agreed to allow WTO manoeuvres on her territory. That Romania was not invaded and was permitted to take so independent a line may be explained by the fact that there was never any suggestion of deviation from Communist policies in her internal affairs, and in addition she occupies no vital strategic position, does not have important industrial interests (especially in the armaments field) as Czechoslovakia has, and she was not actively supported by the West. But the Czech invasion showed that the Soviet Union had her own version of the famous 'domino theory' that drew the USA into such damaging involvement in Vietnam.

Reaction within the WTO was less than happy. Albania withdrew; Romania denounced the invasion, and Hungary was known to have been uneasy at it. Hence the 'Brezhnev Doctrine' on the limited sovereignty of members, and the special bilateral agreements with member countries (including Czechoslovakia) for the stationing of Soviet troops. Clearly, the Warsaw Treaty Organisation is closely tied to the defence strategy of the Soviet Union, and so cannot assume the 'alliance of equals' pose of NATO.

Changes in strategy and strains within NATO

That the Soviet Union was a nuclear power was a major factor in NATO planning. If you are the only nuclear power, the deterrent value of your weapon is overwhelming. If your adversary gains the same weapon, its deterrent value depends either upon your having many more, and the means of delivering them with certainty, or on the realisation of the horrors that would result from having recourse to the weapons – a 'balance of terror', as it has been called. Initially, US policy was to concentrate on developing more, and more powerful, nuclear weapons and to have such a stockpile that a major conventional war would not be attempted, lest the holocaust be unleashed.

But it was no good having nuclear bombs unless one had a reliable means of delivering them to their actual target; and here the USA was far in advance of the Soviet Union throughout the early fifties. Its bombers had the use of NATO airfields, thus giving easy access to all likely targets. This was a guarantee of US forces remaining in Western Europe – if only because their departure might be followed by Russian planes using airfields on the Atlantic coast and having an opportunity, therefore, of reaching US home targets. The vast distances, whether over the pole or across the Atlantic were a partial guarantee against attack, so long as the delivery vehicle was a conventional heavy bomber. (The Pacific seemed to present less risks and was outside NATO areas anyway.) When in 1954 the USA adopted the policy of 'massive retaliation' (launching a great number of nuclear bombs to destroy enemy military capability and survival) as the basis of its deterrent policy (see page 173), it kept airborne a succession of bombers, each equipped with nuclear bombs (to be fused in flight) and always *en route* for their target, but always turning back before entering 'enemy' air space – to be immediately replaced by a relief wave of bombers. So long as the USA kept well ahead in terms of bombs and aircraft, there was less need to worry about the numbers of conventional forces in Europe. Thus the nuclear programme was used both to deter and to compensate for a significantly smaller army under

NATO auspices. Other NATO members were able to 'economise' on their defence commitments, accordingly.

The launching of Sputnik (1957) and the subsequent landings on the moon changed all this. Not only had the Soviet Union demonstrated a sudden leap forward in technological prowess, but she had now acquired a delivery vehicle far superior to a bomber. Terrestrial distance was no longer a problem, and a rocket could, with very great accuracy, reach any target within minutes. There was a sudden major switch to missiles as the new, more certain delivery vehicle (as well, of course, to methods of intercepting enemy missiles). That the US had greater retaliatory power by 1961 was demonstrated by Khrushchev's defeat over the Cuban missile crisis. The Soviet Union began to narrow the gap throughout the sixties and seventies (at the expense of living standards in Russia). Communication satellites added a further dimension to defence policy, and it was apparent that defence planning was beginning to develop on two levels – the conventional and the high-technology nuclear.

But in the very effectiveness of a 'balance of terror' lurked three dangers for

Comparative strategic force advantage, 1965–80

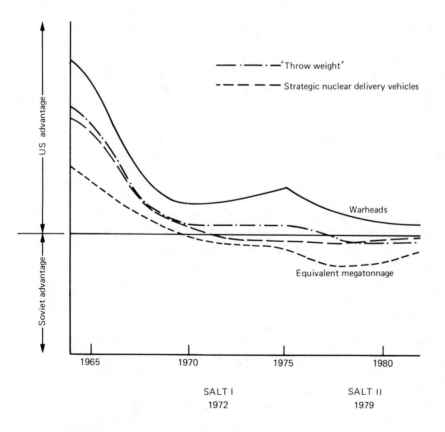

The diagram clearly indicates the rapid Soviet advance after the Cuban Crisis (1962) to 'parity' by 1974. (Source: *NATO Review*, April 1978, p. 22)

NATO. The first was a growing fear that the USA was no longer vitally committed to Europe: European air bases retained a strategic value for US forces but they were no longer vital as the first line of defence. There was less cause for the USA to regard Europe as the 'trip wire' that would check any direct aggression against her, and perhaps she might not respond quickly if Russia attacked Europe alone. Secondly, the control of nuclear weapons was firmly in US hands (for all that NATO was for joint defence) – by the seventies electronic locks were fixed over nuclear warheads. (Nevertheless on 9 November 1979 a nuclear alert was issued in error and war 'by mistake' was only minutes away. The alert was reversed in time – but the whole event took place without consultation with the NATO allies.) In Europe, only Britain and France were independent nuclear powers – and in 1962 Britain had agreed to adopt US delivery vehicles, in particular the polaris nuclear submarine. Thirdly, if a war began and was fought with conventional weapons, the initial battlefields, perhaps the only battlefields, would be in Europe – which would bear the full burden of destruction. Each of these points gave rise to doubts about the effectiveness of NATO.

Significant changes in international relations made it possible for Europe to take a more independent line, for, beginning in 1963, a major rift in Sino-Soviet relations raised the possibility of war between them. Russia might be faced with a war on two fronts – and in 1964 China exploded her own experimental atomic bomb. The West exploited the diplomatic advantage the dispute had given them, and what Khrushchev had called coexistence (a state of mutual tolerance) now emerged into *détente* (a willingness to cooperate to achieve a state of greater stability and confidence). It made possible a game of diplomatic niceties in which considerable gains were possible by balancing the threat presented by rivals. France seized this opportunity and developed an independent policy with an understanding with Soviet Russia that permitted her to withdraw from NATO in 1966 so that her forces might be under French control throughout and she might develop more fully her own independent nuclear strike force – what de Gaulle called the *force de frappe*.

This was a serious blow to NATO and for a little while the effectiveness of the Alliance was in question – the more so as the USA became increasingly involved in Vietnam. Neither the creation of the Nuclear Defence Affairs Committee (1966) nor the Nuclear Planning Group to assist it removed the force of the French objection that the ultimate element in NATO defence was not under NATO control. The Harmel Report (1967) on the future of the Alliance stressed the need to explore *détente* in hopes of finding a basis for stability in East – West relations. The Atlantic Council, meeting at Reykjavik (1968), called for Mutual and Balanced Force Reductions (MBFR) and in 1970 talks began between the USA and the Soviet Union on the limitation of strategic weapons (SALT) – which underlined the degree to which NATO was dependent upon the USA. An effort to overcome this and to promote a closer identity of interests was made in 1968 when, at the suggestion of the British Defence Secretary (Denis Healey), a Euro-Group was formed within NATO. It was a shrewed comment on the work of NATO that after nearly twenty years such a group, dedicated to devising a more concentrated approach to European defence, should have been necessary –

but perhaps it reflected basic changes in weapons technology and global strategy rather than political feebleness within NATO.

Originally the Euro-Group was no more than a loose association of ministers dining together, but its meetings were soon formalised and in the seventies it proved a useful means of deepening intra-governmental discussion within the Alliance. The Euro-Group was not anti-American, rather its existence demonstrated a realisation that the USA could not be expected to defend Europe as she had done in the early days of NATO; but its existence also indicated a degree of strain within the Alliance. There was in the seventies, for example, much concern over what was called 'de-coupling', namely the fear that there might be a break in the spectrum of the West's nuclear defence, between those 'theatre' weapons to be used in Europe and the strategic armoury of the US. It would be conceivable for the Soviet Union to fight a war in Europe using conventional forces and small 'theatre' weapons without calling into play strategic weapons with all their aweful consequences. This could have the effect of dividing the US from Europe in a future conflict: hence the call for medium-range missiles to be sited in Europe. The Euro-Group did much to press forward the European Defence Improvement Programme (1972), increasing the European contribution to defence commitments in the European sector. It was also concerned to achieve greater standardisation of weapons and inter-changeability of parts. It is a severe comment on NATO that so little progress towards weapons standardisation (despite the spiralling cost) had been made in thirty years, for this was one way in which the integrated force that had been projected in 1949 could be achieved. As late as 1978, the *NATO Review*, commenting on NATO's Long Term Defence Programme (1978) with its sharing of costs and moves to standardisation, noted that it would avoid the existing 'fourteen disparate and often over-lapping national efforts, for the most part only loosely coordinated'. There was some suspicion that 'standardisation' in US eyes meant adopting US systems – indeed, there was open talk in 1979 of creating a European integrated arms industry to achieve standardisation and inter-operability independent of US arms. But the Euro-Group's Independent European Programme Group (1976) included France (not a military member of NATO) and had already begun to consider standardisation of weapons. The British and French nuclear capability did not come within their discussions; it would not be shared with other members, but remain as firmly in national hands as the US warheads and bombs. It has been suggested that if the EEC were to assume an initiative in foreign policy and defence, there might be a significant development over standardisation. As it is, the Warsaw Treaty Organisation forces are far ahead in these matters (their weapons being largely Soviet ones) and also in command structure and national force cooperation, centralised in Soviet officers – an area NATO has yet properly to develop.

The Ottawa Declaration (1974) of the North Atlantic Council, whilst reaffirming the Washington Treaty of twenty-five years before, noted 'the strategic relationship between the United States and the Soviet Union has reached a point of near equilibrium'. It was this situation that had changed diplomacy in the seventies and reflected upon NATO, since it raised again those fears that the USA would be less than speedy in coming to the defence of Europe;

and concern was expressed at possible mutual reductions of troops in the Central Sector by the Super-Powers, since this would leave West Germany dangerously exposed. Meanwhile the SALT I negotiations had reached a successful conclusion in 1972 (analysts argued that it was to the advantage of the West). Talks were soon renewed between the two Super-Powers (US membership of NATO notwithstanding) for a SALT II, which took seven years to reach agreement (1979). For the first series of talks they had to rely on US intelligence reports of Soviet forces and equipment; for the second, official Soviet figures were forthcoming. It was a sign of relaxing tension between the two in consequence of their nuclear parity (defined as a state of affairs where neither side is likely to gain from launching a nuclear strike, since the victim would have sufficient nuclear resources to deliver a devastating counter-blow). A further sign of relaxation was the signing in Helsinki (1975), after two years' negotiation, of a complex series of agreements (known as 'baskets') covering defence, nuclear weapons and human rights. This Helsinki 'Final Act' exercised a considerable influence on diplomacy throughout the remainder of the decade, especially in the field of Human Rights (see page 192).

The SALT II Agreement, signed by Presidents Carter and Brezhnev in June 1979, was thought to be marginally favourable to the Soviet Union. The Agreement was vital to both Presidents, to Carter in view of his declining popularity at home and the coming presidential election of 1980, and to Brezhnev

What SALT II permits to each side

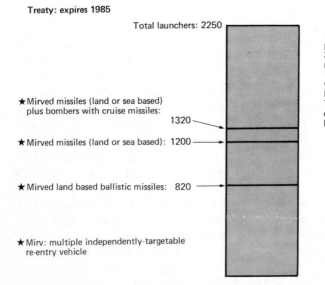

Treaty: expires 1985

Total launchers: 2250

★ Mirved missiles (land or sea based) plus bombers with cruise missiles: 1320

★ Mirved missiles (land or sea based): 1200

★ Mirved land based ballistic missiles: 820

★ Mirv: multiple independently-targetable re-entry vehicle

Russia will be permitted to deploy 308 SS-18 heavy missiles with up to 10 warheads each, within the treaty limits. The United States cannot deploy any heavy missiles.

Protocol: expires 31 December 1981

1 Testing and deployment of mobile land based ballistic missiles are banned.
2 Deployment of land or sea launched cruise missiles with range of over 600 kilometres is prohibited.

(Source: *The Economist*, 23 June 1979)

in order to be able to hold the cost of defence spending and to allow other sectors of the Soviet economy to develop. The Euro-Group welcomed the Agreement, but for some time had felt uneasy about the treaty, partly because of their having no voice in the negotiations, and partly because of the changing nuclear balance in Europe – for example, it might be possible for an advanced Soviet weapon, the SS-20 missile, to penetrate and destroy a NATO command post with little damage to civilian property nearby, whereas the NATO riposte might wipe out a Soviet city and thus provoke that massive retaliation that all would seek to avoid. The proposed negotiations for a further SALT III in the early eighties would include European representatives – a vital point to the Euro-Group because some of the new Soviet missile systems do not fall within SALT II but would be employed in Europe. For this reason, the extended talks at Vienna between NATO and the WTO that had begun in 1973 for mutual force reductions, were expected to make greater progress. However, talks on reducing conventional forces, divorced from nuclear arms, had an atmosphere of unreality and no significant progress had been made by early 1980. In an effort to bring France back into the armaments control talks, Giscard d'Estaing had in 1978 made proposals for realistic disarmament covering Europe from the Urals to the Atlantic (almost in the manner of de Gaulle).

The pursuit of *détente* had helped the Soviet Union not only to the SALT Agreements, but also to achieve some of its long-standing aims in Eastern Europe. East Germany (GDR) was formally recognised, and its frontiers, especially the contentious Oder-Neisse Line, accepted by West Germany through the latter's policy of *Ostpolitik* (see page 115). The reunification of Germany remains still a NATO ideal, but it has been put back in time as a practical policy – and shrewdly altered by the unilateral action of a member nation, West Germany. But *détente* is no substitute for defence policy: it may lead to prestigious treaties, like Helsinki and SALT, but it has not yet reduced the Soviet military programme or stopped Soviet intervention in Africa, nor has it necessarily increased NATO security. At least officially, the Soviet government is committed to the traditional historic Marxist mission towards the West – as Brezhnev put it, 'it does not in the slightest way abolish or alter the laws of the class struggle'. But at least it provides a means of accommodation between two world systems and in a speech reported in *Pravda*, 19 January 1977, Brezhnev summed up the situation well:

> *Détente* means first of all overcoming the Cold War and then a transition to normal, stable relations among states. *Détente* means the willingness to resolve differences and disputes not by force, not by threats and sabre rattling, but by peaceful means at the conference table. *Détente* means a certain trust and the ability to consider each other's legitimate interests.

Clearly, far more was involved in the diplomacy of the seventies than a crude balancing of Soviet fears of China with military preparedness in the West. '*Détente* is a two-way traffic' was how Cyrus Vance, the US Secretary of State, put it. Nuclear parity, and all that it implies, was the main reason for the success of *détente*, and in terms of strategy, ultimately NATO was thrown back on the quality of its conventional forces in Europe – and it was far from clear that it had the advantage in this sphere over Warsaw Pact forces.

Problems of strategy in the later seventies

By the seventies NATO had devised what purported to be a complete answer to any potential aggression from the East. It was based on the 'NATO Triad'. This was the name for a concept of defence strategy operating at three successive stages. An initial attack (NATO always plans on the assumption that it must operate on the defensive against an aggressor) would be countered by conventional forces; if they proved inadequate, then tactical (theatre) nuclear weapons would be employed against the attacking forces. Only if this failed to stop their advance (and so, presumably, to stop the war) would there be recourse to the third and final stage, the ultimate deterrent of strategic nuclear weapons and the probable annihilation of vast numbers of civilians. Superficially, the 'triad' made good sense – but it begged three important questions. First, what if the attacker used tactical weapons at the outset? Secondly, at what stage – and by whom – would the use of tactical nuclear weapons be ordered against a conventional attack, and how would it be possible to prevent this stage moving immediately into the final Stage Three? (In war, things do not always go according to plan, and an excited junior officer might, by an incautious or ill-considered act, set off the holocaust of Stage Three – Herman Kahn noted in 1965, 'once war has started, no other line of demarcation is at once so clear'.) Thirdly, strategic weapons had reached so advanced a point of development that their use would eradicate an opponent, civilians and all. Giscard d'Estaing, the French President, expressed the point succinctly – *'le tout ou rien, n'est pas crédible'*: if the ultimate deterrent were so terrible, then neither side would use it and it would cease to be a deterrent. But the logic of this last point was unacceptable: only the certain knowledge of the capacity to destroy one's opponent would make either side prepared to accept a planned adjustment of armed forces to reach a mutual balance. Nuclear parity assumes a logic of its own. Massive nuclear retaliation was a credible policy for the USA in the 1950s when she had a decided lead; in the later seventies, only the 'neutron bomb' (enhanced radiation weapon, ERW) would make it feasible as an object of deliberate strategy, and that only so long as the Soviet Union lacked a similar weapon, and would be paralysed by the first surprise nuclear strike.

But tactical nuclear weapons are credible, and by the later seventies were sufficiently sophisticated to be operational in a general attack, so that they could be used with great precision against military targets without risking major destruction or problems of massive radioactive fall-out. Both sides have 'mini-nukes' (equivalent to 50 tons of TNT) mounted on 'smart' bombs or missiles (having a zero-error, they will hit their target exactly). In the NATO Central Sector it is not clear that NATO forces have a convincing shield, since both the Soviet 'back-fire bomber' and the SS-20 missile are deployed and neither was covered by SALT II (although their production was agreed to be confined to thirty a year). Also, it is clear that Warsaw Pact theorists argue that in war all

NATO and the Warsaw Treaty Organisation

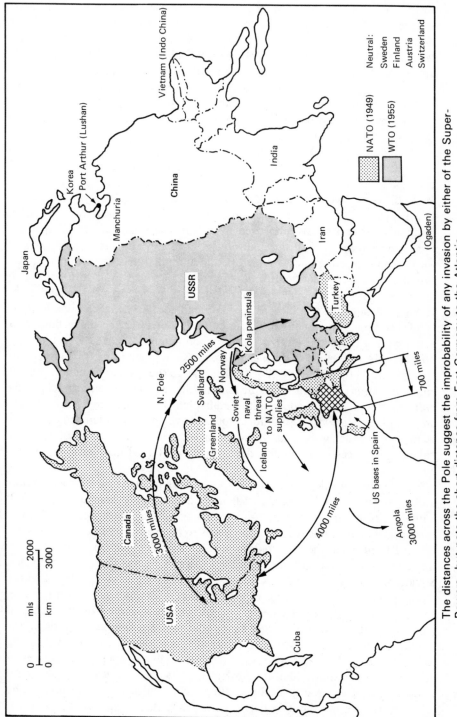

The distances across the Pole suggest the improbability of any invasion by either of the Super-Powers – but note the short distance from East Germany to the Atlantic.

weapons are useable – which casts doubt upon the assumptions of the NATO Triad. By the eighties, it is estimated that NATO would be vulnerable, because its missile bases would be open to pre-emptive tactical nuclear first-strikes—by missiles and low flying aircraft avoiding radar screens—and the Pact has more airfields near to the battle zones than has NATO. But the high cost of these weapons (the Soviet Union has better chemical shells as well) imposes severe strains on the economy and returns planners to conventional forces. The cost of high-technology conventional weapons is also extremely high, and this is a strong factor inducing standardisation of weapons. Ultimately, governments must decide how much may be spent on defence when it must be at the expense of other sectors of the economy.

Much publicity has been given to the considerable advantage in conventional terms held by the Warsaw Pact so far as reported manpower and equipment is concerned. In the autumn of 1979 it was estimated that in the Central Sector 58 WTO divisions faced 28 NATO divisions and that the WTO advantage in tanks was roughly in proportion 2.5:1, in artillery 4:1, and in aircraft 3:2. WTO weaponry has been greatly improved in quality – the Soviet airforce is capable of deep penetration, and is geographically better deployed for attack than NATO forces – and since the mid-seventies, better equipment has been supplied to the support troops in the national armies of the Pact members. But the disparity may not be so great as is popularly presented: Pact army corps tend to be under strength throughout and there is a widespread confidence in the superiority of NATO weapons against superior numbers of troops (though the technological gap is closing rapidly). Thus the heavy preponderance of tanks by Pact forces is offset by NATO defensive missiles. Also, it is contended that NATO forces are more flexible – their training allows fuller play to the '3 Cs' (command, control, communication), through which the local initiative of a field commander can the more readily be accommodated into a main plan. This would give NATO troops an advantage in a combat situation, especially where a main plan had quickly to be modified. Much more than the counting of heads is involved in calculating a balance of forces – though the deployment of Pact forces gives a distinct advantage.

NATO forces are deployed for defence and are stretched from Norway to Italy and across to Turkey. The need to defend the Southern Sector involves some half a million troops and 4300 tanks – forces that could not be moved into Central Europe. Of course, the Soviet Union needs to keep a third of her forces on the Chinese border, but the rest would be available for deployment – and an attack on NATO would depend very much on surprise. It has been calculated that Soviet forces could be increased from an immediate 2:1 advantage to 3:1 within days, and this would enhance prospects of success for any attack. Furthermore, since the principal reinforcements for NATO would come from the USA, it would take at least a week before they could begin to arrive in Europe in any numbers. Thus the likely Warsaw Pact strategy would be for a *Blitzkrieg* aiming to burst through NATO defences and reach the Atlantic ports within a week in order to impede the arrival of the Americans. In such an attack, surprise would be crucial, since any warning time would permit stronger NATO response. The lesson of the Yom Kippur War (1973) was important here, for the Egyptian forces, by effective intelligence deception, were able to keep the defenders guessing until the very last moment. Logistics would be the next problem, and despite difficulties of transport, including a change of railway gauge, Soviet manoeuvres by the Rear Supplies leave no room to doubt their efficiency (witness the 1968 Czechslovakian invasion). Distance and speed of transport of heavy weapons and men may well determine the outcome of World War Three within the first weeks. Against a rapid and successful advance, NATO forces would be in serious difficulties, the more so as her major reserves would be vulnerable to Soviet naval attack (see page 44) as they crossed the Atlantic. For this reason, the USA has established important supply bases in Europe to give immediate short-term support in the form of weapons, machines and ammunitions (more men could come quickly by air) until major reinforcements could arrive. But NATO would not be certain of being able to use French Territory, and therefore its logistic problems would be increased, whilst considerable forces would be locked up in the Southern Sector. The lack of central coordination and the confinement of forces to national commands would prove a further disadvantage.

In any attack, the position of France would be crucial to both sides. NATO could not rule out the possibility of French neutrality in return for a Soviet guarantee of the integrity of her territory; similarly, the Warsaw Pact could not rule out the French use of her nuclear weapons (which would land in West Germany) to defend her territory from intended invasion – even if NATO refrained from using such weapons. Certainly from 1966 to 1975 French defence policy rested on the deterrent value of the certain recourse to tactical nuclear weapons at an early stage. Since 1975, Giscard d'Estaing has modified the policy to lay doubt on the use of the deterrent and to admit the possibility of French troops acting with NATO (but under separate command) in forward positions beyond French frontiers. The nuclear strike force of Britain and France is too small to have any but symbolic importance, but both forces could inflict unacceptable losses on a Soviet *Blitzkrieg* force – and their use could quickly pitch a limited engagement into a nuclear holocaust. In effect, despite public pronouncements, it is unlikely that French nuclear strategy has changed, since it is inconceivable that the weapons would not be used in defence of the country against intended invasion. So far as Warsaw Pact strategy is concerned, a nuclear war would be a distinct possibility at an early stage if the *Blitzkrieg* were checked – since the loss of impetus of advance would give that vital time necessary for NATO to assemble sufficient troops for a counter-attack, and thus the war would have been lost because it had failed within the first week. NATO, for her part, because of the political weight of the prosperous and heavily populated West Germany, is committed to a forward defence policy that (particularly in view of her logistic problems) is militarily untenable.

Current analysis suggests that a Warsaw Pact *Blitzkrieg* would have immediate success, but that it would probably be held at the Rhine (some have argued for an immediate withdrawal to the Rhine, sacrificing West Germany in order to gain the advantages of a major defensive position). Delay at the Rhine would deprive the Pact of victory since, it is argued, the economies and political systems of the West would sustain the strains of a prolonged modern war more

The deployment of Warsaw Pact forces (divisions) in the Central European sector, 1979

	East Germany	Poland	Czechoslovakia	Total
Soviet forces	20	2	5	27
East German	6 (2+4)			6
Polish		13		13
Czech			8	8
				54

The 27 Category One (Soviet) divisions appear to be only 75 per cent manned. The 27 other-member divisions have less-modern equipment, though this disparity is diminishing

Note: Two East German divisions are directly under Soviet command and may well be intended to be held back for the purpose of investing West Berlin.

The balance of forces in Central Europe, 1979

	NATO		Warsaw Pact
Land			
Total soldiers	1	:	1.2
Battle tanks	1	:	2.8
Artillery	1	:	2.7
Tactical aircraft	1	:	2.2
Sea (Eastern Atlantic)			
Surface ships	1	:	1.3
Submarines	1	:	1.5
Tactical aircraft	1	:	1.09

effectively than those of the East. If this position were reached, the problem would simply be whether it would provoke an immediate recourse to strategic nuclear weapons. All this would suggest that an attack on the Central Sector would be unlikely, because the balance of forces and advantage is even. It does not rule out an attack on the periphery (especially the Northern Sector) which may, or may not, be accompanied by a secondary attack on the Central Sector. But any Soviet attempt to increase her power in Europe through intervening in a local incident (in Yugoslavia, for example?) would be unlikely because of the Reykjavik Signal, the severe warning issued by the North Atlantic Council at the time of the 1968 Czecheslovak invasion. (Nevertheless, Soviet military arrangements for Eastern Europe are determined as much by political aims for the area as by the need to match NATO preparedness.)

NATO is committed to the stability of her defensive position; but three major possibilities arise. The first is that the cost of maintaining the existing balance might induce the Euro-Group to accept an accommodation with the Warsaw Pact that would result in the 'finlandisation' of Western Europe (as well as the collapse of NATO) – a position not far removed from the former Soviet proposal for an all-European defence system (excluding USA) in return for dismantling both alliances. So radical a departure from current policy would seem most unlikely. Secondly, that US-Soviet conflicts elsewhere in the world might lead to a conflagration in Europe. Since the Euro-Group (on whose territory such fighting would take place) is more interested in deterring an enemy than in fighting one, it could follow that the USA would fail to carry her allies with her – the French position is clear: 'Europe is unlikely to become a new Vietnam in which the Super Powers can fight wars without risk to themselves'.

The third possibility is more likely – aggression on the Northern Sector (the Southern presents too many logistic and diplomatic complications, as well as the delicate relations between Greece and Turkey; also the Turkish economy is perilously weak and Greece is outside NATO's integrated military structure). An attack on the Northern Sector might be launched either as an independent action, or as the prelude to a massive attack in the Central Sector, once NATO was off-balance. The Northern Sector has a vital rôle to play, not only in defence and as launching areas for missiles, but also as a manoeuvre area for fleets and submarines. A major war could be determined between the Kola Peninsula and the Svalbard Archipelago – it is likely that most of the Soviet nuclear-powered ballistic submarines are on station in the Northern Theatre.

Since the 1960s, the Soviet Union has become a major naval power – Admiral Gorschkov commented that it takes fifteen years to create the global all-purpose Soviet Navy. A Cuban crisis could not have the same result in the later seventies, simply because of the far-flung presence of Soviet sea-power. Already in 1970, the worldwide Soviet naval exercise Okean 1 had demonstrated both her naval capacity and her power to cut NATO sea communications. The 1975 Vesna exercise, simulating attacks on US convoys heading for Europe and including heavy air activity from bases on the Kola Peninsula, demonstrated how NATO Atlantic supplies could be cut. (It is no wonder that the Kola Peninsula is heavily guarded, and that Norway is always extremely careful not to upset Soviet susceptibilities in the area.) The Soviet fleet is well supplied with submarines

Comparison of defence expenditure, 1974–78 (% of Gross National Product)

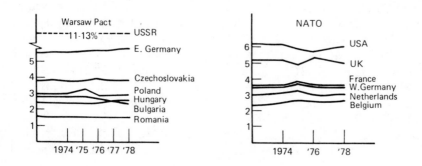

Strategic nuclear forces, 1965–74

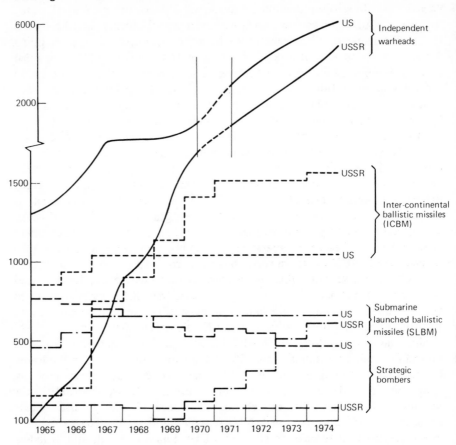

(carrying Submarine Launched Ballistic Missiles (SLBM) and anti-ship missiles probably superior to NATO), support vessels and cruisers. The two ultra-modern Kiev class aircraft carrier cruisers, with both long- and short-range guided missiles and nuclear potential, are stationed off Murmansk (and a giant floating dock, made in West Germany, is there to support them). The fleet is supplemented by a worldwide system of intelligence vessels, and a large merchant marine and fishing fleet. There is also a worldwide system of friendly bases. The naval parity, with its necessary support facilities, has been achieved in a remarkably short time – an object lesson to the West. The global naval presence increases Soviet logistic range: her capacity to handle complex coordinate logistic problems was demonstrated in the later seventies over the intervention in Angola. The old NATO concept of Western Europe as a 'trip-wire' for US defence seems now curiously out of date – and this has implications for the Atlantic and the Arctic as well as for NATO. The capacity of the Soviet Union to offer protection far from its borders is now a reality and Soviet policy choices for the eighties are global in a quite new way – with a flexibility of policy options. At the same time, the naval presence in the Arctic has produced an incredibly accurate survey of the ocean floor, with the potential for exploiting the chemical, geological and biological wealth of the Arctic.

In the Southern Hemisphere, the presence of a Soviet navy is of considerable strategic significance for African politics; and the Soviet capacity for global action was demonstrated by the air-lift during the Angola conflict, and less dramatically during the Ogaden War (1978). During the later seventies, Soviet client states were established in Afghanistan, South Yemen and Ethiopia, and Soviet involvement in Southern Africa, North Yemen and Cambodia points to the global nature of Soviet strategic thinking. It is possible that the West has concentrated too much upon the balance of the Central Sector (another example of the new twilight of Europe, perhaps?). The principal Soviet effort in the late seventies seemed to be concentrated on force reduction agreements (and so on saving money) while maintaining a strategic balance – and acquiring the capacity to make distant force projections. The argument has gone beyond the defence of Europe and NATO. The USA may look more to the Pacific than to Europe in the eighties as a result. But, because global affairs affect Europe directly, the need for continual and comprehensive dialogue between the Soviet Union, the United States and Western Europe remains.

Like the West, the Soviet Union has promoted *détente*, and it is in her interest to maintain it: but secure defence is also necessary. Britain, for example, renewed her Polaris agreement in 1979. But this can only be a short-term policy since the US are phasing out both the Polaris and the Poseidon SLBM, thus depriving Britain of the necessary technical 'back-up' by the nineties. Polaris falls outside of SALT II and was specifically excluded from NATO proposals for arms control (1979) – Britain was clearly adopting the French attitude of defending her own deterrent. She must make preparations now for the preservation of that deterrent in the nineties – such are the demands of defence policy. The two possibilities, the Trident or the C-4 ballistic missile (with a range almost double that of Polaris), would cost some sixty per cent of the entire British defence budget; this would almost certainly involve eliminating some other component of the defence system during the early eighties, the Rhine Army being a likely candidate. Defence costs are so huge that decisions must weigh heavily with all governments – itself a powerful stimulus for disarmament talks.

During the seventies, Western Europe relied upon the US strategic nuclear shield – its own nuclear arsenal, like the French *force de frappe*, being vulnerable to a Soviet first-strike before it became operational. By the late seventies this security had diminished and the idea was widely canvassed that Europe should 'get out from under the US nuclear umbrella'. The Warsaw Treaty Organisation had come to equal, and in certain instances to excel, NATO nuclear defence – and their advantage would remain until the mid-eighties at least (military commentators openly talked of 'the window of opportunity' for the WTO). US defence policy was on the horns of a dilemma. Shortly after retiring as NATO Supreme Commander, General Haigh told a Brussels colloquium (September 1979) that it was unthinkable to abandon the US nuclear guarantee to Europe. 'No American President would survive it', he observed (perhaps with his eye on the Presidential election of 1980). And yet no American President could order massive nuclear retaliation against a limited Soviet aggression.

The answer lay in transferring to Europe an intermediate stage nuclear force (with missiles capable of reaching the Urals, and which were excluded from SALT II). Since NATO nuclear arms were in need of modernisation, the 'window of opportunity' would thus be partly closed. Modernisation proposals were publicised shortly after the two Presidents had signed the SALT II agreement. They involved siting 108 Pershing-11 missiles in West Germany and 464 cruise missiles (having pin-point accuracy and a range to the Urals) to be sited in five NATO countries. All would be under the 'two-key' system, namely under US control, but with the host country being consulted before they were released. The cost of the 572 missiles would be five billion dollars to the US taxpayer, but only five hundred million dollars to NATO allies – merely for constructing the bases. They would fill the gap in the nuclear armoury between theatre and long-range capability and would inflict unacceptable damage on precise targets without necessarily risking an immediate escalation to a nuclear World War Three. In this way NATO could control and limit any theatre nuclear exchange.

Here was a defence policy for the eighties that had many advantages, although the missiles would not be operational before 1983. Yet there was serious division among NATO allies. West Germany accepted the plan, provided the USA retained control of the missiles and actively pursued SALT III. Belgium gave qualified approval, but in December 1979 Holland rejected the proposal to site 48 cruise missiles on her soil. This was a serious reverse for NATO and cast doubts on her unity.

The vigour of the Soviet response to the modernisation programme clearly demonstrated their concern, even though it was assumed that they would have the capability by 1982 to destroy virtually all US land-based missiles at a stroke. There was substance in their complaint that these 'Euro-strategic' weapons circumvented SALT II (although that agreement had allowed Russia to retain her 308 SS-18 missiles each with ten warheads, and to complete the deployment of 140 SS-20 missiles by 1980, which would provide her with just that capability that NATO would only reach in 1983 under the modernisation programme). A propaganda war, even more sharp than that which had been successfully waged against the 'neutron bomb' in 1978, was launched. At a dramatic military parade in East Berlin in October 1979, Brezhnev offered to withdraw some conventional forces and to deploy no more SS-20s (a freezing of the nuclear programme would relieve pressure on the Soviet economy, which had entered a phase of seriously reduced growth, see page 163). Western observers considered the speech must have been decided upon at the highest level, perhaps with the advice of Marshal Ogarkob, and with hopes of inducing the US Senate to approve SALT II (without which SALT III could not begin). A token number of Soviet troops were, indeed, withdrawn from East Germany, leaving Wittenburg on 5 December in a blaze of publicity. In the same month the Warsaw Pact, meeting in East Berlin, put forward a new formula for disarmament and repeated their call of the previous May for an all-European (i.e. without the USA) political conference. There were suggestions on both sides for a nuclear-free Zone in Central Europe. The Soviet Bloc was once more invited to discuss conventional disarmament with NATO at Vienna and more general questions at the projected meeting (Madrid 1980) of the thirty-five nations Conference on Cooperation and Security, the successor to the ill-fated Belgrade conference. But it was clear that the Euro-Group would require a more positive recognition of their interests at any SALT III discussions – if the US would do the negotiating, there would have to be much closer communication with NATO allies than in the previous talks, for if the Soviet Union were to continue to deploy nuclear weapons at the present rate, NATO would be even further behind in 1983, despite the modernisation programme.

There was a further point to consider – if the Soviet Union were capable of a first-strike that would destroy sufficient US nuclear forces and still retain enough for a second strike, then, at the risk of a comparatively small loss (from the few submarine-launched missiles that might penetrate Soviet defences) it might be tempted to destroy the US and so 'gain the world'. Even without risking so dangerous a policy, Soviet nuclear strength is now large enough for them to contemplate an intervention in Latin American affairs, should the occasion arise – there would be no repetition of the Cuban Crisis of 1962. NATO's preoccupation is Europe and the North Atlantic, but this can induce a dangerous myopia: the defence of Europe is no longer a sufficient basis for world security. Events of purely local concern in the Middle East, in Afghanistan, or even in Angola could precipitate World War Three – we have returned with a vengeance to the situation of Sarajevo in 1914!

3

The Creation of the EEC

Reconstruction

In 1945 the allied victors were faced with a trail of destruction that was unsurpassed. Millions of homes had been destroyed and millions more damaged (in Britain as well, although she had not been invaded): of the great capitals, only Paris, Rome, Prague and Brussels had escaped large scale destruction – Berlin 'was like a city of the dead'. Disrupted communications added to the problems – bridges gone, main roads impassable and a shortage of vehicles compounded by a shortage of spare parts and of petrol; the railways were in as bad a state. Food was scarce and the black market flourished; people existed on a calorific intake quite inadequate for manual work. Diaries and press photographs of the time lay great emphasis on the plight of refugees and the civilian population; they shuffled along in tattered clothing, lugging their belongings in home-made carts, waiting at stand-pipes for driblets of brackish water, queuing for potatoes and bread. The victors faced a refugee problem of incredible proportions – over thirty million people had been transported, deported or dispersed and by 1945 some fifteen million awaited transfer back to their homeland, or to new countries if they were Germans or Poles living in the territory east of the Oder-Neisse Line. Europe seemed on the verge of collapse: the loss of life had been great and affected both sexes – it was staggering in the east where Russia lost probably twenty-one million people and Poland more than twenty per cent of her population and Yugoslavia about ten per cent. Industry seemed equally ravaged, and press photographs of bombed and destroyed factories add colour to the tale of woe.

But, while making full allowance for the extent of the destruction and suffering, it is important not to exaggerate it. As the apex of Hitler's New European Order, Germany had done well out of the war until quite late; 'like a gigantic pump, the German Reich sucked in Europe's resources and working population'. Italy seems to have suffered badly; other countries showed a more varied pattern, reflecting the actual battlefields, or the consequence of Nazi exploitation, or of allied reparations. Heavy industrial capacity had increased during the war – a UN Report of 1953 estimated that West and Central Europe's industrial capacity at the end of the war was larger and more suited to its needs than pre-war industry – West Germany, indeed, may have had a greater industrial capacity in 1946 than a decade earlier, a position not substantially altered by reparations and dismantling of installations by the allies (the Russian

Zone was a different story). Yet even in Eastern Europe, where losses were greatest, they did not always exceed the additions that had been made to industrial capacity since 1936. Whatever the appearances, industry in 1945 was not so very ill-placed. Agriculture was in a parlous state, with incredible loss of livestock, agricultural buildings and forests (particularly in Eastern Europe) and of fertility because of the lack of fertilisers in the last years of the war, while in Holland wide acres had been flooded.

On balance, the overall loss of productive assets was much less than is often supposed, although its incidence varied widely, being far heavier in the East. Losses were made good surprisingly quickly and only a few countries continued to suffer major difficulties, though the revival may owe as much to aid recovery programmes as to anything else. Industrial production was very low in 1945, with a shortage of raw materials and spare parts, communications in chaos, and a population generally exhausted and under-nourished. Current shortages were aggravated by world shortages as much as by dislocation of markets and shipping; furthermore, Europe could not pay for essential imports, particularly from dollar areas, the principal source of supply in 1945. Monetary disorder and inflation augmented the difficulties of financing foreign trade. The desperate need for economic aid to establish some element of stability as the new governments struggled to control the situation in the months after the ending of the war in Europe, was incontestable. Here U.N.R.R.A. (United Nations Relief and Rehabilitation Administration) and other organisations did outstanding work, spending some twenty-five billion dollars by 1948 on Relief and Rehabilitation. Without it, many thousands would have died: it was immediate aid to meet an immediate situation, there was no question of it being anything but temporary. In terms of increasing industrial production it may have had only marginal effect and certainly there was neither the time nor the intention to plan the most efficient use of aid for the development of national economies as a whole.

Looming over the desperate problem of reconstructing the economy of Europe were the fears engendered by the possible retirement of the USA into isolationism, as had occurred after the First World War (the prompt ending of Lend-Lease seemed to point in this direction – the resultant gap was made good by loans), and the increasing recognition of the developing rift between East and West. Many voices were raised against the possible return to the protective policies that had restricted the European economy in the inter-war years, but the new governments had to pursue their own interests – even the formation of Benelux was supported as much by the need to stand up to larger trading nations as by the wish to link parallel trading policies. Old attitudes survived, and it was a measure of the extent of the financial crisis that old-style nationalist economies were not promptly restored. The attitude to reparations was itself revealing. The Morgenthau Plan (1944), named after the US Secretary of the Treasury, conceived the draconian idea of industrial disarmament imposed on Germany, transforming her into an agricultural state; it was quickly dropped, and the Western Allies, apart from imposing their armies of occupation, were surprisingly moderate in their policy of removing machinery and cash – one estimate put the value at three hundred million dollars (in contrast to the fifteen to twenty

billion dollars estimated to have been extracted by Soviet Russia from East
Germany, Austria, Hungary and Romania).

A more progressive attitude was abroad; seen, on the national plane, by a
greater willingness than ever before for Western governments to play a directing
rôle in economic planning, with fiscal measures inspired by Keynesian economics,
and extending a direct influence on the economy through nationalising
important sectors of the economy. Internationally, it was to be seen in the
specialist agencies of the United Nations and in the plans to ease world trade and
international payments arising out of the Bretton Woods conference (1944) – the
International Monetary Fund, with its pool of reserves available to members
(not of immediate effect because of the shortage of members' funds, but to
become vital, especially to Britain, in the sixties) and the International Bank of
Reconstruction and Development (World Bank). A further check against the
possible return to pre-war national protective policies with their strangling effect
on world trade was the signing in Geneva (1947) of the General Agreement on
Tariffs and Trade (GATT) by twenty-three nations. The pursuit of lower tariffs
and the substitution of multilateralism for bilateral agreements became a major
factor in the trading policies of the West.

Western Europe staged a remarkable recovery immediately after the war, so
that by 1947 industrial production had surpassed pre-war levels. Agriculture
lagged behind. The severe winter (aggravated by fuel shortages) and poor harvest
of 1947 produced a general crisis that was augmented by inflationary spirals,
over-valued currencies and a seriously weak foreign payments position. Europe's
trade deficit by 1948 exceeded five billion dollars, principally with the USA. It is

Indices of industrial and agricultural production, 1947–51

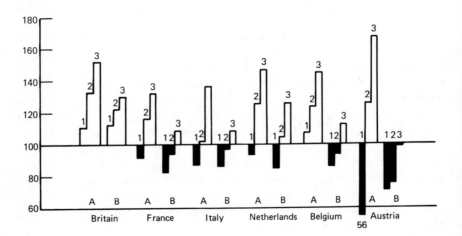

A. Industrial production   (1937/8 = 100)

B. Agricultural production (1934/8 = 100)

1–1947   2–1949   3–1951

easy to see what were the contributory factors to this deficit – the war had shattered normal trade links; traditional markets had been lost for good; an excess of imports over exports arising from the need to import raw materials, food and manufactured goods and machinery to repair war losses; and significantly reduced invisible earnings combined with the liquidation of many foreign assets. Despite all efforts, foreign trade and payments problems put the whole future of the European economy in immediate danger. The effect of this on US trade was a matter of great concern in Washington. President Truman feared Europe's lack of dollars would lead to a serious drop of exports to the USA and to the introduction of high protective tariffs that would induce a revival of economic nationalism and divide the world into trading blocs with 'profound effects upon world politics and the prospects for creating an enduring peace'. An instant solution was to export dollars in the form of aid which would safe-guard the economies of Western Europe and the USA and so strengthen Atlantic links.

The European Recovery Programme

To meet the crisis, the US Secretary of State, George Marshall, produced the Marshall Plan (June 1947) for economic aid to the whole of Europe. The Soviet bloc rejected Marshall Aid as US economic imperialism, and formed Cominform (October 1947) in retaliation. It was ironic that in the previous month the United Nations had established at Geneva the Economic Commission for Europe (ECE) to concert measures for economic reconstruction. Until 1953 the Soviet Bloc offered no realistic cooperation with it.

The US was not disinterested in granting aid. There was some truth in the Soviet assertion that the aid reflected more the US market than Europe's needs, thus only half the 65 000 tractors requested arrived (this would limit agricultural competition), and less than half the rail freight wagons (all earmarked for West Germany) although 65 000 lorries were dispatched. France and Switzerland received 40 000 tons of unsolicited tobacco – which proved a useful black market currency. However, it was a part of the US intention not merely to grant aid, but to promote a degree of close cooperation (if not integration) within Europe to further economic recovery. In April 1948 the Organisation for European Economic Cooperation (OEEC) was created as an agency to administer the European Recovery Programme (ERP), as Marshall Aid was now called. At this stage the French favoured a supra-national authority with a degree of control over national economies (ten years later their views had changed). The British did not support this view and the opportunity to create an effective organisation to direct national economies on major issues, and to advance towards a customs union was lost. Jean Monnet put the point in a letter to Bidault:

> only the establishment of a *federation* of the West, including Britain, will enable us to solve our problems quickly enough, and finally prevent war.

OEEC was controlled by a Council of Ministers, drawn from each of the member states, in which decisions were taken on a basis of unanimity – any member had

The membership of various European organisations

	OEEC OECD	Council of Europe	NATO	ECSC	WEU	EEC	EURATOM	Nordic Council	Balkan Alliance	EFTA	Rhine Commission	European Ministers of Transport
Belgium	█	█	█	█	█	█	█				█	█
Netherlands	█	█	█	█	█	█	█				█	█
Luxembourg	█	█	█	█	█	█	█					█
Italy	█	█	█	█	█	█	█					█
France	█	█	█	█	█	█	█				█	█
W. Germany	█	█	█	█	█	█	█				█	█
Britain	█	█	█	█	█	█	█				█	█
Eire	█	█		█		█	█					█
Denmark	█	█	█	█		█	█	█				█
Norway	█	█	█					█		█		█
Sweden	█	█						█		█		█
Iceland	█	█	█					█		█		█
Austria	█	█								█		█
Switzerland	█									█	█	█
Portugal	█	█	█			○				█		█
Greece	█	●	█			█			█			█
Turkey	█	█	█						█			█
Finland	█							█		Associate		
Spain	█					○						█
Yugoslavia	Observer 1952								█			

● Suspended 1969-74   ○ = Membership actively sought (1980) an effective veto. As with the Council of Europe (1948), despite idealist hopes, this was not the moment for the European federalists. Any commitment beyond basic cooperation between sovereign states lay in the future.

The achievements of the OEEC were considerable, both in furthering a liberalising of trade, reducing tariff barriers and quota arrangements and in promoting organisations to strengthen the infrastructure of the European economy. Chief amongst these was the European Payments Union (EPU), 1950, to facilitate multilateral trade through a multilateral system of payments with creditor finance to promote intra-European trade (it was superseded in 1958 by the European Monetary Agreement, EMA). In 1953 a European Productivity Agency was formed to facilitate the exchange of technical information and new technology; a European Nuclear Energy Agency was created (1957) at a time when there was great confidence in the future peaceful uses of nuclear energy (the costs involved had not at that time been understood) and in the event it was no more successful than EURATOM. There was an attempt to coordinate a transport policy through a Permanent Conference of Ministers of Transport (1953) and a special company, Eurofima (1956) was formed, following the establishment of a Europool wagon pooling agreement, to finance the construction and provision of rolling stock for railways, so that loads could move over long distances without the wagons having to be returned after each journey to the country of origin. But the active rôle of the OEEC was circumscribed by lack of powers, so that it became little more than a body to supply information and publish reports. In 1961 it was enlarged to include the USA and other countries, and its name was changed to Organisation for Economic Cooperation and Development (OECD) with a much broader rôle, looking beyond immediate European problems.

There were other organisations to promote closer cooperation, like the regional groupings such as the Nordic Council (1952) created for consultation between member parliaments and governments, and the Balkan Alliance (1955) balancing it in south east Europe. But agencies for consultation and cooperation, however effective as pressure groups, do not really affect national sovereignty and have not proved to be dynamic institutions establishing a new community of nations. Something more radical was needed if Europe was to move away from old ideas of national rivalry and restrictive trade policies, and its countries were to accept a closer union: as Monnet put it, 'national sovereignty would have to be tackled more boldly and on a narrower front'.

The European Coal and Steel Community

In 1950, France was still prepared to argue in federalist terms for a supranational authority to provide for the unity of Europe. Some have represented the Coal and Steel Community as a limited compromise between the poles of federalist views and the ideas of those pragmatic functionalists who were prepared, at least temporarily, to accept an organisation to direct whatever common action was most urgently needed. But the Schuman Plan had much deeper roots and was of far greater significance than a mere political arrangement. Its roots lay only partly in the wish to take a political 'first step in the federation of Europe'; its roots also lay in *Erbfeindschaft*, the traditional enmity between France and Germany and the fear of German militarism; and there was also the fear of the potential industrial power of the Ruhr that France had failed to secure after the war.

By 1950, the hostility and potential hysteria that underlay Franco-German relations was beginning to be softened by a realisation of the magnitude of the German tragedy. In addition, however much Frenchmen might dislike Germans, they seemed less dislikeable than the Russians. But this provided no satisfactory basis for a Franco-German reconciliation, upon which the future stability of Europe (and so, perhaps, the world?) appeared to the men of the forties to rest. The relative speed of recovery in the Ruhr also prompted many disturbing thoughts. An *entente* with Soviet Russia over the German Question in particular was not practical politics, and the expanding Ruhr steel production (vital after June 1950 to meet new demands arising from the Korean War) threatened to consume the coking coal upon which French steel production, the key to the French Economic Plan, depended. French attitudes were veering towards the traditional hatred of the '*sales boches*': five years after V. E. Day, men were seriously discussing a fresh Franco-German conflict. For Monnet, the vital consideration was to maintain imports of essential German coal and coke and to prevent disputes over the Saar (still French administered) from disrupting relations. Adenauer, the new German Chancellor, however, had declared himself willing to accept the principle of an authority for supervising the mining and industrial areas of West Germany, France and Benelux, and, indeed, to accept any appropriate means of bringing France and Germany closer together, despite public hostility at any suggestion of reconciliation. The solution was to put French and German coal and steel under the same supra-national authority. It would provide France with a steady supply of German coal at favourable terms, reduce wasteful rivalry and provide an opportunity for both rationalisation and diversification in declining mining areas, especially in north east France and Belgium. It would make it difficult for either country to go to war on the other, since coal and steel were essential to a war economy, and both would be under a supra-national authority (it might also help in the ultimate solution to the Saarland problem, since if it were to be returned to German administration, the French would find this more acceptable if the Saar steel were under the same supra-national authority). It was an elegant solution, worked out (but not originated) by Monnet and his aides, Pierre Uri, Paul Reuter and Jacques Gescaul. Enlarged to include Italy and Benelux, it was launched as the Schuman Plan by the French Foreign Minister, Robert Schuman. The draft of the French declaration (May 1950) put the position succinctly:

> Europe must be organised on a federal basis. A Franco-German union is an essential element in it. . . . The French government proposes to place the whole of Franco-German coal and steel production under an international Authority open to the participation of Europe.
> By the pooling of basic production and the establishment of a new High Authority whose decisions will be binding on France, Germany and the countries that join them, this proposal will lay the first concrete foundations

of the European Federation which is indispensable to the maintenance of peace.

Here was a heady mixture of idealism and political realism – the more so as already at this stage was appearing the criticism among West Germans that the whole scheme was a clever French plot to shift German resources into France.

The negotiations were far from easy and the fundamental proposition of the High Authority with supra-national powers was accepted only after both a Council of Ministers drawn from member countries and an Assembly had been agreed upon as checks on its powers. But the High Authority derived its specific powers over particular areas of members' economies from the Treaty, not from these constitutional checks. Monnet put the point: 'we will not build another coalition of governments, we shall unite human beings'. France and Germany would delegate a part of their sovereignty to the Authority and submit to inter-related and reciprocal control over a sensitive area of economic policy. Great efforts were made to draw in Britain, but to no avail (although in 1954 she signed an Agreement of Association). Britain might be excused for her reluctance to be associated in such a new endeavour in 1950 – her coal and steel stood in no need of continental help (indeed, there were fears expressed that the Plan would involve Britain subsidising inefficient continental plant), and her interests at that time were certainly more linked to the Commonwealth and the USA than to Europe. Both major political parties rejected the Plan for the same reasons. Clement Attlee told the House of Commons:

> We on this side are not prepared to accept the principle that the most vital economic forces of this country should be handed over to an authority that is utterly undemocratic and is responsible to nobody.

And at the Council of Europe meeting in Strasbourg in August 1950, Harold Macmillan made the same point more bluntly:

> We will allow no supra-national authority to put large masses of our people out of work in Durham, in the Midlands, in South Wales and in Scotland.

On 18 April 1951, the European Coal and Steel Community Treaty was signed in Paris by the six members, France, West Germany, Italy and Benelux. It was to have a High Authority, with Monnet as its first President, responsible to a Common Assembly; a Council of Ministers drawn from member governments (Benelux insisted on this); and a Court of Law to interpret and enforce the decisions of the High Authority in terms of the Treaty. (These were basically the same institutions as the European Economic Community (1956) was to have, save that the latter was to have its Commission responsible to the Council – a crucial difference.) For all that it was limited to the two basic inter-related industries, the new Community was perhaps a bigger step towards a federal solution to European unity than the Common Market. Adenauer, addressing the first meeting of the Council of Ministers, caught the atmosphere of the moment:

The Council stands at the crossroads of two kinds of sovereignty, national and supra-national. While it must safeguard the national interests of member states, it must not regard this as its paramount task. Its paramount task is to promote the interests of the Community; and, unless it does so, the Community will not develop.

Six years later a greater Union was established: but the EEC was to have a very different atmosphere.

Until its merger with the European Commission in 1967, the High Authority of the European Coal and Steel Community had some achievements to its credit. It established for the two industries a reasonable basis of competition, removing non-tariff barriers (NTBs) to free trade, especially government subsidies and quotas. It directly managed the coal and steel works of the Community (although they retained their separate existence). Help in retraining and rehousing was given to workers affected by the general run-down of the older mines and plant. It was less successful in removing restrictive practices like transport subsidies (notably on rail freight where discriminatory rates were common), and even when backed by the Court of Justice it could not break the government-backed cartels for selling coal, or prevent France re-asserting price control over steel in contravention of the Treaty. Competition from oil (until the altered circumstances of the 1970s) soon revealed the inadequacy of restricting supranational economic planning to two groups of products, however fundamental to industrial economies – and common policies have not always been adopted. There have been difficulties developing a common fuel policy, and the need to obtain the agreement of member countries before carrying out a policy decision has circumscribed even its work to relieve problems arising in areas of declining industry. In brief, the High Authority demonstrated that supra-nationalism (especially when subject to budgetary limitations) was dependent on the consent and cooperation of member governments; and from this experience it looked as though the federalists would lose out to the functionalists in any future extension of European unity, simply because of the political nature of administrative machinery. The national state, seemingly outmoded and disapproved of in 1945, was showing an astonishing virility and fast returning to respectability.

The European Economic Community

The federalists were deceived in supposing that the 1950s would see a great leap forward towards European unity: a further growth in institutions providing for detailed cooperation was no substitute for political unity. It is not enough to establish an institution: what matters is what that institution can and will do.

Economic policy does not exist in a vacuum and the movement of international relations can have more importance than that of trade figures. When the North Korean invasion of South Korea in June 1950 provoked the Korean War there were immediate effects on world trade and prices; more specifically, the problem of the defence of Western Europe assumed a new dimension. What would happen if US forces in Europe were withdrawn to no more than token level in order to meet the needs of the Korean War? There were very genuine fears of this and the demand for a significantly increased contribution to European defence from European forces became a common theme in the speeches of US politicians. To meet this demand, the French Prime Minister, René Pléven, put forward (October 1950) a plan for a European army, in which there would be a West German contingent. This involved rearming West Germany, and that it should be suggested within five years of the Nazi defeat provoked much opposition. There was some opposition within West Germany, and Adenauer rejected the idea of a revived *Wehrmacht*; a German contingent within a European army under a common European command was much more acceptable, however. Britain rejected the proposal since it would mean loss of control over those forces committed to the new European army, and would put a further strain upon her already heavily committed forces within the Commonwealth; it would also damage further diplomatic relations with Soviet Russia, since the European Army could only be understood in anti-Russian terms. France also had imperial commitments – she was fighting a major guerrilla war in Indo-China (Vietnam) – but nevertheless pushed forward negotiations for a European Defence Community (EDC) which would have institutions closely parallel to those of ECSC. The Six signed a provisional treaty in May 1952.

Pooling military capabilities inevitably reduced the opportunities for independent foreign policies and opened the possibility of democratic control over the proposed European Army. In order to promote an effective European Political Community (EPC), the Dutch proposed a juncture of the existing ECSC institutions with those of the new EDC, together with a directly elected European Parliament. From this it was hoped that political unity would follow, and that the limited economic integration achieved with coal and steel would be extended to a general common market based on the free movement of goods and the factors of production.

Five national parliaments approved the scheme, but the French, in 1950 the active patrons of supra-nationalism, now in 1954 rejected the Treaty and thus both EDC and EPC were killed. Many and confused reasons lay behind the French rejection: German rearmament was a very emotive subject with which people did not find it easy to become reconciled. In the event, the prospect of placing a French army under non-French control proved too strong a barrier, and the absence of British agreement played its part. It was a lesson for the federalists. Britain now took the initiative, operating in the more familiar territory of cooperation between nations. The Brussels Treaty Organisation (1948, see page 25) included 'economic, social, cultural collaboration, and collective self-defence'; in agreement with the USA and Canada, Britain proposed to extend it to include West Germany and Italy, and to provide for West German rearmament and her admission into NATO. This was the basis of the new inter-governmental organisation, Western European Union (WEU, 1954) – it met the immediate needs of rearming West Germany (by this time a political necessity to satisfy the USA over Western European contributions to defence) and satisfied the French over British military participation as a guarantee against future German predominance. *Erbfeindschaft* survived: the

The developing EEC

108 other countries are associated with the EEC under the Lomé Convention, the Maghreb and Machrak Agreements and other generalised preferences.

memory of three big wars within eighty years was not easily washed away. (The Soviet response was to form the Warsaw Treaty Organisation, see page 28). There was no intention of creating a new supra-national organisation, although, in effect, this could arise out of the inter-governmental cooperation resulting from the treaty – but the Assembly of the WEU remained purely and solidly consultative.

In 1954 the hopes of federalists for a New Europe had been dashed against the rocks of political pragmatism and national consciousness. Recognising that political union was so difficult to achieve, a new initiative was launched by Benelux aiming to substitute the more simple economic integration as a first step. These proposals called for the creation of institutions for a European Economic Community with a common external tariff (CET). It was discussed and adopted at a conference of the foreign ministers of the Six (Britain sent junior representatives only) in Messina (June 1955), and an inter-governmental committee under Paul-Henri Spaak was commissioned to work out the details. Britain played an active part in the discussions, and major differences soon emerged, principally over the nature of the proposed community. Britain's chief negotiator, Reginald Maudling, put forward the Maudling Plan for a loose free trade area (working perhaps through a strengthened OEEC): the Six, as the Messina Resolution had outlined, agreed on a customs union with supra-national institutions capable of achieving more than mere economic integration. By November 1955, Britain had withdrawn from the negotiations, but the Spaak Committee persisted and its Report (April 1956) formed the basis of the Treaties signed at Rome on 25 March 1957.

Many played their part in the extended negotiations, and Monnet was among the leaders. He resigned as President of the High Authority of the ECSC in order to have 'complete freedom of action and speech in the achievement of European unity, which must be practical and real'. He formed the Action Committee for the United States of Europe, the *Relance*, which reputedly had considerable influence on the Spaak committee.

The negotiations were long and difficult and there were clear differences between France and the other five over the nature of the common tariff (France being protectionist hitherto) and the timetable for arriving at it. The French suggestion that members might withdraw was rejected in return for other concessions, the union being declared indissoluble. Atomic energy proved a major factor in the negotiations. The French seemed keener on establishing an agency for producing atomic energy for peaceful purposes than on the economic community: many saw atomic energy as the great energy source of the future (and some, particularly the French, hoped for a bonus in terms of atomic weapons so that an independence of US defence and foreign policy might be asserted). The French Prime Minister of the day, Mollet, urged the creation of EURATOM as a means of gaining the atomic bomb and so controlling Germany by working jointly with her – it could expedite an independent weapons programme. Monnet, on the other hand, saw atomic energy as an integrating force because the cost of producing the energy would be greater than one country among the Six could afford. It would appear that Monnet's pressure group, Action for Europe, grossly over-rated the importance of nuclear energy at the time in order to get the French Assembly to agree to EURATOM and so to the EEC – oddly enough, the future importance of oil and the consequent dependence on Middle East politics was not mentioned by the *Relance*. Two international events in 1956 had a great impact on the negotiations: the Soviet crushing of Hungary and the collapse of the Anglo-French intervention in Suez. Both events underlined the point that much more than tariffs were involved in the discussions.

It was a sensible proposition to continue the ECSC model, since this was the only European institution to which the parliaments of member nations 'had agreed to transfer sovereignty and delegate powers of decision'. The methods of the Schuman Plan were an additional spur to the French, who wished to join the race for nuclear weapons – the more so as these were specifically forbidden to the West Germans. Louis Armand chose the name EURATOM for an atomic community on the ECSC model.

The signing of the Rome Treaties was a great moment for the growth of Western European unity, and the rejoicing that greeted it was amply justified. But the rejoicing concealed two major points – the extent to which the solutions represented by the Treaties were necessary compromises made between national governments rather than 'European Community' solutions, and the curious anomaly of there now being three distinct community organisations, popularly lumped together under the single title EEC or Common Market. The ECSC had its headquarters in Luxembourg with a definite potential for supra-national action; the EURATOM and EEC were centred on Brussels, established in the shadow of the failure of the EDC proposals, on a less ambitious scale, since in their case the High Authority was reduced to a Commission under a Council of Ministers who had the powers of decision. The Assembly (it assumed the title European Parliament in 1962) had a positive dialogue with the Executive, but extremely limited powers and it was more than twenty years before it was directly elected. Nevertheless, the Rome Treaties remain an object lesson in political realism – and there was abundant room for growth; as Professor Hallstein put it, 'We are not integrating economies, we are integrating politics. We are not just sharing our furniture, we are jointly building a new and bigger house'.

The creation of the EEC coincided with a considerable increase in members' trade, wealth and standard of living. It was a time when mounting affluence became a unique feature of the post-war economy, and this helped the EEC to gain popular acceptance among member nations, and, since EEC growth rate was greater than that of others, to encourage opinion in other nations to consider the advantages of joining the Community.

All governments in Western Europe after the war played a greater part in the conduct of the national economy than had been the case formerly. Changes in economic thinking and the improvements in statistical reporting (particularly as computers began to have an effect in the sixties) helped this tendency. Trade expanded, aided by the lowering of tariffs through the activity of OEEC and GATT, culminating in what was called the Kennedy Round of tariff reductions. Throughout Western Europe, Gross National Products (GNPs) showed a steady growth: the British was sluggish in comparison with that of other European countries, but better than most of the previous decades of the century.

Exports, with a big gain in intra-European trade, played a great part in the prosperity, encouraging a high rate of domestic investment – though it was lower in Britain and this helped to reduce British competitiveness in the long run (by the sixties people were arguing that Britain should join the EEC as a means of restoring her competitiveness through the shock of competition). Inflation, rampant in the forties, returned in the sixties and was partly responsible for a succession of financial crises that plagued Britain, but weakness in the balance of payments was the most obvious factor. The IMF, passive in the fifties because of lack of reserve funds, became active in the sixties and the Special Drawing Rights (1969) helped sterling out of serious difficulties. By the seventies the prosperity was under pressure and the decade saw a severe world recession, connected with the steep increase in oil prices. European Monetary Union (see page 84), frequently advanced as an additional means of effecting closer union, became more seriously promoted as the recession deepened but in the prosperous days of the Community it had not made great progress.

Under the Treaty of Rome, tariffs between member nations were to be reduced until phased out according to a set schedule. Reductions frequently occurred ahead of schedule and the CET was established (later to be reduced along with the world reductions in tariffs). The Common Agricultural Policy (CAP) was finally agreed in detail by the sixties (a significant feature of the growing prosperity was a big reduction in the agricultural labour force and a corresponding increase in tertiary industrial employment). By the late sixties the Community was recognised as an evident success (not so EURATOM). But the success was on the economic plane – and may have owed much to favourable world conditions – whilst on the political front it was a different story. There were numerous political problems arising out of the relationship between the Commission and the Council of Ministers (which proved to be defenders of national interests). Under the Presidency of Professor Hallstein, the Commission tended to take considerable initiative, and the future consequences of this for member states caused some concern, particularly from the French. When the Algerian Revolt destroyed the Fourth Republic and de Gaulle was elected President of the Fifth Republic, France rapidly assumed the rôle of defender of national interests against supra-nationalism. De Gaulle's idea was a *Europe des patries*, an association of national states – it was an interpretation of the Community that stood in the way of close unity or supra-nationalism. 'There can be no Europe other than the "Europe of the States" – except, of course, for myths, fictions and pageants', de Gaulle had announced to a news conference in 1962. The signing of a Franco-West German Treaty of Cooperation in 1963 was treated by some as a triumph of reconciliation; others saw it as an assertion of outworn nationalism, inappropriate to the New Europe, and undermining unity by harping back to the past and by demonstrating a preference for exclusive political alliances.

The issue between the federalist policies of the Hallstein Commission and the nationalist stance taken by France was joined over the Hollstein Plan (1956) to gain an independent Community Budget under the control of the European Parliament (thus increasing the authority of the Parliament and strengthening the Commission). France, who was also dissatisfied over the financial arrangements for the CAP, forced a constitutional crisis by boycotting the Commission. Time was short, for 1 January 1966 was fixed as the moment for ending the unanimity rule: thereafter decisions would be taken by weighted majority vote. But the other five members stood firm. The dispute was resolved by what has been called the 'Luxembourg Compromise' (1966) – arrived at by the Council of Ministers meeting in private without the Commission being represented – by which the Council agreed not to abolish unanimity voting entirely. When a member state pleaded special national interests of over-riding importance, then unanimity would have to be adopted: this was equivalent to blocking integration with governmental cooperation. In effect, a veto was retained at France's insistence. Hallstein resigned to become an outspoken president of the European Movement. The Community survived the crisis, though visibly shaken. However, by July 1968 all internal customs duties and quantitative restrictions had been removed and the CET established nearly eighteen months ahead of schedule, and the three separate Communities were merged into one single Community with common institutions.

Britain and the EEC

Britain's attitude to the idea of the Common Market was not hostile. She approved efforts to liberalise tariffs and reduce barriers to trade, but was not prepared to commit herself to closer association than was typical of the OEEC: cooperation, not integration. She had interests elsewhere and in a famous speech at Llandudno (1948) Churchill had put the point in picturesque phrases by speaking of three interlocking circles of interests: the English-speaking world (primarily Britain and North America), the Commonwealth, and a united Europe. (But in that united Europe Britain was not expected to be numbered.) She continued to regard herself as having world interests that would preclude her joining too closely with Europe – particularly she asserted a special relationship with the USA. Anthony Eden put the point well in 1952:

> We know that if we were to attempt (to join a European federation), we should relax those springs of our action in the Western democratic cause and in the Atlantic association which is the expression of that cause . . . we should be no more than some millions of people living on an island off the coast of Europe, in which nobody wants to take any particular interest.

But with the creation of the EEC, Britain began intensive study through the OEEC of the prospect for a free trade area to include the Six (lest the CET exclude too much British trade). In the fifties and early sixties, of course, the EEC was still more of a customs union than an economic community. Complex negotiations were not helped by the suspicion of Britain's intentions among other European nations: it was widely assumed that the negotiations were intended to torpedo the EEC on the grounds that a free trade area would give many of the initial trading advantages without the need for closer association. Also, Britain excluded agricultural products from negotiations, so that her Commonwealth preference systems should not be upset and her cheap food policy be

British trade by area, 1948–67 ($m monthly averages)

	Exports					Imports				
	EEC	EFTA	OStgA	USA	World		EEC	EFTA	OStgA	USA	World
1948	61	59	264	22	530	1948	63	46	253	63	698
1949	58	58	281	17	540	1949	78	56	258	67	686
1950	65	60	242	27	507	1950	77	35	232	49	610
1951	72	68	306	32	603	1951	120	82	326	89	898
1952	77	64	297	34	603	1952	100	75	335	73	800
1953	89	69	293	37	603	1953	81	77	351	59	769
1954	91	72	310	35	624	1954	91	78	349	66	776
1955	99	73	334	43	678	1955	112	95	366	96	893
1956	112	80	338	57	740	1956	115	90	354	95	774
1957	118	82	350	57	776	1957	115	93	362	113	827
1958	108	77	310	69	783	1958	125	86	295	82	882
1959	119	84	290	89	806	1959	131	92	312	87	931
1960	131	92	309	80	858	1960	155	109	324	132	1063
1961	155	104	299	70	896	1961	158	108	308	113	1026
1962	182	111	284	82	922	1962	165	108	316	111	1048
1963	208	121	306	85	988	1963	180	118	353	117	1125
1964	225	134	322	100	1065	1964	220	147	396	152	1329
1965	229	143	345	121	1143	1965	232	156	381	157	1345
1966	243	160	375	152	1122	1966	258	168	420	169	1389
1967	237	163	352	146	1198	1967	290	186	408	185	1476

OStgA = Overseas Sterling Area (Commonwealth).

EEC trade almost quadrupled in this period, but Sterling Area trade grew very slowly (even though it accounted for a high proportion of British trade). Again, this was interpreted as an argument for Britain's entry into the EEC. The trend shown here continued in the 1970s.

endangered – against this the Six regarded their CAP as vital. Negotiations failed, but it proved possible to create a second trading bloc, the European Free Trade Association (1960), an arrangement that imposed few conditions and permitted Britain to retain her Commonwealth preferences.

Already, however, Britain had begun to re-appraise her position. The Suez episode (1956) had revealed brutally her incapacity for playing the rôle of a world power. More than this, Britain failed to maintain a properly independent military deterrent after Blue Streak (1960), and with the failure of Skybolt (1962) because of its escalating cost Britain fell back upon the use of US Polaris submarines, thus committing Britain to US defence policy. President Kennedy made clear his wish that Britain should join Europe: that 'special relationship' with the USA was fast passing away.

It was ironic that de Gaulle should veto Britain's first application for membership of the EEC (1962) on the grounds that her Commonwealth interests and her relationship with an Atlantic Community indicated that she was not yet prepared to become sufficiently European to qualify for admission. In addition, a serious sterling crisis (1961) shattered the ill-founded confidence of British prosperity and underlined Britain's sluggish performance in contrast with that of the EEC (significantly enough, the government adopted some of the French

Comparative growth, Britain and the EEC 1958–66

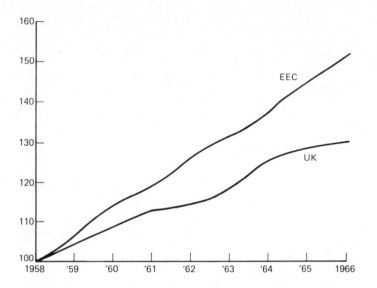

Britain's performance was sluggish (if better than during most of the decades of the century): the EEC was expanding more rapidly. The case for Britain joining the EEC, on the basis of the latter's prosperity, grew stronger as the decade advanced.

methods of indicative planning, for example the National Economic Development Council, 1962). Finally, the overseas sterling area was falling significantly in terms of Britain's overall trade. In 1950 it accounted for 48 per cent of total trade, by 1960 it had dropped to 30 per cent and 27 per cent by 1970. It no longer afforded the same preferential advantages, moreover, as new Commonwealth countries gained their independence and the traditional Commonwealth links became weaker.

Two of Churchill's interlocking circles had ceased to be of major importance: this itself was a sound reason to seek membership of the EEC, albeit from a position of weakness, and the evident prosperity of the EEC provided a significant inducement. The major obstacles were Britain's farming policy that did not coincide with CAP, Britain's declining Commonwealth preference, and the critical point of supra-nationalism (when Britain eventually joined the EEC in January 1972 she had to accept 42 volumes of Common Market law which appeared to diminish the authority of Westminster).

The negotiations following Britain's first application for membership were extremely detailed and quite failed to capture the popular interest. De Gaulle's veto (a common interpretation is that he feared Britain would reduce French influence in the Community and might open the door to US influence, too) did not diminish the political significance of the bid for admission and it remained a live issue, especially among those who sought British membership in order that the Community might wield a greater influence in world affairs. A second application was announced in 1966, but negotiations were overtaken by another severe sterling crisis which was widely interpreted as showing basic weaknesses in Britain's economy. But for the second time de Gaulle effectively vetoed the application (1967) although it caused sharp resentment within the EEC. It was presumed that France would not agree to enlargement of the Community until the CAP financial arrangements were complete.

The serious strikes and 'non-revolution' of 1968 and de Gaulle's resignation in the following year opened the way to British membership, and negotiations were opened after the Hague Summit meeting of Heads of Government of the EEC in December 1969. Britain joined in 1972, but a new Government in Britain insisted on re-negotiation, particularly over Economic and Monetary Union, CAP and the Community Budget, and the following year a referendum was held in Britain to determine popular acceptance of the new terms of entry (which still included acceptance of CAP). Denmark and Eire also joined in 1972, making the Six into Nine. Norway joined, but after a referendum which rejected membership, withdrew – the referendum campaign proved very sharp and raised heated passion. This was not the case in Britain, where the referendum scarcely ruffled the political surface. It was by no means the constitutional innovation that its opponents claimed and it produced a clear, if unenthusiastic 'Yes' by an almost two-to-one majority. It occurred at a time of gathering monetary crisis of world proportions arising out of the Yom Kippur War. Britain's industrial perform-ance fell back further whilst her rate of inflation shot ahead – no doubt this had a bearing on the result. It was not a vote for any radical new departure but for a newly established *status quo*: as Sir Christopher Soames put it, 'This is no time for Britain to consider leaving a Christmas Club let alone the Common Market'. An immediate result of British accession was that the Free Trade agreements with the surviving non-member EFTA countries were continued, effecting something not unlike the Maudling Plan (1956) free trade area scheme. This seemed more feasible to the original Six in the seventies, because of enlargement and because economic integration had advanced among them – the Kennedy Round of tariff cuts had made their impact, too, for tariffs were lower.

The other alternatives open to Britain were to secure a free trade agreement comparable with those negotiated by the surviving EFTA countries who did not join, or to adopt a 'siege economy' with complete control over tariffs but without free trade agreements: this would have been possible but would have involved considerable changes in import patterns and might have had incalculable effects on the British balance of payments and the strength of sterling. Wisely, the opponents of the Market sought to maximise the 'No' vote rather than to enter into intricate argument about the merits of these two rival possibilities.

The 1970s

The prosperity of the sixties was followed by a world recession aggravated by continual increases in crude oil prices. It was a decade of stress for the newly enlarged Community, and it was notable that the EEC did not respond with a European solution, but rather each member sought individual means of reaching economic stability. The attempt to launch European Monetary Union in 1979 (see page 84) did not end economic uncertainties, indeed, its introduction appeared as much a political act, to instil vitality into the Community's flagging morale, as an economic measure to facilitate intra-European trade and finance.

On the political front, a number of constitutional issues have been raised, indicating signs of stress, as well as institutional advance. Efforts to improve political cohesion have not always been successful, and there have been signs of concern at the lack of progress in building a Community awareness. At the beginning of the decade, the Davignon Report (1970) recommended regular exchanges between Community officials and ministers of the six member countries to strengthen solidarity by promoting harmonization and coordination. Six-monthly colloquies between ministers and members of the Political Affairs Committee of the European Parliament were also advocated. The feeling of lack of progress led to the Tindemans Report (1976) on European Union; but

The Gross Domestic Product of the EEC (average) and some of its members, 1960–77 (1970 = 100)

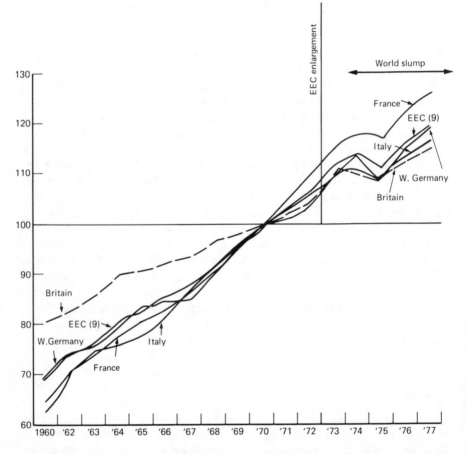

Taking GDP as a measure of prosperity, Britain failed to increase in prosperity at the same rate as the EEC during the 1960s, but kept in line with the EEC average in the 1970s. The onset of the world slump, together with a serious sterling crisis, makes comparisons between the two decades far from easy.

it was somewhat overshadowed by the mounting difficulties of the energy crisis. Its call for a single decision-making centre to strengthen the political side of the Community did not meet with a response. Meanwhile, the European Parliament, as it approached the end of its days as a delegate assembly of national parliaments, became progressively more vigorous in pressing its demands for greater political powers: disputes over control of the Budget and the Regional Fund led the Council of Ministers to compromise with the Parliament. The new European Parliament, now directly elected and capable of speaking with a more weighty voice than its predecessor, would have to assert itself if it were to gain any additional powers: and if it does not do so, the value of its existence might be called in question. 1979 saw the first European direct elections: a moment of great significance for federalists in particular, and for the Community in general. The early sessions of the new Parliament gave no impression of vigour or a determination to enlarge its influence, but by the end of 1979 it had begun to assert itself strongly (see page 79).

The seventies, on both economic and political fronts, were not happy years for the Community: indeed, the most successful development was one that strengthened national governments. This was the increased importance attached to the occasional meetings of Heads of States from the Community: a new feature of 'summitry' appeared that challenged the Council of Ministers in terms of political influence within the Community. In 1975, Monnet commented:

> We were wrong in 1952 to think that Europe would be built with the High Authority of the Coal and Steel Community as a supra-national government. What matters now is that the Heads of national governments meet together regularly in the European Council. That's where the authority is. It's a very big change.

It is a change that does not aid the cause of federalists, but rather the supporters of de Gaulle's '*Europe des patries*'. Heads of States may commit their governments more effectively than even senior ministers in the Council of Ministers: they may not be provided for within the Treaty of Rome, but their political power could serve as a powerful counterweight to any Community policy with which they disagreed. The uncertainty of the position is illustrated by the occasional incidents at their formal meetings, when the President of the Commission is clearly treated not as a Head of State, but rather as a functionary: such public wrangling over precedence speaks volumes as to the political situation. The change appeared most notably at the Hague Summit of 1969, which agreed, among other things, to consider the British application for membership, and also to embrace, not later than 1980, the idea of Economic and Monetary Union. That these were matters for the Council of Ministers did not alter the position. The 1972 Paris Summit underlined this monetary goal (although initial efforts in the mid-seventies failed) and recognised the need for a Regional Development Fund, and for a new initiative on social and industrial matters. It was not that Heads of State should not discuss and decide about such matters, since they directly concerned their countries; the question was simply that their action overshadowed the Council of Ministers, by-passed the Commission and left small room for the Parliament. At the 1974 Paris Summit, it was agreed that Heads of State might meet formally up to three times a year, and where necessary might meet with the Council of Ministers. They assumed the title European Council and their meetings were institutionalised – occasionally they meet in private session without officials and administrative staff. The European Council is a development of considerable importance to the future of the Community and of the balance of power within it.

4

The Institutions of the EEC

Prosperous years of expanding trade followed the launching of the EEC, and its success as a prescription for the problems of Western Europe seemed assured; but the experiences of the seventies were not happy ones for the Community and in the face of a deepening world recession that threatened the stability of the US dollar member nations returned to older national attitudes. To the evident distress of proponents of a federal Europe and of Community civil servants with their *communautaire* attitude, a 'European' answer to common problems rarely emerged. It was unfortunate that the enlargement of the Community from Six to Nine occurred against a background of economic crisis. Boldly, the Hague Summit (1969) had announced the imminent birth of measures leading to European Monetary Union as the prelude to a new dynamic growth: it was launched in a very uncertain manner in 1979. Even the first direct elections to a European Parliament (1979), arguably the most important political development since the Treaty of Rome, were conducted in an atmosphere of unreality with a far greater concentration on national concerns than European. As the Community entered the eighties there was lacking that confidence with which different leaders had entered the previous decade. Far from progressing, the Community had stumbled through the seventies, uncertain, and unwilling to experiment with policies of closer unity. The growth towards greater cohesion, which Monnet had predicted, was taking longer than had been imagined. In judging the seventies, and making full allowance for economic adversity, our grandchildren may well question the clarity of our vision and the depth of our commitment to a New Europe.

Forms of Economic Cooperation

Unquestionably, the Treaty of Rome had a political purpose, but it was expressed in economic terms:

> The Community shall have as its task, by establishing a common market and progressively approximating the economic policies of Member States, to promote throughout the Community a harmonious development of economic activities, a continuous and balanced expansion, an increase in stability, an accelerated raising of the standard of living and closer relations between the States belonging to it. (Article 2).

This bold, idealist aim could be achieved through economic means because of the close connexion between economic and political life: it is a fact of life, in advanced communities, that government, both as a major employer and as the ultimate controller of the economic system, must lead the business community. Governments today, whether in the East or the West, regard the maintenance of prosperity as perhaps their primary concern: and prosperity depends not merely upon the successful management of a national economy but also upon the mutual advantages that arise from international trade.

The nineteenth century had had a vision of world prosperity and of peace. Remove artificial barriers to trade (like tariffs), they argued, and a major cause of international antagonism would evaporate, whilst trade, allowed to find its natural limits, would expand, bringing prosperity and contentment. In a Free Trade world, where there was neither protective tariff nor any other artificial barrier to trade and production, the most efficient producers would specialise in particular products that they would be able to sell not merely to the local market but to the world. Producers of raw materials would have a world to supply and could rely on that market to supply them with manufactured goods. In this way economies of scale and the advantages of international specialisation would combine to maximise the potential market and thus expand wealth to natural limits. The dream was never a reality and by the end of the century protective tariffs were widespread, not only to protect new home industries, but to control as much of the supply of raw materials and manufactured goods as was possible. Germany was a leader in this respect, developing what was in effect a policy of national *autarky* – making the national economy as self-sufficient as possible. The widespread use of tariffs between the wars increased the severe strains from which the capitalist trading system suffered and it is not surprising that the reduction of tariffs became one of the prime objects of GATT after 1947.

Removal of tariffs does not by itself induce international cooperation. But if a stable pattern of trade existed, it would be possible to strengthen it by offering preferential treatment to certain countries through adjusting tariff levels, allowing goods from one market to enter your own at a low tariff (or no tariff at all) whilst other countries would have to pay a full protective tariff. The arrangement could be reciprocal and could be raised to the level of a trading system – witness the Ottawa Conference (1932) which launched Commonwealth Preference. These preferential arrangements were very advantageous to Britain (though not always to Commonwealth countries) and proved a major difficulty during the negotiations for entry into EEC – they were wound up in 1975. A similar, less developed, system was adopted by the EEC in the Yaoundé Convention (see page 95).

The system could easily exist between sovereign nations who agreed to remove all tariffs and other non-tariff barriers (like quotas and price arrangements) between themselves, but to maintain their own tariffs against other countries. This would be a free trade area – a concept that inspired the unsuccessful Maudling Plan proposed during the early discussions about the Common Market in 1956, and the European Free Trade Association (EFTA, 1959) which Britain launched in response to the EEC.

A Free Trade Area: how others take advantage

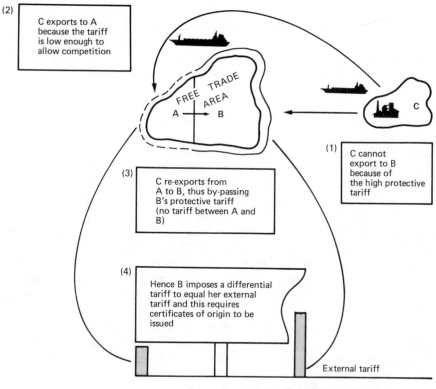

(2) C exports to A because the tariff is low enough to allow competition

(1) C cannot export to B because of the high protective tariff

(3) C re-exports from A to B, thus by-passing B's protective tariff (no tariff between A and B)

(4) Hence B imposes a differential tariff to equal her external tariff and this requires certificates of origin to be issued

External tariff

A common external tariff would obviate the need for the differential tariff and exclude C's goods.

A free trade area may be successful economically, but it does not necessarily advance political unity and it also has serious disadvantages. Tariff barriers are removed between members, but there is no agreement as to the barriers members raise against other third-party countries. A non-member, excluded by a high tariff from selling in one member country, might be able to enter that country through a second member country whose tariff against him was much lower. In this way the protective effect of the first member's tariff would be undermined, and that member would have to impose a differential tariff on goods coming from the second member country: but, to ensure that only goods from non-member states paid this tariff, it would be necessary to insist on 'certificates of origin' for goods imported. All this would add to administrative costs and cause, no doubt, much ill-feeling, perhaps even disturbing international relations.

The solution would be for member countries to adopt a common external tariff (CET) which is the feature of a customs union (like the Prussian Zollverein, 1833). Agreement on the level of the tariff and on enforcing it throughout member states could involve a loss of sovereignty, in that it would be necessary to place a certain degree of control of one's trade in the hands of an authority composed of all member nations. Clearly, this has political implications, and it could be used as the basis of a political union. Article 9(i) of the Treaty of Rome states:

> The Community shall be based upon a customs union which shall cover all trade in goods and which shall involve the prohibition between Member States of customs duties on imports and exports and of all charges having equivalent effect, and the adoption of a common customs tariff in their relations with third countries.

This is a common market and the EEC began in this way – but it determined to go beyond. In theory, the customs union permits a maximising of the potential market within it. In practice, there are still barriers to free competition arising from government regulations or freight agreements or employment policy and the like, which effectively raise non-tariff barriers against other member states. In order to prevent this and so produce conditions of fair competition, members must adopt common policies and harmonise all relevant regulations. In this way the common market becomes an economic union (or community) adopting measures to integrate the policies of member states, both in a positive (adopting common policies, e.g. on agriculture, transport energy and monetary policy) and in a negative sense (getting rid of tariffs and other forms of discrimination between members). This involves surrendering a significant part of national sovereignty by agreeing to abide by important decisions arrived at by some central authority. It also implies that one cannot vary these conditions unilaterally, nor withdraw from the union, since this would automatically upset the balance created within it. It is the purpose of the EEC to establish just such a union, adopting common policies on major social and economic matters and harmonising members' laws and regulations upon them.

The political implications of this are immense. It is also likely that all major decisions will be compromises between members' particular interests – and in the negotiations leading to the decisions, a great deal of horse trading will have to take place. If it is vital to the interests of a member that a particular decision be taken, it is likely that a whole series of concessions on other, often unrelated, matters might have to be made to secure agreement on that one vital matter. Integration is a highly complex matter involving a hundred minor adjustments to arrive at a particular major aim. The EEC cannot be understood without recognising the force of this. As Professor Hallstein put it, 'We are not in business at all; we are in politics'. It makes of an economic community something totally different from a free trade area.

The Treaty of Rome was greeted as the possible beginnings of a European federation. But the progress to integration has been very slow, the Community adopting a pragmatic, almost functionalist approach, dealing often with one problem at a time in the hope that, taken together, the solutions would result in ultimate unity of system, and aware that gradual progress along a well trod path would be more productive of effective integration than the shock of a sudden and great change. This 'Community Method', recalling that of the Fabians, has been described by David Coombes as 'a process of unification by which "supra-national" institutions, acting initially within limited sectors, are expected to have wide-ranging effects on political behaviour and by this means to provide an impetus for growing political union.' It was taken a step further by the Davignon Report (1970) proposing systematised meetings between ministers and senior civil servants of member countries.

Decision-making institutions of the EEC

The Treaty of Rome lists the principal institutions of the EEC as the Commission, the Council of Ministers, the Court of Justice, the European Parliament and the Economic and Social Committee. Diagrams are often reproduced to illustrate the relationship between these institutions; but it is one thing to show a structure and sometimes quite another to show what actually happens in practice. In politics it is the latter that really matters.

A basic purpose of the Community is to achieve free and fair competition. This meant removing tariffs between members (whilst adopting a CET) over a transitional period of time, and also the removal of a whole range of agreements providing disguised protection and restricting competition (Article 85). It involved preventing large companies abusing their position (Article 86) and ensuring that mergers did not injure the public interest. The Commission was the instrument of this basic policy, which clearly gave it considerable political power. Some saw the Commission as the motor power of a future European Union, and the development of the Community has centred round the relationship between the Commission and the Council of Ministers in terms of wielding political influence and power.

The Commission is the appointed guardian of the Treaties and exponent of the Community interest; it is also the executive arm and has the right to initiate Community policy. Since 1967 it has been the single executive of the three communities, following the Merger Treaty of 1965. There are thirteen commissioners nominated by member states for renewable terms of four years, the president and his five vice-presidents are appointed for renewable terms of two years. Great care is exercised to achieve a balance of member nationals as commissioners, but the president (following the Tindemans Report, 1975) is consulted over the appointment of new commissioners. Each commissioner takes an oath of loyalty to the Community and to accept no instructions from his government; he appoints a personal *cabinet* (private office – generally of his own nationals) and his *chef de cabinet* will deputise for him. There are twenty administrative departments, varying in size according to their special task (the largest is Agriculture and Fisheries), under a Director General who is a career civil servant. Having power of initiation, the Commission can determine the moment at which to launch a measure – ideally when the ground for a 'community solution' has been well prepared – and thus it is the Community's strongest pressure group as well as its executive. Many regulations are delegated to it for enforcement in the interests of the Community as a whole (Article 155), and it is ideally placed to assist disputing member states to reach an agreement – its potential power behind the scenes is considerable. In order to act as a check on the Commission the Council of Ministers instituted the *Comité de Gestion* (for agricultural matters) and *Comité de Legislation* (for other matters), deciding by weighted majority on draft Regulations – for as part of the right of initiative the Commission drafts all proposals for legislation which are then presented to the Council. In the task of drafting, the Commission consults as many interested parties as it may in order to arrive at what it interprets as the community interest.

The Commission might have become the nerve centre of the Community; but from the outset it was clearly not intended to assume the supra-national rôle of the ECSC High Authority, for it can only make proposals and administer policies delegated to it. Its effort to extend its influence, especially under Professor Hallstein, was one of the factors in the constitutional crisis of 1965 (see page 62). Since then its influence has been reduced by the growing importance of the Committee of Permanent Representatives (COREPER) (see page 76) whose existence was recognised in the Merger Treaty, and the success of the Heads of State in making the European Council (so called after the 1974 Summit) an effective instrument within the Community (see page 77). In a sense, the Commission's unsatisfactory position results from the gradualist functionalist approach that has typified the development of the Common Market, for the question of political responsibility (deliberately?) was not settled in the Treaty. It is not the central motor it might have become, and shows no great signs of becoming it. The national states retain their identity and their powers. This is underlined by disputes over the precedence to be accorded the President of the Commission – he is not treated as an equal by the Heads of State at the European Council and at other diplomatic meetings.

The Council of Ministers clearly controls the Community and makes Community Law, but it also strongly defends the national interests. It meets monthly but does not have a fixed membership (itself a limitation if it sought to act as a 'government'). Different ministers attend according to the agenda, although Foreign Ministers (oddly enough the Community has not developed a common foreign policy, and the French early vetoed the idea of Community ambassadors) and Ministers of Agriculture tend to meet about once a month. Chairmanship (a crucial office) rotates alphabetically every six months. Although the purpose is to arrive at consensus, there is a voting procedure allowing broadly a two-thirds majority (forty-one out of the fifty-eight members) weighted according to the size of members' populations – although a member may still effectively veto a measure if it affects a special national interest. This arises out of the Luxembourg Compromise (1966, see page 62) which made explicit what previously had only partly been perceived, namely, that the transfer of power from national to community level would be inhibited by the refusal of governments to subordinate 'vital national interests' to the collective interest of the Community (France dictated the compromise, but it seemed not unwelcome to the other Five members). In consequence, voting rarely takes place in Council and the reconciling of views tends to be arrived at through inter-governmental committees rather than through the Commission – itself a significant point. The Council reflects to some degree de Gaulle's 'Europe of the States', and where a peculiarly sensitive issue arises (transport policy for the Dutch, import of citrus fruits for the Italians, the CAP for Britain), national governments can be expected to insist on their position. However, there has developed since 1975 a greater tendency for some decisions to be taken by qualified majority vote.

Decision-making in the EEC

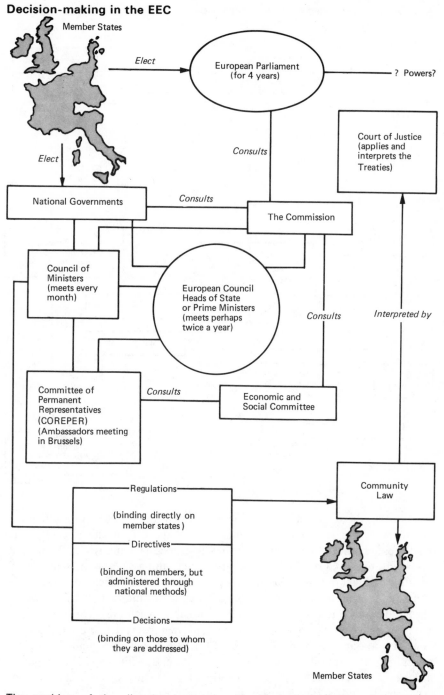

Member States

Elect → European Parliament (for 4 years) → ? Powers?

Court of Justice (applies and interprets the Treaties)

Consults

Elect

National Governments — Consults → The Commission

Council of Ministers (meets every month)

European Council Heads of State or Prime Ministers (meets perhaps twice a year)

Consults

Interpreted by

Committee of Permanent Representatives (COREPER) (Ambassadors meeting in Brussels) — Consults → Economic and Social Committee

Community Law

— Regulations —
(binding directly on member states)
— Directives —
(binding on members, but administered through national methods)
— Decisions —
(binding on those to whom they are addressed)

Member States

The position of the directly elected European Parliament within the EEC remains to be determined. The Commission, though it has rights of initiative, is not the determiner of policy.

The Council of Ministers formally makes the Community Law, but its relationship with the European Council and national governments remains ambiguous.

A 'proposal' becomes an EEC Regulation

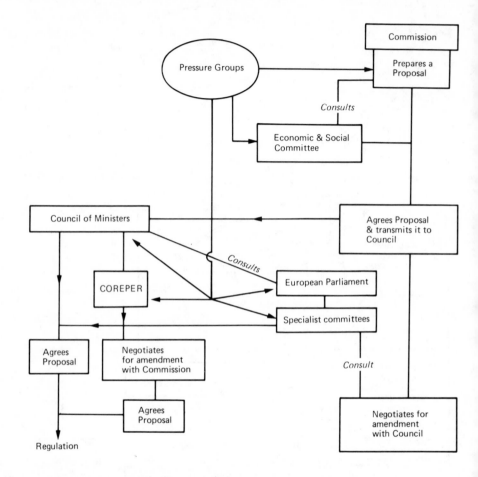

To assist the Council (its business impeded by its lack of permanent membership and infrequent meetings – quite apart from members having portfolios at home to look after!) there has developed a Committee of Permanent Representatives (COREPER) who are either ambassadors or senior civil servants of high prestige. At first there was considerable jealousy from the Commission, the more so as COREPER duplicates the Commission's work, since it also seeks advice as extensively as possible to achieve a consensus (save that it does so from the point of view of national member states). Few drafts go to Council without first being vetted by COREPER, whose potential political power in the Community structure is obvious: the discussion may not be in public and the influence of COREPER may detract from a truly 'community solution' to problems – indeed the compromises that emerge tend to make the pursuit of a positive policy peculiarly difficult. The chance of reaching supra-national solutions seems to have given way to discussion at inter-government level (which the Davignon Report, 1970, seemed to support), while the importance of the

European Council underlines the preference for an inter-governmental approach. It is scarcely to be wondered at that in 1975 two reports, produced independently by the Commission and the European Parliament, both urged the creation of a single decision-making centre within the Community, responsible to a directly elected European Parliament. Such an institution may appear in the 1980s if the Council of Ministers permits it.

In order to ensure that as many different interests as possible are consulted, the Economic and Social Committee was established (Articles 193–8). It serves both the EEC and EURATOM and, since 1961, it may officially discuss with the Consultative Committee of the ECSC. It is composed of 144 members drawn from a wide spectrum of business and public life. They are appointed by the Council for four years, which may be renewed, and they undertake not to be bound either by their national government or any particular interest group. It is consulted, as required by the Treaties, but it receives very little publicity, and pressure groups have direct access anyway to the Commission, COREPER and Parliament. Effectively, it is no more than a convenient sounding board that differs from *ad hoc* bodies and specialist committees in that its existence is provided for in the Treaties. But, as an officially recognised body, its opinion, particularly if the political circumstances are right, could be as weighty as that of the well organised and successful pressure groups that have secured the CAP. This was illustrated in 1979 by the part it played in the campaign to enlarge the 1980 draft budget in order to make more money available for sectors other than agriculture (see page 79).

The European Court of Justice sits at Luxembourg. Its predecessor was that of the ECSC, and it champions Community law. It is an international court in that it may regulate relations between member states but it also gives access to the Commission and to individuals within the Community; it gives rulings on the rights and duties of institutions as they arise out of the Treaties, and it is an administrative court in the manner of French administrative law, protecting individual rights. It has nine judges appointed from member states for six years; the appointments are renewable, and to preserve continuity a partial re-appointment occurs every three years. There is no requirement detailing national origin of judges.

The court is principally concerned with enforcing the Treaties and many cases arise out of Article 9 concerning the removal of all customs duties between members, 'and of all charges having equivalent effect'. Clearly, the Court applies Community rules with a primacy over conflicting national rules. It implies a principle of non-discrimination to underwrite the Community aim of fair competition – foreign companies and multinationals working within the Community are subject to the same rules. The Court ensures that all firms and member governments fulfil their obligations, of which it is the sole interpreter. Disputes between individuals and the Community may come before the Court and it has an impact in the social field in enforcing the principle of freedom of movement and equality of treatment of nationals of all member states. The CAP, the only policy to achieve integration, gives rise to numerous cases, principally against traders. The Court is not concerned with harmonising the structure of national laws into a common body of law, but with applying the Treaties in the relevant commercial and social fields: as the scope of the Community widens, so will the authority of the Court.

The Assembly of the Community (it assumed the name European Parliament in 1962) provides the best example of the gap between the vision conjured up by the name, and the reality in practice. If, in Spinelli's words, 'the Commission proposes and the Council disposes', the Parliament is merely consulted – some would argue that it is no parliament at all. In origin it comes from the Common Assembly of the ECSC when it was transformed into a single assembly for all the three Communities, but with minimal involvement in the legislative process. It has the right to be consulted over legislation and for this purpose it divides into twelve specialist committees (usually meeting in Brussels, whilst the Parliament meets in Strasbourg or Luxembourg) which do effective and serious work upon proposed legislation. Much resentment is voiced at the time and money wasted in the frequent movement of members and staff between three cities (two without a major airport). In November 1979, it was officially estimated that two million EUA per annum would be saved if there were only one meeting place. But powerful vested interests, not merely for the prestige and local employment that arises from sessions, urge a continuance of the present arrangements – new buildings of appropriate size and quality are now available in Luxembourg and Strasbourg. The opening in February 1980 of 'Euronet Diane' a high-speed computerised information system linking the capitals of each member country, may relieve some communication problems. However, the lack of an established base making possible daily physical contact with the leading administrators of the Community throughout the year, is a bar to the growth in power and significance of the European Parliament. Arrangements that were felt to be inadequate when it was composed of representatives from national parliaments are not suitable now the assembly is directly elected. Its powers are strictly limited – by a vote of censure it may dismiss the whole thirteen-member Commission (not an individual commissioner). This is so radical a power that it could only be used in the greatest of crises, which might, indeed, result in the break-up of the Community (although the power was threatened in 1972 and 1976). It has no control over the selection of Commissioners who are the nominees of member governments (though in early 1980 it was proposed that Parliament should take an active part in the selection of the new President of the Commission in 1981), and no control at all over the Council, the effective power within the Community, so that no concept of individual ministerial responsibility can be enforced. Legislation is presented to the Parliament for its opinion, and the Council under the Treaties must consult with it, but amendments need not be accepted by the Commission; furthermore COREPER decides whether a matter is of such importance that it must be determined by the ministers themselves. Clearly, the position of the European Parliament in the decision-making process was never logically worked out. Despite increasing evidence of a wish to assert a political will of its own in the last couple of years before direct election, it had clearly not matured as a political institution, indeed, its rôle was not greatly superior to that of a significant pressure group.

The European Parliament may come to exercise a very considerable influence on major policy developments through the power of the purse. In 1975 it gained the power to amend the small (twenty per cent) non-compulsory part of the Budget (i.e. the part not specifically provided for in the Treaties); it was a minor concession, but an important one for the future when the Community (after 1979) should become self-financing from its own resources (principally VAT). In 1978, when it obliged the Regional Fund to be enlarged, it gained the right to reject the Budget as a whole (a power then deemed as unlikely to be exercised as the dismissal of the whole Commission). After a sustained crisis the new directly elected Parliament rejected the 1980 draft budget on 13 December 1979. It did so with an overwhelming majority (288 for rejection, 64 against, one abstention) and so comfortably cleared the two hurdles erected against the rejection of major policy votes, namely that the vote should be a simple majority of the 410 members of the assembly, and also be a two-thirds majority of the votes actually cast (Article 203, viii). It was a vote that demonstrated that the Parliament had become a serious political force to be reckoned with – direct election was having its effect. It was a vote directed against the spending priorities of the Commission and the Council of Ministers (nearly three quarters of all EEC cash was to go to farmers); having only a consultative rôle in EEC law-making, the Parliament was using its budgetary powers to influence policy. The CAP (see page 85) was the policy particularly involved, especially the refusal of the Council of Ministers to concede cash limits to the prices offered to farmers for crops in considerable surplus (for example, the subsidies to finance the 'wine lake' agreed by the ministers for 1980 would have been £540m – 800m ECUs). But other policies were at issue, like Parliament's demand for increased expenditure on regional, industrial, social and energy policies, which the Council had habitually rejected, and also that the raising of loans to help Community industries in difficulties (the 'Ortoli facility') and the European Development Fund (for aid to the Third World, see page 94) should be included in the budget – and so be under parliamentary control.

Article 204 requires that, in the event of the rejection of the Budget, the Commission may spend only one twelfth of the previous budget each month until a new budget is agreed: this would mean a substantial cut-back in real expenditure, and no settlement of the outstanding points of dispute. The whole crisis was symptomatic of a serious division, not only within the structure but within the EEC as a whole. Progress towards a 'tighter' Community could only be made if member nations would be prepared to compromise their entrenched positions and the Council of Ministers allow Parliament to become a serious rival. In the old parliament, usually it had been enough to secure agreement by making small concessions of extra money to particular appropriations to 'keep people happy' – it was popularly known as 'pocketmoney for the kindergarten'. The new parliament was demanding a share in control – which could involve a radical revision of sections of the Treaty of Rome. The battle between Parliament and Council was not over money (sufficient agreement could easily have been effected by moderate readjustment of appropriations): the battle was about the sharing of political power. Negotiation over the 1980 draft budget dragged on into mid-1980. The issues at stake proved difficult to resolve, and the demand that Parliament should play a part in determining the Budget from the outset was made forcibly.

Until 1979 members were representatives selected from national parliaments and therefore at best had a dual loyalty. However, political parties on a European basis have begun to appear – indeed, in the ECSC Assembly, members sat in party rather than national groupings. In the mid-seventies federations of European Parties appeared, beginning with the socialists (1974) who have always shown great sympathy for international groupings. Parties use a whipping system, but discipline so far has been weak. The principal change in Parliament's fortunes came in 1979 with direct elections.

This was a change of tremendous significance. Not only does it produce a Parliament whose members may claim an electoral mandate, but their moral standing, as against members of national parliaments, is greatly enhanced. A directly elected Parliament can claim to speak for Europe in a way that not even the Council of Ministers could challenge. As a basis for arriving at 'European' solutions, the new Parliament could not be better placed – but this is not to say that it will thereby be permitted to assert a different influence. Direct elections by themselves will not further the cause of European unity, and the Community will continue to function throughout the eighties primarily through cooperation between member governments. Whilst this is a disappointment for the federalists, it remains a fact that the vision of federal unity has not captured the popular imagination. The 1979 election campaigns largely reflected national party positions, and engendered small enthusiasm at that. Partly this arose from the fact that in some countries the size of the European constituencies was so much larger than the parliamentary constituencies that candidates and electorate alike experienced a sense of remoteness; partly it was because prominent national leaders (there were a few very notable exceptions) have preferred to continue their careers solidly within national politics; partly it was because the European Parliament up to that time had made little impact.

Several anomalies need to be settled during the life of the first directly elected parliament – two in particular are the system of election (it is likely that the next election will operate with some mandatory system of proportional representation), and the presence of a dual mandate (a member may be elected to the European and in some cases a national parliament, which imposes both a physical burden and a division of loyalties that may well outweigh any advantage arising from having a voice in both chambers). The major tasks for the new European Parliament must be that of asserting a more significant position in Community politics, becoming more involved in Community law-making, and increasing its minimal powers. However, both Britain and France have made it clear that they are opposed to the idea of Parliament acquiring supra-national powers or legislative competence – and any increase in Parliament's powers would have to be granted by the Council, where national interests are paramount. The idea of Parliament forming a sort of Upper Chamber on the analogy of the West German *Bundesrat* (see page 112) has not gained favour, and it does not seem likely that increasing powers as a federal institution will prove an immediate way forward.

Parliament has, indeed, begun to extend its influence. From 1975 'concertation procedure' has strengthened its consultative rôle with the Council agreeing to meet Parliament over difficulties involving finance in a 'conciliation' committee.

The use of the Parliamentary Question (especially as demonstrated by British members) has increased the prospect of its exercising a supervisory rôle. An area for increasing parliament's budgetary powers might be certain items of 'compulsory expenditure' under the Treaties. This could only be at the expense of the power of the Council – and the sovereignty of member states. The question of where political power does – and ought to – reside within the Community has yet to be fully faced, and at least a part of the conflict resulting in the rejection of the 1980 draft budget was due to the dissatisfaction at the lack of political direction within the Community as it entered the eighties. Goodwill and tolerant *'communautaire'* attitudes are no substitute for legislative power and executive authority – and the Community lacks these. Neither the Commission nor the Council can act as the government of the Community: neither is yet in a position to look at European problems as a whole. But at least the new European Parliament, directly elected and no longer tied to national parliaments, has made its name.

The Budget

The Parliament and the Council are the Budgetary Authority under the Treaties, but the Council has the last word. The ECSC is self-financing, so the Budget relates to the other two Communities, and was at first met by quotas paid by member states. By 1970 agreement was reached upon making the Community financially autonomous with *ressource propre* (revenue from its own sources) drawn from customs duties and levies and the national contributions were phased out in exchange for revenue not exceeding one per cent of the product of VAT (cost of collection being met by a refund of ten per cent). This arrangement strengthens the Community as against the national parliaments, since it provides a basic source of income. The Budget is calculated in European Units of Account (EUA) first introduced in 1978 representing a 'basket' of the nine members' currencies 'floating' according to their current value (in 1977 the European Council agreed that budget contributions might be made either in national currency or EUA, the resulting 'hole' being made good by member governments in the same proportions – paying in sterling saved Britain some £200m and cost West Germany some £70m in 1978).

The Budget is divided into 'compulsory expenditure' arising directly out of the Treaty (agriculture, energy, social policy etc. amounting to about eighty per cent of the total) and 'non-compulsory expenditure' (including, from 1977, the Regional Fund). Parliament has control over the latter, except that it is restricted by the Commission to a pre-determined ceiling, the 'maximum rate'. In 1975, also, the European Council agreed to a concertation (conciliation) procedure of joint meetings of Parliament, Commission and Council of Ministers to review the budget in the light of current problems over a period of three months – effectively, this gives Parliament a three month veto over the Budget if necessary. Expenditure on new policies under the non-compulsory heading (e.g. industrial, regional and social) has recently increased because of parliamentary pressure, but since the budget is relatively tiny – equivalent to under one per cent of total Gross Domestic Product (GDP) of the Community – and the CAP accounts for

British Treasury estimate of the cost of Britain's EEC membership (in million ECUs: 1 ECU = £0.664 at 1978 prices)

	Net Budget Gain	Agri-culture Gain	Fisheries Gain	Trade Gain	Total gain from British membership	As % GNP
West Germany	+600	+40	+20	+30	+690	+.14
France	+400	+75	+75	+25	+615	+.17
Italy	+190	+35	+0	+15	+240	+.13
Holland	+120	+35	+25	+20	+200	+.20
Belgium/ Luxembourg	+100	+5	+5	+15	+125	+.16
Denmark	+40	+10	+25	+5	+80	+.18
Ireland	+10	+50	+10	+10	+70	+.74
EEC (8)	+1500	+250	+150	+120	+2020	+.16
Britain	−1500	−250	−150	+120	−1780	−.74

In June 1979 the British Treasury prepared a memorandum outlining the extent of the estimated cost to Britain of her membership of the EEC. The argument was that while all other members made a net gain, Britain (with the largest contribution to the Community Budget) made a net loss. (Source: *The Economist*, 23 June 1979)

over seventy per cent of it, these sums are ridiculously small. It is through the 'power of the purse' that Parliament is likely to augment its influence. In both 1977 and 1978 Parliament was in conflict with Council over the Budget, and rejected it in 1979.

The Commission supports Parliament, arguing that 'the budget today in no way measures up to the part it is expected to play in the move towards greater economic integration. The deepening of the Community requires a major expansion of the financial resources available to it'. The huge size of the agricultural payments not only distorts the budget but is a shrewd comment on the failure of the Council of Ministers to respond to the other needs of the Community. Both Commission and Parliament are urging a redistribution of the budget to permit more policies to be effective. A reasoned and concerted study of Community needs as bases for budgetary planning would promote closer integration through Community financed policies paid via the Social and Regional Fund. Since it was necessary to prepare also for the future enlargement of the Community in the 1980s, a new fund of 20m EUA was established for 'crises in certain industrial sectors' – by 1979 the Commission was already beginning to use the budget as a dynamic tool for future Community policies. But present sources of revenue for Community policies will not meet the needs of the 1980s and a progressive system of budget financing is being studied, for by 1981 Community revenue will no longer cover its expenditure, as calculated in 1979.

Britain has a special interest in the Budget. She is the largest contributor to it, although one of the poorest members and receiving proportionately little in direct benefit. Italy is in a similar position. The Budget is doubly biased against Britain since a large part of Community income is from taxes on imports from outside the Community which hits Britain particularly because of her heavy import bill; on the expenditure side, some seventy five per cent goes on farm price support, most of which goes to farmers in other member countries. Britain's contribution problem has been aggravated by this apparent inequality – the Labour government actually contemplated withdrawing from the CAP in 1978. The Budget costs add significantly to Britain's overseas debts and a formal demand for a redistribution of budget expenditure to permit Britain to enjoy a larger return for her contribution was made in 1979. But the European Council, meeting in December 1979 in Dublin, failed to reach any acceptable solution: even the suggestion for a 'corrective mechanism', a sophisticated formula by which a member country might claw back a significant proportion of its payments as receipts under various Community Funds, failed at Dublin. Neither was the problem resolved at the April 1980 Luxembourg meeting of the European Council. The meeting ended in acrimony and it was recognised that the community faced a major crisis. This was avoided in June when an agreement was reached to reduce Britain's budget contribution by £1570m over two years, but with increased prices for farmers despite the efforts of the Commission to reduce them. In fact no final solution had been reached, despite the suggestion that the whole community system of financing might be reconsidered.

If, on the political front members were showing small signs of determination to reach acceptable solutions, there was progress on the administrative front. The Treaty amendments of 1975, increasing the power of the Parliament, also set up the EEC Court of Auditors (largely at Parliament's insistence). This is an independent body with a full-time panel of nine members to scrutinise all Community revenue and expenditure and financial administration. Its first meeting was in Luxembourg in 1977. It may demand documentation from all member states to facilitate its enquiries and also check or analyse particular accounts that are still in operation. Within the Commission efficiency has been increased by placing routine financial matters under one Commissioner, and the coordination of Community Funds and various Community intervention appropriations for financing structural policy under another.

European Monetary System

If the Community failed to move beyond inter-governmental compromises it would never achieve that degree of integration needed to create a true economic community. Monetary union is the most fundamental of the policies needed for this end, for decisions on monetary policy pervade society. Politically, monetary union involves, at least theoretically, the surrender of sovereignty to a central decision-making supra-national body, whose decisions would cover fiscal policy, harmonising of taxes, free convertibility of currencies (if not devising an actual European currency), control of balance of payments and influence over policies to achieve price stability – in effect, a single economy and a single currency with centralised economic decision-making. A Central Bank would hold the

Community's reserves of gold and foreign currencies and make loans to member governments. Monetary union could only be introduced gradually, but its consequence would be to create a community somewhat closer to that federal union of which the Resistance dreamed than to de Gaulle's '*Europe des Patries*'. It would cement political union and help the efficient expansion of industry, be a powerful tool to control inflation and (if the central authority were sufficiently powerful), it could provide a stimulus for growth (and thus employment) and promote better regional distribution of work and wealth throughout the Community. As a significant trading area, it would provide a major international currency capable of inducing stability in world trade and rivalling the dollar (or even displacing it).

In 1969, Raymond Barre (to become Prime Minister of France in 1976) produced a plan, and the principle of European Monetary Union (EMU) was adopted as an aim for 1980, at the Hague Summit (1969). A compromise method of achieving it was proposed by the Werner Report (1970) and in 1971 the Council of Ministers launched stage one by creating the 'Snake' (the exchange rates of member currencies were allowed to fluctuate within defined limits, with support for those that temporarily fell outside the margins). Greeted as a great step forward, it was almost immediately overwhelmed by events and several major countries had to withdraw. EMU had failed. The world recession of the mid-seventies demonstrated that the Bretton Woods system, which had brought at least some stability to international finance since the Second World War, had collapsed and the US dollar ceased to be a strong international currency. Member countries were subject to all the short-term hazards of exchange rate problems and their consequent effects on internal economic policies. But by the end of the decade, a sufficient degree of confidence had returned to try again, as much to avoid exchange-rate crises as to attempt to curb inflation and reduce unemployment. That intra-Community trade was so significant a part of members' trade was an added inducement. But there was much disagreement as to method, the more so as estimates of the cost of launching EMU were as high as seven per cent of total Community GNP, although a proportion of that sum would be in terms of payments transferred from national to Community funds.

In 1979, following a dramatic false start and much horse-trading to secure Italian and Irish acceptance, the Council launched a new European Monetary System (EMS) linking exchange rates with a permitted fluctuation of 2.25 per cent. A European Monetary Fund was to be established and a new European Currency Unit would be introduced at the same value as the European Unit of Account, so that the new EMS would not merely be a glorified 'snake'. Britain remained apart, convinced that a central authority regulating monetary supply throughout the Community was essential (since EMS cannot work unless backed by economic coordination) and that it would seriously affect the government's attempt to control inflation: the new scheme was less a system than a 'basket of adjustment mechanisms'. Although expressed in terms of practical objection the real issue was ultimately one of sovereignty. Dr Vaubel suggested launching a convertible parallel currency, which would avoid the hegemony of the Deutschmark implicit in the present arrangements. There was no disagreement over the ultimate benefits, only over the immediate methods and cost. It was widely acknowledged that Britain would be vulnerable to declining competitiveness if parities were locked in EMU, and only a gigantic financial crisis could induce a currency merger all at one time.

The European Council, rather than the Commission, had been the principal motor of events in the creation of EMS, and at the Dublin meeting (1979) it was decided to move forward towards stage two, when the ECU would become a genuine reserve asset with a European Monetary Fund and a coordinated dollar policy.

The Common Agricultural Policy (CAP)

It is no exaggeration to say that the only common policy that has been properly developed by the Community is the CAP. Its cost is phenomenal – over seventy per cent of the annual budget – and it is under severe attack because it favours the producer against the consumer, fails to stabilise production and tends to raise prices. By protecting the producer it ensures that the Community can grow about ninety per cent of its necessary food; and a prosperous agriculture preserves the balance of rural society. The basic principles of the policy were written into the Treaty (Article 39): to increase agricultural productivity, ensure a fair standard of living for the agricultural community, stabilise markets and assure supplies which would reach consumers at reasonable prices.

Ideologically, farming was well suited to become the major example of a common policy. It implied uniform prices for producers over the whole Community, and so a centralised system for determining the prices and controlling the market mechanisms to produce them. All member countries protected their farmers in various ways: a common policy would make fair competition possible and preserve rural society. There was also a powerful inducement in the likely straight interchange of manufactured goods from West Germany and surplus grain from France. Negotiations were extremely long and arduous, justifying the claim that the CAP is more the sum of the protective agricultural policies of the Six than a Community policy. Once established (1968) it became a positive major cohesive element within the Community – an example of the will to succeed (other common policies also written into the Treaties have yet to be achieved). In 1958 only the Dutch had successfully developed agriculture into a major exporting industry: in the other five it was heavily labour-intensive with a multitude of small farms and a low rate of mechanisation and modernisation. A policy of inducing efficiency through amalgamation of holdings and the adoption of modern methods and machinery within a guaranteed price and market could only lead to increased production, exports and surpluses.

The CAP is a support system guaranteeing a set price to farmers and protecting them from the wide fluctuations of world prices. The price is maintained partly by an external tariff excluding low-priced competitive agricultural imports, and partly by buying up any surpluses within the Community. The surpluses have caused a major problem: they can be stored for release into the market to preserve price levels if supplies are affected, or exported (often at a loss – although the big rise in world commodity prices in the seventies

Civilian employment in the EEC by sector, 1960/1975

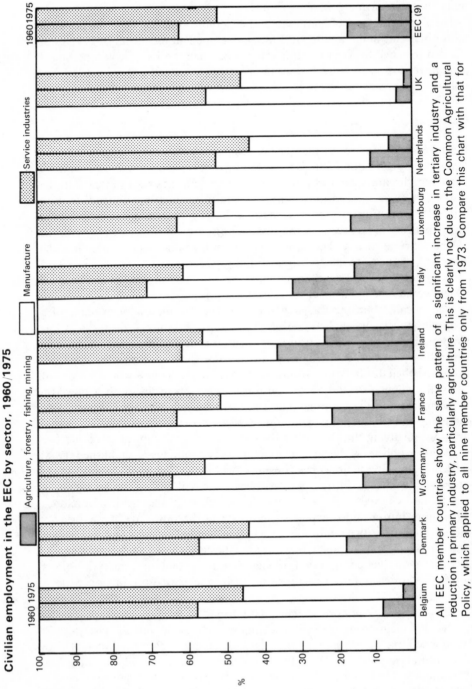

All EEC member countries show the same pattern of a significant increase in tertiary industry and a reduction in primary industry, particularly agriculture. This is clearly not due to the Common Agricultural Policy, which applied to all nine member countries only from 1973. Compare this chart with that for COMECON countries (p. 123)

has ended the era of cheap food). The export of dairy produce, especially to the USSR, at very cheap rates caused a major protest in the mid-seventies, and in 1977 the disposal of fruit and vegetables (in some cases the destruction of produce) cost the EEC taxpayer £16m. It has become a common thing to talk of wine lakes and mountains of unwanted butter and powdered milk.

The methods for pricing differ with each commodity, but that for soft wheat illustrates the system well. Duisburg in the Ruhr is selected as the centre having the least adequate supplies and the price annually calculated for Duisburg gives the target price (that for other commodities is similarly derived from other selected centres). The price guaranteed to the producer is the intervention price, as close as possible to the target price, and is maintained by the Commission's agents purchasing surpluses (or releasing stored supplies to maintain the price level). To finance this the European Agricultural Guidance and Guarantee Fund (FEOGA) was created in 1962, the Guarantee section dealing with price mechanisms and the Guidance section (tiny in comparison) dealing with structural improvements in farming. There is a proviso that all production in excess of thirty per cent of the estimated production is to be exported. A threshold price is calculated daily to protect against cheap imports, which can only enter at the threshold price and do not undercut Community prices. When the product is exported by producers an export refund is available to the farmer so that he sells at the world price (commodity price increases in the seventies made this unnecessary and instead a tax was imposed to discourage exports when world prices were temporarily higher than in the Community – thus stability of supplies was encouraged). After the French devaluation of 1969, the Community was forced to adopt a 'green rate' in determining agricultural prices, the difference between it and the actual exchange rate being made up in monetary compensation amount (MCA). As a currency fell in value, a difference between it and the 'green rate' appeared which in effect was a subsidy to the consumer. In 1976, following the devaluation of the pound sterling in 1975, British consumers were subsidised to the tune of £1.5m daily.

Structural reform (through the Guidance section of FEOGA) was outlined in the Mansholt Plan of 1968, but there has been little major progress through the Fund – which underlines the essentially political nature of the CAP. In practice, the Policy has dominated the Community Budget throughout and so great a proportion of available funds has been absorbed by guaranteeing prices that little has been available for restructuring farming. Surpluses in milk and dairy produce, meat, sugar, olive oil and wine have become a serious political – and practical – problem. By the end of the seventies, the CAP, which has been described as a new version of Hitler's New Economic Order, was under severe attack for paying vast subsidies to efficient farmers to produce vast surpluses of unwanted food at ridiculously high prices – and poorer farmers seemed to benefit less than the already rich. The Commission was vainly proposing reforms to the Council of Ministers, and was supported by the out-going Parliament. (The Council stood firm and increased prices marginally against Commission advice.) There was an urgency about the demands for reform, for it was predicted that by 1981 the Budget would be incapable of financing the CAP and both Britain and West Germany had made it clear that they would not contribute more funds. The Council's refusal to make adequate readjustment for other Funds at the expense of the CAP provoked the rejection of the 1980 draft budget. Clearly, the whole agricultural policy is shot through with members' vested interests: it suffers from being the only genuine common policy (unless one counts the simple dismantling of intra-Community tariffs) and is particularly vulnerable to the impact of currency crises which the absence of EMU exaggerates.

The policy survived the seventies because world commodity prices rose steeply and Britain was expected to absorb much of the surplus produce as a big importer of food. World price rises slackened off at the end of the decade – and the prospect of the enlargement of the Community (see page 96) by three strongly agricultural countries made reform a pressing issue.

A common fisheries policy (CFP) was agreed in 1970 allowing all EEC fishermen equal access to each other's waters. There was no great problem until the British, Danes and Irish joined, making the policy unworkable. Partly to conserve fish stocks, the UN Law of the Sea Conference (1976) allowed countries to claim an exclusive fishing zone of 200 miles. This decision raised serious problems for Britain, whose Channel and North Sea fishing grounds thereby became common to several nations. Fishing is a declining industry and the very real problems associated with it have yet to be resolved. The defence of members' particular interests in this connexion, as in other matters, makes for unhappy relations within the Community.

Transport policy

The creation of a common transport policy (excluding sea and air traffic) was another major concern of the Treaty of Rome. Without a common policy, specifically prohibiting 'rates and conditions involving any element of support or protection in the interest of one or more particular undertakings or industries' (Article 80), fair and undistorted competition was not possible. Transport is fundamental to any advanced industrial community both as a means of securing raw materials and extending the market and as contributing directly to the expansion of employment and industry. The concern of national governments to strengthen their transport systems, either overtly through nationalising railways or constructing motorway systems, or covertly through special rates and rebates and freight quota arrangements underlines the importance they attach to them – and explains the Community's failure to develop a common transport policy. Such a policy would extend beyond arrangements for particular sectors of the transport industry to methods of coordinating an integrated policy covering all major transport sectors and determining their expansion or contraction. An indication of the relative importance of each sector was given by a US study in 1972, estimating the distance in miles per ton (or gallon) as follows: pipeline: 300; waterways: 250; rail: 200; road: 85.

A revolution in road transport has occurred in the lifetime of the Community: to the advantage of flexibility has been added the speed possible over long distances on motorways, and great technological developments in the production of juggernaut lorries. This has been at the expense of railways. Although a licensing system was introduced giving rights of *cabotage* (picking up loads in any member country), each country has different regulations as to axle weight and wheel base (reflecting the activity of pressure groups rather than prevailing road conditions), which leads to considerable discrimination between national industries. The forces of cohesion in the Community, powerful in agriculture, do not extend to transport. Britain, particularly, opposes proposals for increasing the size of juggernaut lorries. Their effect on motorway wear was underlined by a Transport and Road Research Laboratory report (1979) forecasting that increased axle-weights would increase damage to motorway surfaces by 340 per cent by 2005. Existing motorways were built for lighter lorries than currently use them: new ones would have to be much stronger – and more expensive (and the wear caused by very heavy lorries is not confined to motorways). The proposal to increase permitted axle-load to forty tonnes was not acceptable to Britain: however, her representatives on the Economic and Social Committee suggested a European Road Repair Fund to assist governments in strengthening roads and bridges. This would help towards a common policy on road transport, but it would involve additional expenditure by the Community Budget.

There are many examples of cooperation between nations over transport policy. Free navigation of the Rhine was secured with a Central Rhine Commission in 1815–reconstructed in 1963, but as a separate organisation from EEC transport policy. Schemes for an integrated transport system were worked on by the Allies' European Central Inland Transport Organisation (1945) and the United Nations' Economic Commission for Europe (1947) – which planned the E route motorways for Europe. Railways have been reorganised and modernised, with carefully arranged international agreements over rolling stock and routes. Waterways have enjoyed a revival, both with the construction of links between the Rhine and Danube systems and the Rhine and Rhône systems, and by canal enlargement to carry loads of up to 1350 tons. But this does not amount to a transport policy, still less an integrated policy, which implies some rationalising of routes and types of transport (water, rail, road) according to circumstances. Nor has serious account been taken of the impact of the growing number of bulk pipeline supply routes.

The Commission has not been idle in its endeavour to reach a basically competitive solution to transport matters (which is not a substitute for an integrated transport policy), but progress has been slow, even with the threat of the Commission taking governments to the Court of Justice over failure to end restrictive transport policies. By 1977, however, the Council of Ministers had agreed to harmonise state regulations relating to hours of driving and the use of the tachograph, although Community driving licences, 'symbolising the reality of the Community for the individual', have not arrived, nor has harmonising extended to summer-time arrangements. By 1977 it was clear that shipping and air transport were being included in arrangements and discussions. Additionally, from 1975, a combined road/rail goods transport system (*ferroutage*) was developed for long-distance heavy freight (including Austria and Switzerland) – but it is not run by the Commission. Transport is still the jealously guarded preserve of governments and private enterprise.

Regional policy

The Treaty of Rome did not specify any Regional Policy for the Community; but it was clear in 1956 that substantial regional differences existed and any process of integration would be likely to exacerbate them and possibly lead to tensions that could have a politically disruptive impact. The problem has grown – and threatens to become very significant when Greece, Portugal and Spain join the Community in the 1980s. Of the original Community, the Italian Mezzogiorno (the south, including Sicily and Sardinia) presented – and still does – the most serious problems of rural poverty, structural unemployment and migration of young people in search of jobs elsewhere. Western and southern France showed similar signs, and the old industrial areas of the Nord, the Belgian Borinage and parts of the Ruhr presented problems of urban and industrial decline. The accession of Britain and Ireland increased the regional imbalances.

Partly as a consequence of the Werner Report and the decision of the Hague Summit (1969) to go for EMU by 1980, a common policy on regional aid began to emerge in the seventies. Until then the Social Fund of the ECSC, the Guidance Section of FEOGA and the European Investment Bank had made some contribution, especially towards retraining and rehousing of redundant workers; but it was on a small scale (some 2.6 billion EUA between 1958 and 1972). One problem of course, was that each member nation already had active regional policies and the Council tended to the view that it was the member's own concern. Britain secured the creation of the European Regional Development Fund (ERDF) (1972), which was regarded as a means of correcting the imbalance she would suffer between her future contributions and her likely benefits. It was not a substitute for a regional policy, but an instrument to meet an eventuality; as Professor Swann put it, 'the Regional Fund might do for Britain what the CAP had done for France!'. The Thomson Report (1973) identified the prime regional problem areas as the Mezzogiorno, Ireland and Britain – which by and large had an average national income per head below the Community average (West Bavaria, the poorest region of West Germany, has an income per head higher than the most prosperous areas of the UK), and proposed that the ERDF, financed from the Community Budget, should aid regional development programmes. These began in 1975, on condition they were additional to existing national schemes. 1975 was economically a bad year for the Community. In 1977 the European Council renewed the Fund for three years – not making it permanent nor allowing it the funds recommended by the Commission. The path to Regional Policy is long and stony. The impact of EMU would be likely to increase regional disparities and increase the migration of labour from poorer areas, adding to existing employment and social problems in both rich and poor areas alike. A failure to adopt a satisfactory common regional policy will have serious political implications not only in the regions themselves but in terms of the gains and contributions of member nations. Only if the policy were genuinely *communautaire* would problems be likely to be eased. A new phase may have been started by the Budget of 1979 more than doubling the size of the Fund.

Social policy

Among the many changes that so sharply distinguish the present century from previous ones is the emergence of the Welfare State. Once again, this is the concern of individual member states, not of the Community itself, although it has significant implications for Community policy, notably in the movement of workers. State provision of social and health services and education vary in method and level, reflecting differences of attitude, but all member states have social services of a similar nature.

The section on social policy in the Treaty of Rome is not concerned with Welfare State matters, but with employment matters and equal conditions of pay and work. Following closely the experience of the ECSC, it established a European Social Fund (Article 123) 'to improve employment opportunities for workers in the common market and to contribute thereby to raising the standard of living'. It refunded up to fifty per cent of the cost of rehousing and retraining workers displaced by Community policies. Such limited aims were recognised as inadequate: integration implied European policies on a wide front and the social policy was considered by the Hague Summit (1969) in its connexion with EMU. The Paris Summit (1972) acknowledged that the pursuit of economic expansion was not a sufficient aim of the Community, and that attention should be paid to the quality of life (including the protection of the environment) and to the reduction of disparities in living conditions. It was described as 'giving the Community a human face'. In 1972 a New Social Fund was launched financed from the Community's own resources and able to allocate funds in advance wherever the need was greatest (although it was still restricted to matters related to employment and re-training). The Commission's *Guidelines for a Social Policy* (1973) still retained the narrow definition of the Fund, although it laid emphasis on greater worker participation in the conduct of firms' decision making, and improvement of working and living conditions. Spiralling inflation and the world recession in the mid-seventies brought a growing unemployment problem throughout the Community. Active measures to assist youth unemployment and promote equal opportunity for men and women (Article 119 had not been enforced in twenty years) were taken, and a new development was a scheme to assist member states to eliminate deprivation, if only on a minor scale. The Commission had begun the task of leading member states towards a harmonising of social welfare policies – for such policies, though the responsibility of individual states, nevertheless had a Community implication, if only from the need to assist free movement of workers and their families by securing equivalent social services, or at the least no loss of social benefit, when moving from one country to another. The Tindemans Report suggested a broader aim:

> The task of the present generation is to seek a transition to post-industrial society which respects the basic values of our civilisation and reconciles the right of the individual with those of the Community. . . . A new type of economic growth displaying more respect for the quality of life and the physical and human environment, and better able to reconcile economic and social objectives.

In 1976 the Commission produced a European Social Budget showing in comparative terms members' expenditure on social insurance benefits and welfare. It came as a rude shock to Britain, founding father of the Welfare State, to see that expenditure on social services was higher in nearly all the other member countries. The bare statistics concealed predominant attitudes, and a closer analysis revealed that Britain distributes social security resources more evenly and provides a more effective safety net for the poor, while the continental practice takes better care of the ordinary working man and his family. Differences in the incidence and levels of member nations' schemes are so great as to present a serious barrier to harmonisation – but the significant difference between the British method of universal benefits and the common continental practice of selective benefits has grown much less in recent years. Escalating costs have affected health provision particularly, and there are big differences in the method of raising the money required – notably in the incidence of the burden as between employer, private taxpayer and the patient. Private medicine, with resulting widely differing standards of health care, is much more widely accepted on the continent.

Poverty remains a problem throughout the Community, and the Commission's Action Against Poverty Programme (1974) represents a new departure regarding groups of people in a social context rather than as cogs in an economic machine, defining the poor as 'an individual or family whose resources are so small as to exclude them from the minimum acceptable way of life of the member state in which they live'. Migrant workers have perhaps suffered the most during the recession of the seventies. Intra-Community migrants are covered by the Treaty of Rome, those from outside the Community lack this security. Encouraged to enter in the expansive days of the sixties, and usually taking low-status jobs, their numbers (at least ten million) present a serious problem in times of recession. Restriction on the entry of non-member migrants began in 1974 and existing migrants found it increasingly difficult to renew their work permits. Repatriation schemes are not always successful and migrants contribute a significant proportion to the Community's unemployed. Member states have been unwilling to extend to resident non-Community migrants the same rights and security as others. The Community Action Programme seeks to overcome this problem.

Education policy

An education policy for the Community began to emerge after the Janne Report (1973) and the appointment of Ralph Dahrendorf as Commissioner for education. A widely ranging programme, both at national and at Community level, was launched in 1975. In order to facilitate movement of workers and their families, special reception classes were to be organised in the principal language of the host country and the whole range of the educational and vocational training systems were to be opened to children of migrant workers. For professional workers, freedom of movement depends on the recognition of qualifications between member states. Student mobility between universities is established and teacher mobility at all levels is accepted in principle. Again, within certain conditions, doctors and nurses may now move freely between appointments in different member countries but this does not apply to all health workers. The EEC directives on State Registered Nurse training (1979) enlarged the course to include compulsory community nursing – and the cost of the three year training falls squarely upon the health service of each member state – it is not a matter for the Community Budget.

There is some way to go yet before the equivalence of professional qualifications as a whole is established throughout the Community. The learning of at least one foreign language is an obvious necessity if movement of workers at all levels is to be freely available, but education ministers have yet to agree on the ways of making this possible. Although the organisation of schools within the public sector has tended to move towards the comprehensive principle in member countries, their courses are still the responsibility of different authorities and they differ widely in content and style. Efforts are being made to ensure that both sexes have equal educational opportunities. The tendency for children to remain longer at school has produced the '*explosion scolaire*' which exerts pressure on scarce resources at secondary and tertiary levels – although middle-class youth still predominates at universities. Cooperation between countries on educational matters is made the more difficult by the different administrative systems – the problems are much the same, but there is a lack of common machinery to tackle them. As with other areas, Community education policy is regarded as merely supplementary to existing national policies. There seems to be a logical inconsistency here, since the CAP has absorbed existing different national policies for agricultural support; to distinguish between this and other policies – transport, regional, social, educational, energy – appears somewhat arbitrary, if not merely a matter of politics.

Energy policy

The Second World War demolished the established framework of energy supplies in Europe, and the political division after the war did not help to restore it (notably, Polish coal was no longer available in the same quantities). US efforts at organising energy supplies were taken over by the UN Economic Commission for Europe, and coal experienced a revival. When the Community was formed there was far less awareness of the significance of energy supplies than in the seventies (no one imagined an international energy crisis could develop within twenty years). EURATOM was viewed as a potential federating force because of the cost of developing power from nuclear energy (see page 59) and also because it was hoped that it would supply the main future energy needs. But nuclear energy has not achieved the heights that were once expected of it. Oil rapidly reduced coal's share of the energy supplies in the sixties, especially because of its cheapness – but the Yom Kippur War brought a dramatic change in price and the West during the seventies became acutely aware of the energy crisis. North Sea Oil proves a useful addition, but it does not supply all Community needs. Cost, radiation hazard and the problem of disposal of waste (which remains radioactive indefinitely) has reduced the emphasis put on nuclear power (the conversion of coal into natural gas seems cheaper). Yet, as in other areas, the

EEC energy sources (percentages from each source)

	Oil	Coal	Natural gas	Primary electricity	Lignite
1972	59.5*	21.5	11.6	4.5	2.8
1976	55.5	19.5	16.7	5.6	3.2

* 10 per cent in 1950

Community has developed no common policy, even in so fundamental an area as energy.

Efforts to do so had been made in the sixties, as much to preserve coal against the competition of cheap oil, as to secure supplies. But the crisis of 1973 forced action and an Energy Committee was appointed at the Copenhagen Summit (1973) and a scheme to reduce oil imports by thirty per cent over ten years, and to diversify energy sources was accepted in 1975.

The reaction to the energy problem was not to turn to a Community solution, however, but to pursue national ends. France pursued a lone policy and Britain, understandably, refused to share North Sea Oil with her Community partners – the theoretical specialisation of free trade has clear natural, national and strategic limits! But EURATOM was probably saved because of the need for all avenues to be kept open – a Joint European Torus (JET) scheme for producing nuclear energy was begun at Culham, Berkshire (1978). There were other projects – solar energy and wave energy – particularly as the crisis was deepened by further price increases in 1977 and 1979 and the severe reduction in Iranian oil after the fall of Shah in 1978. It is easy to blame the Community for not developing a common policy – perhaps the energy crisis is not a sufficiently severe one to oblige the cutting through of the mass of vested interests that surround energy policy.

The deepened energy crisis of 1979 concentrated attention on means to reduce Community dependence on foreign oil, especially OPEC, though this reflected more an *ad hoc* reaction to political necessity than a new *communautaire* attitude to energy problems. The European Parliament in November urged a thorough-going common energy policy to include the coal industry, but this was not taken up. Instead, there was widespread interest in further developing nuclear energy, despite the costs and the much publicised accident at Harrisburg, USA. At its meeting in Strasbourg (June 1979), the European Council endorsed this interest: 'without the expansion of nuclear power generating capacity in the coming decades, economic growth and higher employment will be hard to achieve'. Major expansion in nuclear energy was projected in France, Britain (where it was expected to provide forty per cent of all electricity by 2000) and even in West Germany, despite the growing importance of the ecology 'Green Party' that opposed the expansion of nuclear power and was expected to have considerable impact on the 1980 election. There was small attention paid to a common energy policy – which might include coal liquidisation; indeed, some observers pointed to the likelihood of over-capacity and excess production within a few years in each of the larger Community countries. Nationalism continues to exact a high price.

The Community and the Third World

In the 1950s the colonial empires still survived. France and Belgium still retained substantial colonial empires in Africa and had free trade, or preferential trade relations between colonies and mother country – a relationship that was partly carried forward into the EEC by the principle of Association (Article 131). Holland, Italy and even West Germany also maintained economic relations with former colonies. By the 1960s colonies had become independent, but former Belgian and French colonies were linked as Associate States to the EEC through the Yaoundé Convention (1963). This trading agreement, which has been called 'myopic and paternalist', allowed for trade between the EEC and the Associate States, with reciprocal preferences except where products competed with the CAP. There was also provision for development grants, channelled through the European Development Fund (EDF) and supplemented with loans via the European Investment Bank (EIB). A novel feature was the creation of joint institutions to enable a continuous dialogue to take place. At the head was a Council of Association, composed of Ministers, with powers of initiation and decision; it delegated most of its business to a Committee of Association composed of ambassadors. There was also a parliamentary conference of member states and an Arbitration Court of the Association. These institutions (there is some comparison with those of the EEC) have been enlarged to accommodate the subsequent admission of new member states, and they continue under the Lomé Convention – but they are not in continuous session, nor does their existence guarantee cooperation between members.

A second Yaoundé Convention (1969) increased development funds and lowered the CET on tropical products. In 1966 Nigeria had gained similar treatment by signing a treaty of association, and the Arusha Agreement (1968–9) extended it to Kenya, Tanzania and Uganda. The several agreements were re-negotiated in the five-year Lomê Convention (1975) which was extended to include former British colonies (by 1979 there were fifty seven members drawn from Countries in Africa, the Caribbean and the Pacific – and therefore known as the ACP). The Lomé Convention allowed free access to the EEC of most agricultural exports from the ACP (special arrangements applied to sugar) without reciprocity, but in return the ACP allowed most-favoured-nation entry for EEC products – it was something like a free trade area, but it was not out of line with the general reduction of tariffs that were taking place in the seventies with the encouragement of GATT. A big innovation was a stabilisation fund (STABEX) to compensate ACP in the event of losses on their export of basic products due to price fluctuations or world slump or natural disaster. Financial and technical aid was increased. When the Convention was being re-negotiated in 1979, the level of this aid was thought by the ACP to be unrealistically low, even when it was raised to £3.6 billion (5.6 billion EUA). STABEX (System for Stabilization of Export Earnings) was to be extended by a new fund (SYSMIN, System for Safeguarding and Developing Mineral Production) to cover mineral products and the European Investment Bank (EIB) was to help finance mining and energy projects. Negotiations ended in some confusion over the details of the aid and whether a reference to Human Rights ought to be included: several ACP states clearly thought the Community too concerned with its own self-interests. But if Lomé II earned less commendation than its predecessor, much store was set by the Joint Consultative Assembly in which MEPs and representatives of the ACP states could meet for a regular exchange of views.

In addition to these trade agreements, what can only be termed a Mediterranean policy began to emerge after the Paris Summit (1972). Negotiations were hastened by the oil crisis following the Yom Kippur War and resulted in the agreements with the Maghreb Countries (Algeria, Morocco, Tunisia) in 1976 and the Machrak Countries (Egypt, Jordan, Lebanon and Syria) in 1977 for development aid and free access for products (other than the CAP). Like the Lomé Convention, these agreements also provided for an annual meeting of a Cooperation Council of Ministers with a committee of plenipotentiaries to provide for a continuing dialogue: in the words of the preamble, the agreements were

> a new model for relations between developed and developing States, compatible with the aspirations of the international community towards a more just and more balanced economic order.

Clearly, the Commission has developed a worldwide network of agreements (there are trade links with Eastern Europe and China) by which the CET is reduced and trade and cooperation increased. The several agreements are in line with the resolution of the UNCTAD (United Nations Conference on Trade and Development) meeting in 1968 – although access to the EEC market is not unlimited under the general preferences arranged and the trade balance (oil apart) tends to be favourable to the EEC. In its relations with the Third World, the Community is not merely altruistic – a view apparently confirmed by the largely unsuccessful meeting of UNCTAD V at Manila (1979) where the developed world was accused of protectionist activity.

Further enlargement of the EEC

Since the late seventies active negotiations have been conducted to enlarge the Community from Nine to Twelve, with Greece (with whom negotiations first began in the 1960s) signing a Treaty of Accession (1979) for full membership in 1981. Spain and Portugal seek entry in 1983. There have also been serious suggestions about Turkey joining. Each of the prospective members is in Southern Europe and until recent years all were under political dictatorships. Membership would strengthen the democratic institutions within them, as well as their internal stability; also it would serve to extend the Community across much of Europe. The chief reasons for admitting new members are unashamedly political. Their entry poses much more serious problems than the enlargement of 1973 – problems which would, initially at least, put serious strain on common policies and strengthen those tendencies in the Community to make it a looser *Europe des Patries* than the economic community that was originally envisaged. In particular, each of the prospective members has a large agricultural element (in Greece 34 per cent of the labour force, in Portugal 30 per cent, in Spain 23 per cent) which produces Mediterranean crops already in surplus. Spain is the foremost producer of olive oil, of which the Community is already 65 per cent self-sufficient and her wine production is 20 per cent that of the Community's total. Some see this as a political weapon to force a renegotiation of the CAP.

Northern-temperate farming would no longer be predominant in the Community and French and Italian producers of citrus fruits, preserved fruits and vegetables, as well as wine and olive oil, would be adversely affected. Each of the applicant countries is relatively poor and this will put severe pressures upon the emergent Regional and Social Funds, and upon arrangements for the free movement of workers. British arguments for bigger transfers of resources from richer to poorer regions would be reinforced by the enlargement. The anticipated increase in intra-Community trade might well be cancelled out by the increased payments needed in the Budget. Although there exist good opportunities for enlarging the market for consumer goods, there is already with the new applicants an adverse trade balance (Portugal's was £500m in 1978), even with existing protective tariffs: free trade could have serious repercussions for a series of industries in the Nine that are already under pressure. It is no wonder that the negotiations proceed slowly and that the admission of Spain and Portugal in 1983 appears to be in doubt.

An increase to Twelve members will put great strain on the Community's decision-making process – it was designed for six reasonably homogeneous nations and is already under pressure with Nine. There would be three additional languages, which would add to the cost of administration and increase the time taken by meetings. The work of the Council of Ministers would take longer and the threat of a veto under the Luxembourg compromise (see page 62) would be unacceptable. Various suggestions have been made to overcome the problem of a member nation of a Community of Twelve being faced with a decision felt to be against its national interests: weighted majority voting has been strongly urged, and the idea that a vetoed proposal might be referred to the European Parliament has been floated. The admission of Greece emphasises the importance of political and economic relations with Yugoslavia which could become a transit-country for intra-Community trade and so shrewdly affect the diplomatic balance in Europe. There is the further possibility of the admission of Turkey (already a member of NATO, and with whom an agreement of association, ultimately envisaging full membership, was signed as early as 1962, and a protocol added in 1973 intended to lead to a complete customs union by 1995). Greek relations with Turkey, even without the delicate issue of Cyprus, have been far from happy and a possible Greek veto of a Turkish application could not be discounted. Turkey would benefit quite as much as the other three Mediterranean applicants in terms of strengthening her democratic institutions, of her trade, of financial aid to agriculture and industry and of the right of free movement of migrant workers – all of which would increase the burden of costs on the existing Nine members.

It would be naïve to view enlargement as a simple extension of an economic area – the idea of a two-tier system of new applicants being merely 'associate members' (an idea reminiscent of the Maudling Plan of 1956) seems to have been discarded. Economic and political advantages for both the Community and the applicants arise from enlargement, but the financial cost to the Nine would be great. In administrative terms, enlargement will place incredible strain upon present institutions and policies and may point the Community away from that degree of integration that was originally envisaged. Admission of the three Mediterranean applicants will go further than merely increasing internal Community stresses, it will involve a reconsideration of the economic and especially political relations with Turkey, the Maghreb and the Machrak countries (see page 96) – a very sensitive area for world diplomacy. Certainly, the balance within the Community and its place and purpose in the world would be shrewdly altered in the 1980s.

The lessons of the 1970s

The political integration envisaged by the founding fathers of the EEC lies still a long way off. Economic crises have led to institutional ones, and the hopes for restructuring Europe's industry have given way to the 'crisis management' of declining industries. Even in the high-technology industries (aero-space and computers) there has been no great European leap forward. The 1970s have not been a happy decade for the Community – and it cannot all be laid at the door of the oil crisis.

The development of the Community seems to be polarising towards a reassertion of the importance of the national state. The Community has always been a matter of nicely balancing interests with an eye to the immediate future. Where there is a strong convergence of interests between members, common policies seem possible (witness the CAP and the moves in 1979 to devise some form of energy policy), but the absence of such policies from other areas, especially where there appears no urgency, suggests a very minimal sense of European unity among political leaders. The Community, after all, has been with us for over twenty years. Direct election of the new European Parliament presages a change in the relationship of the institutions at the centre of political power in the Community (although the disappointingly low turn-out for the direct elections does not enhance the moral stature of the new European Parliament). It may be that a new centre of political decision-making is required, for the institutions of the Community are at base those that emerged from the small homogeneous ECSC: they may be far from adequate to meet the needs of a Community enlarged to Twelve members in the 1980s.

In 1975 the Tindemans Report made some very modest proposals for reform: they caused a storm, suggesting that the Community even then was not poised for a 'great leap forward'. A 'Three Wise Men' Report (1979), on means of improving efficiency in anticipation of enlargement, made no radical proposals apart from recommending weighted majority voting in Council in place of a veto (which would increase the pressures for 'horse-trading' compromise agreements). But to continue to exclude from the direct concern of the Community the vital areas of security (defence) and foreign policy would suggest that ultimate unity is not the wish of member governments. To introduce defence, making the Euro-group of NATO the defence committee of the Community (with France and Norway as associates) would introduce an institutional imperative into Community affairs that would induce a strong political centre. Without such a centre, it could be doubted whether the Community would grow in cohesion as it grows in membership. Clearly, the EEC has gone beyond the stage of a customs union: the need for cohesion through common policies becomes more pressing. Social and Regional policies are obvious areas – the more so as they will be of vital concern to the new member states – and energy is a vital area too, for North Sea oil will not survive the century, and nuclear reactors have a long way to go before they can supply a major part of our energy needs.

The seventies were not easy years for the Community. The lessons point on the one hand to a concentration upon immediate problems, with the Community making grants to member countries to help deal with their particular difficulty. This would not lead to closer unity and would limit the Commission, for example, to the management of trans-national matters. On the other hand, the lessons could point towards a streamlining of existing institutions and a strengthening of central powers, especially through the new European Parliament as against the Council of Ministers. The institutions of the 1950s may well be insufficiently sophisticated for the 1980s: the major problem is how to make central institutions powerful enough to develop and control major areas of Community policy and yet retain the confidence of the general electorate. For the general electorate may have lost faith in the capacity of central institutions to provide a ready answer to their problems – in this, there is some comparison with the world of Eastern Europe. The Community is an evolving institution. It has a part to play in the development of Europe: but it has also a world rôle to play. Modification and change are needed to preserve its vitality and capacity to meet future challenges. And in all this, the choice still lies between Monnet's vision of an integrated Community, secure against poverty at home, against war within it, and against the great trading empires of the world; and the contrasting vision of de Gaulle, of a '*Europe des patries*' in which Europe, led by France and others, asserts a world presence against the Super-Powers.

5

France and West Germany

France

France rivals Britain in the history of Western democracy, but her tradition differs in that it stems directly from the French Revolution of the 1790s and its culmination in the régime of Napoleon. The ideological conflicts arising from that Revolution are with us still, joined today by those stemming from the Russian Revolution. No view of French politics can escape the force of the revolutionary tradition, nor fail to acknowledge the strong presence of central government with its traditions going back to the *ancien régime* and to the more centralised forms of Napoleonic France. Even more than in Britain, history casts a deep shadow over French politics and the experience of more recent crises – the *dégringolade* of 1940, Vichy, the defeat in Indo-China, Algeria and the fall of the Fourth Republic, the 'non-revolution' of 1968 – has helped to mould the outlook of the present political leadership.

One of the strongest principles that have inspired French constitutions has been that of a 'republic, one and indivisible' – a principle that strengthens central authority, and has a fundamental importance where supra-national authorities are concerned. Even so, there is a tradition of distrust of strong central executive power, and this is partly the explanation for the institutionally weak ministries which changed so frequently under the Third and Fourth Republics that they induced at times almost a state of political ineffectiveness (*immobilisme*); this, the Fifth Republic (1958) hoped to end. The 1958 Constitution is presidential, in that it places the president above parliament and provides him with the opportunity of taking the leading rôle in politics and government. It was once popular to argue that it had been cast in this presidential form to allow de Gaulle (President 1958–69) effective control of the executive. But, in fact, the Constitution was a compromise and de Gaulle failed to secure the overriding authority which the President of the United States enjoys. Instead, it made him the arbiter, not the leader of French politics, and it preserved sufficient of the traditional checks by the legislature for some to call it parliamentary. It also preserved the administrative structure dating back to Napoleon, together with control of the higher civil service (*grand corps*) by the 'technocrats' trained in the prestigious *grandes écoles* like the Polytechnique (1795) or the Ecole Nationale d'Administration (E.N.A., 1945), which ensured a continuance of the centralised state even after the 'events' of 1968.

The President

Under the Constitution, he is Head of State, but more concerned for maintaining the stability of France and her place in the world, than for daily affairs of current politics. He is elected for seven years by universal suffrage (amendment of 1962) with a system of second ballot (if no candidate has a clear majority, a second ballot is held between the two leading candidates two weeks later). He has no actual power of veto over legislation, but has an implicit veto in that he may ask Parliament to reconsider a law. He appoints the prime minister and the latter's choice of ministers and he is chairman of the Council of Ministers and Commander in Chief of the armed forces: thus he has powers independent of the National Assembly and of the prime minister, but his decisions must be countersigned by the prime minister, who then takes political responsibility for them. Each of the three presidents has tended to adopt a personal rôle in decision-making.

The president has certain reserve powers. In the event of political deadlock, he may dissolve the National Assembly (having first consulted with the prime minister and the presidents of the two chambers) – but only once in any year. This has occurred in 1962 and 1968. Secondly, he may appeal directly to the people by means of a referendum, and insist on a referendum on certain bills. De Gaulle made fairly frequent use of referenda in order to assert a presidential policy – it gave him a direct link with the people against parliament (but it was not infallible, since the 1969 referendum on local government reform produced an unfavourable result and he resigned). Since 1972, when his successor, Pompidou, used it over the accession of Britain to EEC and there was an abstention rate of forty-five per cent, recourse to referenda has fallen out of favour – the presidential style of Giscard d'Estaing is decidedly different from that of de Gaulle. Finally, in a national emergency, the president may assume full powers (Article 16). This was originally designed to avoid any repetition of 1940, when a weak president gave in to the defeatists. Potentially, it is of great significance, but its use is circumscribed by having to consult the prime minister, the presidents of the assemblies and the Constitutional Council. It was invoked in 1961, following the generals' *putsch* in Algiers, but it proved cumbersome and has not been used again, even in the serious situation of 1968.

The Prime Minister and his government

The prime minister is supported by the Constitution against the president (who cannot dismiss him) and the government is his responsibility: but the government has a collective character, and this is symbolised by all major decisions being taken in the Council of Ministers, normally under the chairmanship of the president. If a vote of censure is passed, the resignation of all ministers must follow; but a feature of the Fifth Republic, unlike its predecessors, has been the stability of governments (ministers may resign, but governments have not changed frequently). The vote of censure procedure (Article 49) can be utilised to preserve the life of a government, for a prime minister may stake the life of his government on a particular measure and thus manage to get a majority for it from members who regard the measure as less of a threat to their interests than the possibility of a general election or at least the fall of the government. It was intended as a device to be used very occasionally, but in November 1979 Raymond Barre used Article 49 to force through changes in social security payments and made it abundantly clear that he would have recourse to the same mechanism throughout 1980 – the socialists complained that he was using Article 49 'like a machine gun'.

Ministers must resign their seat in Parliament upon appointment (Article 23), securing a substitute in their place, which avoids too many by-elections – and ministers need not be members of parliament at all, a number are successful career civil servants or businessmen. This reduces the influence of Parliament (ministers may speak – not vote – in the Chamber to advise on a particular policy or measure). Each minister chooses a *cabinet* of advisers, who need not all be civil servants although many of them are, and their *esprit de corps*, begun in the *grandes écoles*, is of inestimable advantage in settling problems of administration. While they are members of the *cabinet*, their salaries normally continue to be paid either by their ministry or the firm from which they come – not only is great prestige involved, but other advantages may arise from having a 'friend at court'. The importance of the *cabinets* has increased; many decisions tend to be taken as a result of consultation between *cabinets* rather than in the Council of Ministers. They have been attacked for usurping the function of parliament, whose powers have diminished under the Fifth Republic and ministers are able to manipulate the chambers, particularly on technical matters, through their *attaché parlementaire*. In the rivalry arising out of the ambiguities of the relationship between president and prime minister the *cabinets* also play a crucial rôle.

Parliament

There are two chambers: the Senate, or upper chamber, is elected for nine years (one third of the senators retiring every three years in order to achieve continuity) by indirect voting by local authorities in order to ensure adequate representation of the local authorities as a whole. An electoral college, composed of delegates from municipal and rural authorities, elects senators on a départmental basis. There is a very heavy rural bias which generally results in a Senate of a different party complexion from the National Assembly, and considerable tension results from this. De Gaulle had hoped to change the composition of the Senate by his proposed local government reforms which were defeated in the 1969 referendum.

The deputies of the National Assembly (lower chamber) are elected for five years by direct universal suffrage of all citizens over eighteen. In order to avoid the evident inequalities that result from a simple majority (the British system of 'first past the post'), a two-stage ballot occurs. Candidates gaining a clear majority on the first ballot are declared elected: otherwise, a week later (elections are held on Sundays), all candidates who obtained more than ten per cent of the votes on the first ballot may stand again, and the one with a simple numerical majority is elected. (Numerous electoral deals take place during the week in hopes of influencing the second election.) Psephological evidence suggests that this *ballotage* system does not so much give an opportunity for a more equitable

1978 French election results

Centre and Right:		
	Gaullists	153 (*173*)
	Giscardians	137 (*127*)
		290 (*300*)

Union of the Left:		
	Socialists	104 (*95*)
	Radicals	10 (*13*)
	Communists	86 (*74*)
		200 (*182*)

(figures in brackets for previous parliament)

result as reinforce the first result with an electoral bias towards the right wing.

The experience of splinter groups and ministerial instability under previous Republics led to the 1958 Constitution allowing less powers to Parliament; in particular, it lacks the power of legislative initiative, has only limited power over government legislation and, in any case, sits for only about half the year. The government may exercise closure on discussion of a measure (Article 44) by requesting each chamber to vote by a single vote (*vote bloqué*) on the text under discussion, and may promulgate the budget by ordinance if it has not been passed within seventy days. By adopting a motion of censure, however, the National Assembly obliges the prime minister to submit the resignation of his government to the President (Article 50). Power to adjudicate between government and parliament lies with the Constitutional Council, but the Constitution tends to lead the Council towards favouring the executive against the legislature.

The Fifth Republic has not had a smooth parliamentary history, and much criticism has been raised against the Constitution for being weighted against Parliament. In the National Assembly, however, perhaps the most significant development since 1958 has been the concentration of splinter parties into four principal party groups (indeed, from 1972–78 the Communists and Socialists combined in an uncertain alliance on a Common Programme).

Local Government

Unlike Britain, France has a strong tradition of central control in local affairs, with the government working for the general good through civil servants of high status, imbued with a high sense of public service. This tradition of *étatisme* enjoys a considerable reputation. But there has always been tension between local and central government since at least the time of the Revolution, when the 1790 reform sought to break down local provincialism by dividing France into new *départements*. As in other countries, there is now considerable pressure for local government reform, but also considerable local resistance, and despite the measures of 1964 and 1972, a situation amounting almost to *immobilisme* exists today. But increased pressure for revision of the rural-biased local government system appeared during the sixties and seventies in response to changes like the creation of a modern transport system with inter-connecting motorways, the partial dispersal of industry and a considerable movement of rural population to urban centres.

France is divided into 95 *départements*, each with a *conseil général* directly elected for six years, but under a government-appointed senior civil servant, the *Préfet*. The department itself is sub-divided into electoral districts (*cantons* and *arrondisements*) and a large number of *communes* (there were 37 700 in 1958) each with its *conseil municipal*, elected by universal suffrage for six years, although it has only minor functions and is controlled by the mayor who is elected by the *conseil* from among their members. The *Préfet* is the executive agent for the department but is appointed by, and responsible to, the central government: he is a career civil servant who does not come from the area – and, indeed, is moved on frequently lest he become too 'involved' – and whose career frequently depends to a considerable degree upon his capacity to keep the local administration running smoothly. The *Préfet* perpetuates the dependence of local authorities on central government: his general supervision is known by the word *tutelle* – tutelage.

Reform of local government was a major topic of debate in the sixties – it was, indeed, the cause of de Gaulle's defeat in 1969. Demands for reform covered a number of topics, as for example, larger, more effective local units; more participation in decision making (this was a major theme in the 1968 troubles); rationalisation of powers and greater decentralisation of powers and financial resources. There were reforms: regionalisation was the theme, on the argument that the larger the unit the more likely it was to be efficient. At the lower level, an ordinance (1959) allowed multi-purpose syndicates of communes, and in 1966 four large urban communities (Bordeaux, Lille, Lyons, Strasbourg) were created, taking over the function of communes in their areas. At the upper level, there was the creation of the District of Paris (1959) and the decree (1960) grouping departments into 22 Regions for administrative coordination and economic planning, followed by the appointment (1964) of Regional Prefects and of official Regional Development Boards (CODER, Comités de Développement Economique Régional) together with advisory councils (DATAR, Délégation à Aménagement du Territoire et à l'Action Régional) after the style of the Monnet 'concertation' principle (see page 105). The referendum defeat of 1969 prevented this potentially significant reform going further, and although President Pompidou and President Giscard d'Estaing were known to favour reform, there were no major steps forward. The 1970 relaxation of tutelage changed little, and the Local Government Act (1971) encouraging the merging of communes had little effect (in 1979 there were still some 36 300 communes of which 22 500 had fewer than 500 inhabitants). The high water mark of regionalism was reached in the 1972 Act creating Regional Councils – they were criticised as outposts of central government, allowing little local initiative. Similarly, DATAR, also criticised as reinforcing centralism, has not made that impact that was hoped for. The regional problem remains, now compounded by a new development, for people are less prepared to quit a run-down area for the dubious attraction of Paris and its environs. Real devolution has not progressed in France – it has been argued that this may be partly because in Italy and Spain it has led to left-wing local power bases. By 1978, it was clear that regionalism and further local devolution of powers was out of favour – the President himself was quoted as telling an assembly of Regional Prefects, 'I am here to defend the unity of the country: Corsica has made enough trouble already'. The socialists continued to encourage *autogestion* (local self-government) and to urge regional councils elected by universal suffrage – but they lost the 1978 election. *Immobilisme* seems to have overtaken local government in France.

The Plans – and their demise

The tradition of strong central control provides a backcloth to the 'indicative planning' that has been a feature of French economic development since the war. Indicative planning differs from 'directive planning' as practised in the Soviet Union (see page 151) in two fundamental respects: it works within the constraints of a free market economy by the government leading large organisations towards specific ends (*dirigisme*) and the specific ends are agreed by consultation between the government and all interested parties. It is a form of planning that has proved popular in the West, and is best seen in France where it has promoted by Jean Monnet as part of the programme of Reconstruction after the war.

In order to appreciate Monnet's achievements in the late forties (both in organisational and in economic terms) it is necessary to recall the serious situation in France in 1945 (see page 48) with many people still subsisting on less than 2000 calories a day. Vigorous action was needed, and the recent experience of total war made central direction psychologically acceptable. Fairly extensive nationalisation of basic utility service industries and economic and industrial planning were easily introduced. The idea of central planning centrally imposed by bureaucrats, however, would have provoked opposition, since it would have savoured too much of Soviet Gosplan methods. It was Jean Monnet's achievement to devise a method that made central planning, if only in specific and restricted areas of the economy, both widely accepted and generally popular. The key lay in *concertation*, in bringing all parties involved into extensive discussions to achieve consensus in terms of objectives of the Plan (the *Conseil économique et social* (1946) helped here). This was no mean achievement, even allowing for the favourable atmosphere of the time for Monnet was intent on changing the French economy so that a country with a tradition of protection might prepare itself for a leading rôle in the competitive integrated European Market that he desired: 'Modernisation and reconstruction must go hand in hand'.

The *Commissariat Général au Plan* (1946), from its inception as an independent government organisation under the prime minister, had an immediate impact. It combined ministers and leading public figures and set about forecasting the immediate needs of the economy. Modernisation commissions (on coal mines, electricity supply, steel, building materials, transport, farm machinery and later petrol and nitrates for farm fertilisers) were established, comprising administrators, businessmen and trade unionists, to act as a means of communicating the Plan to the administration and to the public at large. They were later developed into a veritable network, both in vertical (sectoral) and horizontal planes – by the Seventh Plan there were twelve of the former and seven of the latter, involving a total of some 3500 people. The commissions also received, as part of the dialogue, advice and information from all interested parties, so that the 'spirit of the Plan' might reflect the economic and social forces of the nation. Once adopted, the Plan became quasi-contractual, with the State offering financial aid to contributing firms – but the Plan, of course, was a guide line only, subject to any necessary later changes. As Monnet put it

> The Plan is essentially a method of convergent action and a means whereby everyone can relate his own efforts to those of everyone else. It is concerned as much with orientation as with control.

The First Plan of Modernisation and Equipment (the 'Monnet Plan') lasted from 1947 to 1953; it was essentially a long-term austerity plan and was a conspicuous success – although, in the inflation of the later forties, it was Marshall Aid that kept it alive. It suited the French *étatiste* tradition. The Plan was indicative, not mandatory, resting on 'concertation' not subordination – '*ni libéralisme, ni dirigisme*' – and perhaps its biggest offshoot was the pooling of information and forecasts, as a result of which sounder investment and planning decisions could be made – the process was 'de-politicised'. It was, as it were, a basis for a permanent exchange of ideas between the administration and the country in an *economie concertée*, a partially corporative approach to planning that operated as much among those actually involved as among the politicians. But the limitations of the Plan must also be remembered: it was sectoral, covering only certain major industries, and it was the concern of the large enterprise, rather than the small. Furthermore, the actual preparation of the Plan remained a confidential stage in the hands of technocrats – concertation did not mean joint decision-making: the interest groups consulted were there for discussion and advice, not decision.

There followed a succession of Plans of greater complexity: the Second (1954–8) and Third (1958–61) were concerned for growth in industrial production and domestic consumption and concentrated on the problem of allocation of resources in the economy. Inflation overtook both Plans, but already a new dimension was appearing – how to restructure the French economy to fit into an international framework within the EEC. The Fourth Plan (1962–5) had the outright backing of de Gaulle, who spoke of '*l'ardente obligation du Plan*'. This was the time of considerable interest in regional development, and of the birth (1964) of DATAR and CODER. The Fourth Plan was more comprehensive than its predecessors and contained detailed projections for output – it was becoming more political and *dirigiste*; it had not changed the economic system, but had helped its progress, as de Gaulle put it, it 'compensates for the inconveniences of freedom without losing its advantages'. It attracted a great deal of interest abroad, and was the inspiration for the National Economic Development Council (NEDC, 1962) and the ill-fated British Plan of 1966. The Fifth Plan (1966–70), following the 1963 economic crisis, concentrated on strategic planning with priority targets and proposals for industrial restructuring. It was overwhelmed by the 'events' of May, 1968 – although it saw the creation (1969) of the *Institut du développement industriel* (IDI) for state aid for the concentration of firms to improve their competitive position. This was a sign of the times: the much heralded mid-term planning was being transferred to the Treasury and so back to government control. By the Sixth Plan (1971–5) the central planning aspects were in something of a retreat, for it was more a 'frame of reference' than a projection of output targets – people began to talk of the demise of planning and the shrinking of concertation. However, this Plan for the first time made use of a fully formalised model (FIFI) based on the impact of foreign competition and proposing that the particular sector exposed to competition (for this was the time of the 1972/3 enlargement of the Community) would have its prices determined for it by the foreign competition itself, thus a new emphasis on competition was present in both the Sixth and the Seventh Plan. The trade unions took little part – and less in the discussions for the following Plan, which became much more of a government proposal. If the sixties had witnessed a French 'economic miracle' with a growth rate rising to 6.2 per cent between 1968 and 1973, opinion nevertheless was challenging both the secrecy with which the preparation stage was surrounded, and the limited range of the Plan's content. This Sixth Plan fell dramatically short of its growth target, and the suggested target of 5 per cent of its successor seemed scarcely serious.

The Seventh Plan (1976–80) confirmed the impression of a turning away from Monnet-type planning. It was prepared at incredible speed and in the wake of the oil crisis, and although touching on problems of unemployment and expectations concerning the quality of life and the reduction of social inequality, it was sketchy in detail and its attempts to strengthen the competitive position of the small family firm were not part of a developed integrated plan. A new feature was the establishment of twenty-five Priority Action Programmes (PAPs) for specific and limited planning objectives, although, taken together, they do not constitute a coherent development policy. A new institution, the Central Planning Council (1974), was created, with President Giscard d'Estaing in the chair, to strengthen the links with government, but it appears to short-circuit the concertation process by taking decisions before the process had had time to run its course.

A change of attitude towards planning had taken place; the Sixth and Seventh Plans were now 'Plans of Government', limited, specific and more controlled; there was less concertation and more formalised government planning. It is an indication of the increased politicising of the planning process, for the uncertainty of the international climate, especially with regard to energy supplies, made any form of economic planning wait upon political decision. At the same time as the Seventh Plan was launched, it was rendered effectively redundant by the new Prime Minister, Raymond Barre's, Stabilisation Plan (1976). Direct government intervention, if only in terms of crisis 'fire-fighting' (like the drastic pruning of the steel industry in 1979 which provoked serious riots at Denain) seems to have replaced the Monnet approach, and the experiences of 1979, with continued economic depression and inflation, confirm the impression.

Originally, the French model of the Plan implied a limited centralism – that this process might be strengthened and extended to other countries was one of the reasons for promoting the EEC and for encouraging Britain (who would follow the French Plan method) to seek entry. By the later seventies, a different atmosphere had appeared, much more pluralist and closer to the original German model, allowing greater independence to the individual firm. At the same time, French planning was beginning to wither away – a victim of inflation and international economic disturbances, or a failure of political will to take central planning further.

Education

The French tradition in education policy has been one of central direction of schools, curriculum and pedagogy. French educators have placed a high premium on knowledge and on its necessary accompanying requirement of rote learning, although the ultimate purpose is the development of the intellectual faculties of the child. A major change, in effect a logical result of the 1968 troubles, was marked by the Haby Education Act (1975) which began to take effect in 1977–8. It provided for a juncture of the different types of secondary schools and the pursuit of a common curriculum taken in unstreamed classes – in effect, it introduced comprehensive schooling and also allowed parents the opportunity to influence class teaching through a series of meetings and committees. The old *Lycées*' formidable examination, the *Baccalauréat*, was to be reformed from 1983, when it would be divided into two parts, the first taken in basic subjects at the end of formal schooling (age 16) the second in optional subjects two years later. This major change in French education provoked considerable opposition from the teaching profession and appears (1980) to have had less impact than was expected. Streaming (if in disguised form) appears to be widespread, although the curriculum reforms continue, and parent pressure groups appear to have more political muscle than in Britain. The *Baccalauréat* reform also appears to have been deferred – although M. Barre had concluded, in the aftermath of the 1968 troubles, that the old-style examination had already become an anachronism.

The academic pressure survives the change of system and bears more heavily on those of less ability in that French school children have the shortest school year in Europe – 310 half-days (compared with 400 half-days in Britain): clearly, parents are expected to support teachers and supervise work at home. Indeed, since the 1968 troubles, the government has instituted a system of school and class councils on which parents and pupils are represented (though, with the head teacher in the chair, doubts have been expressed about their utility). It is no longer the practice for pupils to repeat a year's work if they fail to reach the required standard (unless parents specifically request it); extra classes may be available for those in need, or those wanting more advanced work. At sixteen the *Lycée d'enseignement général* takes students to the *Baccalauréat*, and the *Lycée d'enseignement professionnel* to professional qualifications. The class councils continue, with parents represented, and routine discipline is in the hands of the school council.

French universities are regional (Paris is an exception) and some, like Lille, have recently been rebuilt on new sites. More so than England, university

The educational system in France

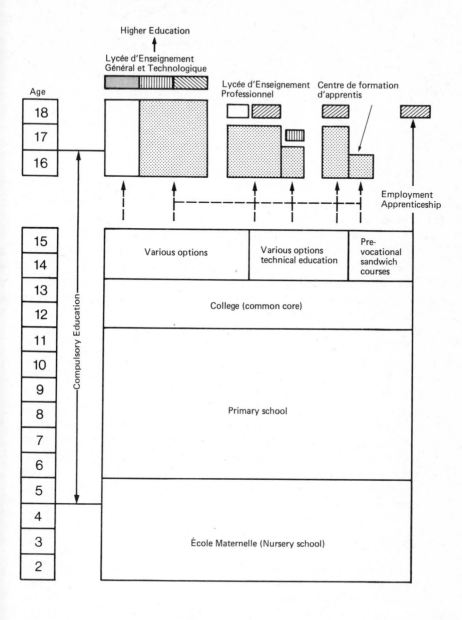

Higher Education

Lycée d'Enseignement
Général et Technologique

Lycée d'Enseignement
Professionnel

Centre de formation
d'apprentis

Age

| 18 |
| 17 |
| 16 |

Employment
Apprenticeship

| 15 |
| 14 |

Various options | Various options technical education | Pre-vocational sandwich courses

| 13 |
| 12 |

College (common core)

| 11 |
| 10 |
| 9 |
| 8 |
| 7 |
| 6 |

Primary school

| 5 |
| 4 |
| 3 |
| 2 |

École Maternelle (Nursery school)

Compulsory Education

Baccalauréat

Brevet d'Études
Professionnelles

Brevet de
Technicien

Certificat
d'Education
Professionnelle

Certificat
d'Aptitude
Professionnelle

Technical
education

students tend to be middle class with strong professional connexions. Beyond the universities are the world famous training schools, where a common educational background (especially with a degree in law) and experienced in the *grands corps* open a career prospect beyond government administration, in politics and in private corporations: here the Polytechnique has a rival in the Ecole Nationale d'Administration (ENA) created in 1945, whose pupils (*énarques*) have done much to mould the Fifth Republic. The most brilliant future secondary school and university teachers are trained at the Ecole Normale Supérieure.

West Germany

The birth of West Germany was not an occasion for rejoicing. Three zones of occupation of the Western Powers were grouped together and the new state survived because of the determination of the allies, because of Marshall Aid, of natural resources, and of a population enlarged by refugees. Its constitution rests on the *Grundgesetz* (fundamental law) of 1949: it is a federation (*Bund*) of ten states (Länder) – the Saarland became German after a plebiscite on 1 January 1957 (see page 20). The capital is Bonn: West Berlin is an anomaly. A symbol of the desire to reunite the two Germanies, it has remained an isolated prestige outpost – the autobahn linking it with the West is maintained throughout by West Germany. It sends twenty-two representatives to Parliament, but these are not elected, they are chosen from members of the West Berlin city parliament, and at Bonn their votes are separately recorded. The 1971 Quadripartite Agreement (see page 116) sanctioned the close ties that exist, but West Berlin is not quite a full member of the *Bund*. The ties go beyond sentiment and involve considerable subsidies from the Federal Republic to maintain the city's economic viability. However, it is a 'dying' city in that the young people tend to leave for West Germany and the working population is maintained by immigrants who receive considerable inducements to work and settle there. The economy of the city is a continual worry and some firms have transferred to West Germany. There are fears that it may become something of a capitalist white elephant. Vast stocks of food and essential materials continue to be maintained lest it be once more besieged.

The Länder

The *Länder* are modern creations: only the *land* city state of Bremen and of Hamburg, and the south German state of Bayern (Bavaria) have survived post-war territorial changes (Bayern actually rejected the *Grundgesetz* on the grounds that it was insufficiently federal). Whatever the motive of the Allies in creating quite new *Länder*, it coincided with a psychological rejection of the Nazi period with it, evident centralisation and the cataclysmic ending of the Third Reich (the 'German catastrophe', as Meinecke put it), a rejection contained in the concept of the *Stunde null* (absolute zero). There have also been profound social and economic changes that underline a break with the past – even agricultural Bayern is fast developing a mixed economy.

Each *Land* has its own parliament (*Landtag*) and the elections, even though federal issues overshadow local ones, generally result in a different pattern from the federal Parliament. Each *Land* has a government under a Ministerpresident, which is responsible for the normal range of government services (for the *Länder* are in part independent) save for foreign affairs and defence. (The city *Länder* have a similar pattern.) Each *Land* raises its own taxes (the *Bund* subsidises the poorer *Länder* with the richer contributing to an equalisation fund through the 'horizontal equalisation system'. As costs rise and the field of government extends, a pattern similar to the 'cooperative federalism' of the USA has developed bringing federal and *Land* governments closer together; this is evident in education, health and hospital services, and urban renewal, whilst regional economic planning comes under a joint commission. Below the *Land* government level, however, there is a confusion of local and district authorities of all sizes. These are the *Gemeinden*, jealous of their self-governing status – but considerable inroads into their autonomy have been made by both federal and *Land* governments. In 1975 there were some 11 000 *Gemeinden*, about half of which had less than 500 inhabitants (although sixty-four had over 100 000). Local pride remains an important factor, but rationalisation of local government divisions is an urgent problem. Small rural *Gemeinden* are linked with the *Landkreis* (rural district) and very large towns are divided into *Bezirke* (districts). The *Landkreis* are controlled by the *Regierungsbezirke*, into which the *Land* may be divided.

The constitution of West Germany

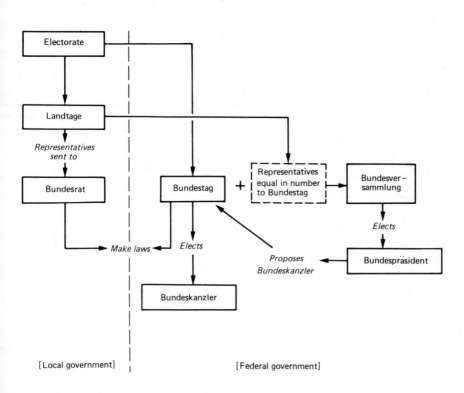

Federal government

The *Länder* exercise a certain influence on the federal government through the Upper House, the *Bundesrat*. Its members are appointed by the *Land* governments and vote according to their instructions (each *Land* has between three and five members according to population) casting their votes as a single bloc. The majority in the *Bundesrat* may differ from that in the Lower House (*Bundestag*) and in the event of conflict between the Houses a joint mediation committee is held. The conflicts have increased to the point of positive obstruction by the *Bundesrat* in the seventies.

The *Bundestag* is elected by universal suffrage (all adults over eighteen) for four years, though it may be dissolved between elections if it refuses a vote of confidence to the Chancellor. The *Bund* is divided into 248 constituencies of about 240 000 people (the boundaries being periodically adjusted to take account of movement of population). The electoral procedure is highly complex. Each voter has two votes; the first is cast for a candidate in his own constituency

The distribution of seats in the Bundestag, 1965–76

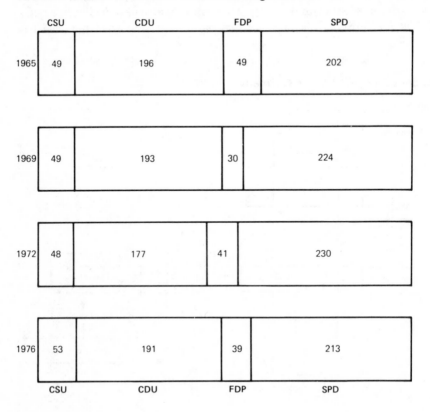

There has been a remarkable stability in the balance of parties in the Bundestag (496 deputies)

(*Wahlkreise*) who wins by simple majority on the 'first past the post' principle. This accounts for half of the members of the *Bundestag*; the other half is chosen from candidates appearing on party lists separately compiled in each *Land*, and the second vote is cast for a party list. The results of this second vote are shared out proportionally after counting all the votes cast for the party lists in all the *Länder*. The seats gained by the first (constituency member) vote are deducted from the total number of seats due to the party in each *Land*: the greater the success with the first constituency vote, the less chance have candidates on the party lists. The voter, of course, may vote for one party in the constituency and another on the party lists (the SPD seems to benefit from this practice). The highly complex system provides a great many opportunities for skilful electoral practices. For example, the proportional representation system could result in a party gaining a member in the *Bundestag* although it gained none in the constituencies – but to avoid the splinter group parties that plagued the Weimar Republic between the wars, only those parties polling at least five per cent of total valid votes in the whole *Bundesrepublik* may be represented in the *Bundestag*. This secures the position of the major parties – only four have been represented since 1961. There is also a certain stability between the representation of the two major parties, the CDU and the SPD, indeed, under Dr Kiesinger's Chancellorship in 1966 a Grand Coalition between CDU, CSU and SPD was formed.

German political parties have a legal status under Article 21 of the *Grundgesetz*, and a further act concerning parties (*Parteiengesetz*) was eventually

Party finances in West Germany

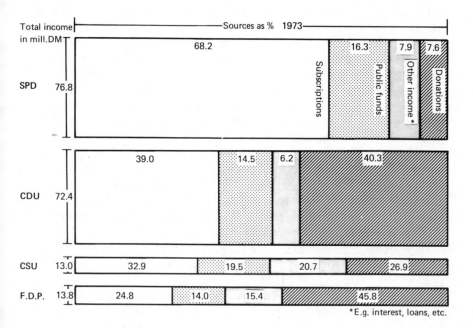

*E.g. interest, loans, etc.

passed in 1967 and amended in 1969, governing their organisation and finances. There is no limit on election expenditure (the 1969 federal election cost some DM 115m) and the *Parteiengesetz* provides for public funds to cover election expenses at federal and *Land* level (in 1974 the subsidy was fixed at DM 3.50 per registered voter, provided the party gained 0.5 per cent of all second votes cast). Subsidies for the 1974 election amounted to DM140m. Two parties, the right wing Socialist Reich Party (in 1952) and the Communist Party (in 1956) have been banned as endangering constitutional order (the ban against the Communists was lifted after 1968).

The experience of the Third Reich left West German political parties with a desire to avoid the extreme. In this they have been aided by the rapid economic expansion in the fifties and early sixties and the absence of major ideological divisions – the appearance of the New Left and various terrorist movements in the seventies was a matter for intellectuals and students, rather than the mainstream of political life. Two kinds of coalition have dominated the politics of the seventies, each striving to occupy the middle ground and so achieve a majority; there were the Social Democrats and Free Democrats (SPD and FDP) on the left centre and the Christian Democrats (CDU and CSU) on the right centre. By the end of the seventies, there seemed to be a movement in politics towards greater differentiation between the two groups and Herr Strauss, leader of the small Bayern party of the CSU, emerged as leader of the right-centre coalition with a distinct programme opposing *Ostpolitik* (which he condemns as an error and a deceit, arguing that to attempt to reconcile Marxism and democracy is 'tragic schizophrenia'). He favours a West German nuclear deterrent (a major departure, this) and the neutron bomb, together with closer relations with the Chinese Republic as a strong counter-weight to Russian influence. West German politics seemed to be polarising and the 1980 election campaign had begun by mid-1979. (A cynic might point to the agreement to study the British complaints over the size of their contribution to the EEC Budget (see page 83) as a clever means of avoiding crisis within Community politics and deferring a contentious item that could reverberate on national politics until after the election.)

The Head of State is the *Bundespräsident*, elected every five years by a specially convened assembly of the *Bundesversammlung* comprising both *Bundestag* and *Landtag* members. The *Bundespräsident* is a figurehead and has few powers, although the right to propose a candidate for the Chancellorship could be important in certain circumstances (Adenauer first became Chancellor by voting for himself – a majority of one). Similarly, there is potential power in the right to dissolve the *Bundestag* if a Chancellor fails to win a vote of confidence (though the initiative must come from the Chancellor); and he may wield some influence through his power to appoint federal judges, senior civil servants and officers in the armed forces. He promulgates laws passed by the federal parliament and has to decide upon their constitutionality. He is not to be compared with the President of France – or the USA.

The real power is wielded by the Chancellor. He can only be defeated by losing a 'constructive' vote of no confidence (Article 67) by which the *Bundestag* must at the same time agree upon a successor. He chooses his own ministers and may dismiss them himself – and since there is no cabinet responsibility, his powers are increased. He is the effective executive power, although the federal government is checked by the independence of the *Länder*, even though that independence is waning in the face of economic pressures. The aloofness with which Adenauer exercised the Chancellorship (1949–63) – despite the scandal of the Spiegel Affair (1961) that tarnished his personal reputation – has added a special aura to the office that the more homely style of later Chancellors, notably Brandt (1969–74) and Schmidt (since 1974), has not wholly dissipated.

Ostpolitik

In 1969 the SPD took office and rapidly brought to fruition a policy of *Ostpolitik* with which it had been concerned during the Grand Coalition (1966–9). Berlin is a symbol of German reunification (under a West Germany, of course), and officially the West remained committed to reunification as an ultimate solution to the German Question (even, indeed, to the point of supporting frontier alterations over the Oder-Neisse Line with Poland). But twenty years of progress in both East and West Germany had made it increasingly clear that there would be no hope of a peaceful reunification. Despite the invasion of Czechoslovakia (1968), which showed that the Soviet Union would fight rather than lose an important member of the Soviet bloc, relations between the two Germanies had been growing more stable throughout the seventies – East Germany, indeed, through the common frontier in Berlin, was enjoying considerable trading advantages with the EEC. To acknowledge the *status quo* would further ease relations and might even ultimately lead to some basis for reconciliation: certainly, the international situation, with its accent on *détente*, was favourable to a normalising of relations between the two Germanies.

This was Brandt's policy of *Ostpolitik*. There were four problems: the Oder-Neisse Line and the 'lost' lands in Poland, the position of German families who had fled from former German land after the war, and the problem of Berlin (which directly concerned the Four Allied Powers). Each problem touched sensitive areas of public opinion and international relations. It was not merely a German matter, for the division of the country symbolised the ideological division between East and West. More than this, it prevented the emergence of Europe as a single power bloc (with or without the Soviet Union). Again, any move towards re-unification had serious implications for NATO: it would shrewdly affect the balance of power in Central Europe, and it had military and strategic implications (particularly after the French withdrawal of 1966, see page 34). A reunited Germany could not be neutral – which side would it favour? And could either of the two sides risk the loss in terms of prestige and military preparedness that would follow the absorption of their half of Germany? Even to contemplate some form of accommodation between the two showed how far opinion and the realities of politics had changed since the dangerous moments of the Cold War. Europe was no longer the centre of the Super-Powers' attention, and they had come close enough to a balance to be able to seek ways of further reducing tension between them – SALT I talks (from 1971) were about to begin (see page 177). Again, there was the position of the two economic communities, the EEC and COMECON, to consider, if anything beyond the acceptance of the *status quo* was contemplated. Finally, things had changed sufficiently by the late sixties, for a capitalist state to have direct dealings with a Communist one, intra-German trade had extended considerably and, despite the building of the Berlin Wall (1961), personal contact between families in the two Germanies had increased.

Negotiations to reach some accommodation between the two Germanies advanced rapidly, and the three Treaties that crowned the *Ostpolitik* policy were a tribute to the political realism of all concerned. The Treaty of Moscow (1970) between the Federal Republic and the Soviet Union officially recognised West Germany and acknowledged the territorial integrity of all the states of Europe, but in particular recognised the inviolability of the Oder-Neisse Line as the western frontier of Poland (Article 3). Quietly, this ended a chapter in East-West relations – any re-unification of Germany, if such were to occur, would not be at the expense of Poland. The Warsaw Treaty (1970) between the Federal Republic and Poland, officially recognised the Oder-Neisse Line as the inviolable western frontier of Poland and normalised relations between the two states. The *Bundestag* ratified both treaties in May 1972: a very considerable change in diplomatic policy had taken place and the movement of German families desiring to leave Poland (or West Germany) was made easier. A 'Basic Treaty' between both Germanies followed in 1972 – a diplomatic reinforcement of the *status quo* – respecting the 'independence, autonomy and territorial integrity, the right of self-determination, the protection of human rights and non-discrimination' of both Germanies (Article 2), and affirming 'the inviolability now and in the future of the frontier existing between them' (Article 3). The very fact of a treaty between the two Germanies underlined a new recognition of the division between them.

The ideal of German re-unification was not rejected by these treaties; on the contrary, on the occasion of the signing of the Moscow Treaty the West German President presented a letter to the Soviet Foreign Ministry stating that 'this Treaty does not conflict with the political objective of the Federal Republic of Germany to work for a state of peace in Europe in which the German nation will recover its unity in free self-determination'. German re-unification remained a lively political issue in West Germany (so central a policy could not be dropped overnight), and the SPD had officially to reaffirm its commitment to re-unification for the 1975 election, and, as part of his campaign to extend the electoral influence of the CSU beyond Bayern, Herr Strauss laid emphasis on the policy of re-unification. His *Freudeskreise* (journalists call them 'Strauss fan clubs') had some impact in the rest of West Germany, so that in 1979 he was able to assume leadership of the CDU/CSU coalition as their candidate for the Chancellorship in the 1980 election.

Diplomatically, the problem of Berlin was beyond the powers of either Germany, but a Quadripartite Agreement on Berlin was signed by the Four Allied Powers in 'the building formerly occupied by the Allied Control Council in the American Sector of Berlin this 3rd day of September 1971' (Part 111). It reaffirmed the separate existence of the two Germanies, but provided for increased cooperation in a wide variety of fields, and by acknowledging the close ties of West Berlin with West Germany, the Soviet Union had made a major concession to the West. The Agreement was a tacit acknowledgement that both sides had retired somewhat from their traditional positions (on the West, regarding Berlin as a bridgehead within communist territory to achieve a German re-unification on Western terms, or, on the Soviet side, the squeezing out of the Western presence within East Germany). Berlin, and the whole problem of German re-unification, is a matter that steps beyond the German nation and involves the relations of both NATO and the Warsaw Pact, and of the two Super Powers of East and West. Nor does the Agreement take the Berlin Question out of political controversy: it is still used as a point of pressure.

In June 1979, East Germany announced the incorporation of East Berlin into the German Democratic Republic by abolishing the special status of its sixty-six parliamentary deputies – they would in future be directly elected to the *Volkskammer* (Parliament) instead of being nominated by the city council. There were Western protests at what was regarded as an infringement of the 1971 Four Power Agreement, and protests within the SPD/FDP coalition and by the West German opposition. Berlin remains a point of tension, as was evident by the vigorous and hostile reaction of the West to the well-publicised military parade in East Berlin, with Mr Brezhnev present, to mark the thirtieth anniversary (1979) of the founding of the Democratic Republic.

Economic recovery and planning

The German 'economic miracle' (*Wirtschaftsordnung*) by which West Germany was transformed from the destruction and distress of 1945 to the prosperity and confidence of the 1950s and 1960s, has become something of a legend. A full analysis has yet to be made, but among the factors bearing on it were the initial dependence on Marshall Aid; ample labour supply from the flood of refugees; the political concern of the West to maintain and defend a new régime; the strong influence of business-orientated banks; the impact of ECSC and the EEC; the natural resources of an industrial power (relieved of the dragging effect of the poor agricultural Eastern lands); the popular stereotype of the (north) German capacity for discipline and hard work. From the outset, full emphasis has been laid in official policy on the private sector with the free play of market forces, and the consequent production of consumer goods as much as capital goods.

In the 1950s, liberal ideas prevailed in a 'social market' economy typified by free enterprise and unrestricted competition safeguarded against abuse by Ludwig Erhard's Cartel Act (1957). Alone among the original Six members of the EEC, West Germany refused to establish an Economic Council for the purpose of multilateral bargaining and cooperation. But a change in official policy came with the slackening pace of growth after the 1966–7 recession, and the pressures of inflation and labour shortages. German trade unions, hitherto somewhat docile, became more assertive in wage negotiations and in demanding a greater share in rising prosperity. The principle of co-determination (*Mitbestimmung*) – worker representation upon company boards at supervisory and local management level – did not guarantee against labour troubles, although the principle was extended to all works with 2000 workers by the Workers Constitution Act (1976).

An 'enlightened market' economy, associated with Karl Schiller, emerged in the later sixties, typified by the Act for Promotion of Stability and Economic Growth (1967), a product of the Grand Coalition. It coincided with the EEC Commission's conversion to long-term planning of economic development, emulating French experience of indicative planning. Schiller's view contrasted with Erhard's in that it sought a new pragmatism, relying on a combination of liberal free competition together with a federal macro-economic policy. The federal policy was arrived at by a dialogue between governments and pressure groups – a pluralist view of the state, seeking equilibrium in the economic and political field (though it tended to ignore social antagonisms). The Stability and Growth Act allowed for federal government intervention in the economy, following consultation with interested parties – but the secrecy that shrouded the consultation and the nature of the selection of those interested parties led to extensive criticism, particularly as the Bundestag was not directly involved. A classic case of what was called 'government by monopolistic groups' was the Ruhrkohle AG amalgamation (1968) of 26 Ruhr companies. Other major cases of government-promoted concentration were in petroleum (1968) and in the advanced technical industries like aeronautics, computers and nuclear energy. However, the Erhard doctrine of fair competition had clearly given way to a belief in the benefits of concentration and oligopoly in dominating any given market. A positive rush of mergers typified the early seventies, producing the larger units needed for long-term competitiveness (the Cartel Act, 1965, was amended to facilitate 'cooperation' between small and medium-sized firms). This was in conflict with the EEC Commission's wish to promote trans-national concentration as being far more effective for the Community – promoting a 'European' rather than a national market. Although the case for federal aid for ailing industries was not contested, there has been a rising feeling of unease at the degree of concentration during the seventies in West Germany.

The SDP had ambitious plans in 1969, which laid emphasis on redressing social inequalities, and encouraged a wider acceptance of the principle of government planning and influence. But, although the principle of state intervention in economic and social life appears to be advancing, schemes for extending the planning staff in the Chancellor's Office in order to assist long-term projects have had to be reduced. West Germany retains its faith in economic liberalism.

Education

Constitutionally, the *Länder* have responsibility for all aspects of education from kindergarten to university. This, perhaps their most important function, has led them increasingly into cooperation with the federal authority, if only because of finance (expenditure on education rose from DM 16.8bn in 1965 to DM 38.7bn in 1972). University building projects are now subject to federal grants-in-aid by a constitutional amendment (1969). Student grants and other sectors in education may also attract federal aid, particularly through the Council of Arts, Science

The educational system in West Germany

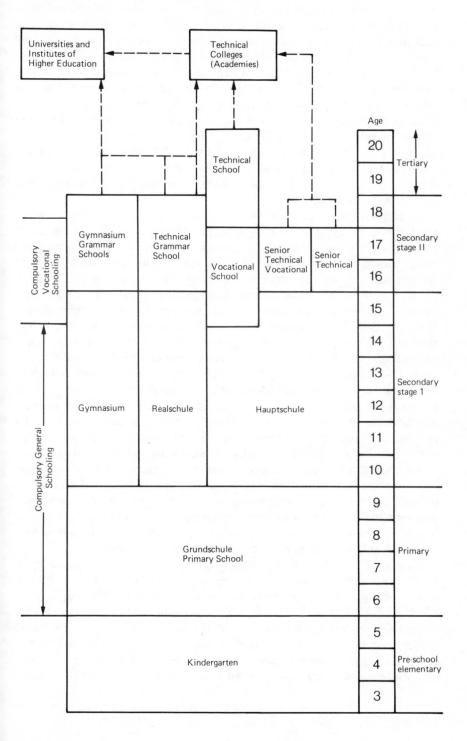

and Research (1957). Major proposals for federal aid and influence on education policy have passed the *Bundestag* in the early seventies, but are strongly resisted in the *Länder* preserve, the *Bundesrat*. There is no fully effective national education policy, but there is a growing tendency for an inter-linking of federal and *Land* resources for education with coordination of education policy and research in the hands of federal ministers advised by a standing conference of ministers of education from the *Länder*. In 1970 a joint committee for educational planning was established which produced the 1973 Comprehensive Education Development Plan covering structural reorganisation, curriculum reform and expansion of education services to promote equality of opportunity – but it has not been implemented in many *Länder*. However, in education, perhaps the closest of local policies, the reaction against centralisation, which has so strengthened local government since the war, has begun to weaken; the federal hand grows steadily stronger.

To an even greater extent than in France, parents are expected to play a positive rôle in educating their children, particularly as full-time schooling is generally on a half-day basis (proposals for parent-teacher-pupil councils are being considered by several *Länder*). The *Kindergarten* fall outside the state system; there are only a few of them and barely fifteen per cent of the age group can find a place. The primary school (*Grundschule*) is generally for four years from the age of six, and is organised on comprehensive lines: its curriculum is gradually changing, especially in maths. In secondary education, different systems operate according to the *Land* concerned; the traditional pattern is a tripartite division. In rural areas, particularly, the *Hauptschule*, taking all pupils to age fifteen (often closely linked with the *Grundschule* as a *Volkschule*) tends to concentrate on more practical education and training. The *Realschule* provides more academically demanding courses leading to careers in lower management. The *Gymnasium* provides the normal route through to universities and the professions. Parents make a choice when their children are ten years old, advised by the *Grundschule* – and confirmed by a probationary period of up to two years in the school of their choice. The SPD particularly criticises this early selection procedure and favours the *Gesamtschule* (comprehensive school) which exists in certain *Länder*, especially in large towns – although there are still only a small number of them. Curriculum reform at secondary level has serious implications for the traditional organisation of secondary education, and by implication points towards a return to a more centralised education system.

Vocational education at secondary and tertiary level is provided by a multitude of institutions that offer separate certificates. Student numbers at universities have trebled since the early 1950s and pressure on places has imposed selection of candidates (itself a violation of the tradition of free access to learning and training on which West Germany prides herself) and the old practice of having freedom to lecture, or to attend courses of lectures, according to personal choice, has been seriously eroded. Pressure for university reform, particularly from students, has resulted in a number of structural changes during the 1970s.

6

COMECON

Neither the advancing Russian armies, nor the new frontiers imposed on Eastern Europe guaranteed a 'new communist order' after the Second World War. Only in Albania and Yugoslavia did communist governments assume immediate control: they had won this through their own war of liberation (and both were to remain upon the fringe of the Soviet world). In Bulgaria and Romania the monarchy survived for over a year. In Hungary and Poland and in the Russian Zone of Germany, communist parties did not seize control immediately, and Czechoslovakia was only secured in 1948. But the whole area, and especially the former Axis members, despite the devastation that had been suffered, had to bear the loss of raw materials and productive industry despatched to Russia as reparations. In 1946 this tribute rose as high as twenty per cent of national production: some of the grosser consequences, particularly with regard to the Soviet Zone, were prevented by Voznesensky, chairman of Gosplan until 1949. But reparations were not terminated until 1953 and covered an estimated $20b, of which $12b came from East Germany.

The new governments in Eastern Europe were at first dominated by Moscow. A pronounced feature of their trade policy was its 'radial' pattern by which each was linked to Moscow rather than permitting trade links, even of a bilateral kind, to develop between themselves. The pattern was strengthened as the Cold War developed, for in 1950, encouraged by NATO, a Coordinating Committee (COCOM) was set up in Paris to enforce an export embargo against Eastern Europe and China, on any products likely to assist a war effort. This obliged a policy of *autarky* and helped to give a greater appearance of unity to the Eastern Bloc, an appearance furthered by the economic policies adopted by the new governments. Each adopted (by 1950) the centrist programme that Stalin had built up in the 1930s, with the state acquiring the means of production and centrally administering a 'command' economy. But the appearance of unity was deceptive. The West represented Eastern Europe as a dragooned group of satellites obliged by the presence of the Soviet army to follow policies determined by Moscow. That this was not the whole truth was demonstrated by the slow progress to a communist government in the several states and by the rift in the 'iron curtain' occasioned in 1948 by Yugoslavia's insistence on following an independent course towards its own version of socialism – a profit-orientated syndicalist ideology that was to have some influence on neighbouring states in the 1960s. Yugoslavia was 'excommunicated' (but not invaded); yet it was not alone

Economic recovery in Eastern Europe, 1938–65 (1958 = 100)

	1938	1948	1953	1959	1962	1965
Bulgaria	11	22	55	121	170	238
Czechoslovakia	31	44	64	112	143	159
East Germany	38	27	66	112	137	159
Hungary	28	38	84	111	149	177
Poland	16	28	61	109	145	182
Romania	25	22	63	110	168	243
Yugoslavia	29	43	53	113	150	217
USSR	23	40	58	111	146	184

A transformation of the economy in Eastern Europe has taken place (cf. p. 123) – remarkable in view of the low state of development in most of Eastern Europe before the Second World War.

'By 1970 COMECON accounted for some 30 per cent of world industrial output as against 18 per cent in the early 1950s' (M. Kaser).

among the communist states in showing positive signs of independence. The Soviet bloc was not that monolithic creation of Western legend.

Eastern Europe had been created out of the lands of the Austro-Hungarian Empire. Its frontiers did not satisfy the complex national and linguistic groupings that characterised much of the area, and its cultural roots differed from those of the West. Between the wars it had a strong tradition of central government influence and encouragement of industry. They had suffered badly from banking failures and were less opposed to state control than the West supposed – particularly as nationalisation of land and collectivising of farm holdings (the whole area being heavily rural in the 1940s) was by no means as extensive as might have been expected of communist régimes under Moscow orders. Yugoslavia and Poland were particularly averse to collectivisation. Each of the countries of Eastern Europe had suffered badly in the war, and experienced severe economic disruption and inflation in the years immediately following. Yet by 1949 (East Germany apart) they had surpassed pre-war industrial production, an economic recovery impressive by any standards.

By 1950, each country had adopted the directive system of a 'command' economy (see page 151), with a State Planning Commission controlling the economy centrally and preparing five-year plans which concentrated on heavy producer goods, iron, steel and machinery, to the disadvantage of other sectors of the economy. Enterprises were required to keep to targets set by central planners, who also controlled prices and investment policies. Stability was aided by artificially balancing supply and demand through pre-determined targets. A number of state cooperatives were establishd with direct Soviet membership of their management committees. Consumer rationing and control over trade unions helped the first plans to work, and in agricultural areas there was a significant improvement in the standard of living. This was not reflected in industrial areas and there were serious disturbances in Hungary, Czechoslovakia

The changing composition of Gross National Product in COMECON countries

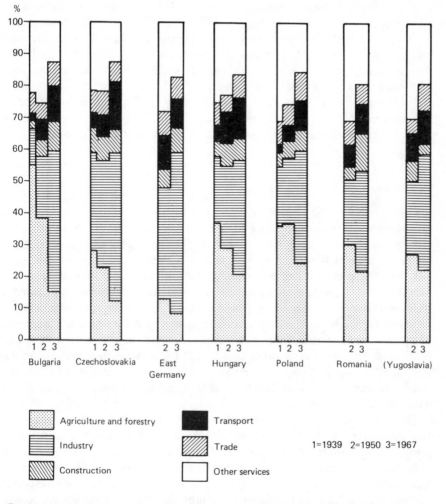

Rapid development in the post-war period brought a transformation of East European economies: their structure begins to resemble that of Western economies. Compare this chart with that for EEC countries (p. 86). (Figures adapted from M. Kaser, *The Socialist Economies of Eastern Europe*, p. 213)

and Poland in the fifties – the Polish riots had serious political repercussions, like those of the seventies. For some twenty years there was little comparison with the West in living standards, but this reflected the socialist order of priorities – investment at the expense of consumption. There was diversity, however, even in the planned economy. Yugoslavia rapidly moved towards a social democratic pluralism permitting the influence of ordinary market forces; a syndicalist approach to industrial management was adopted and by 1950 factories were to be managed by elected works councils. A different model was developed in

Poland following the riots of 1956; central control remained, but the enterprise was allowed to respond to local market conditions once its production targets were met. Incentives were introduced and an allowance made for an enterprise to make a profit reflecting the manager's ability. Prices were controlled but tended to reflect market conditions and the pressures of the relevant industrial associations. The model has strongly influenced later developments in the DDR, Romania and the USSR itself. By the seventies only Albania retained the original pattern, and this only in a decentralised form. Throughout Eastern Europe, however, the Communist Party in each country effectively controlled the whole system of government and administration, giving an impression of unity, although the parties differed in the details of their internal organisation.

Formation of COMECON

Stalin's control of the Communist bloc and the politics of the Cold War have more to do with the origin of COMECON than economic policy or plans for integration between like-minded countries. The rapid deterioration of relations between East and West pushed both sides into entrenched positions (see page 24). But the possibility of Hungary, Czechoslovakia and Poland accepting Marshall Aid to assist them in their programme of Reconstruction, caused a sharp reaction. Stalin condemned Marshall Aid as US economic imperialism and unwarrantable interference in interference in internal affairs of other countries, and communist countries refused the Recovery Programme – clearly, there was concern in the Kremlin that other members of the communist bloc might go the way of Yugoslavia (Dimitrov's Balkan Federation project, initiated by the Bulgarian and Yugoslavian Treaty of 1947, had been stopped by Stalin in the name of national sovereignty).

There was need of a political cementing force. COMECON (Council for Mutual Economic Assistance, called CMEA) provided it, but it was launched in January 1949 with no more than a brief statement.

Between 1949 and 1954 it held a very few *ad hoc* meetings: for ten years it lacked even a Charter, and it was clearly intended by Stalin to serve no especial purpose beyond strengthening the Communist Bloc. There was a strong emphasis on national recovery and national *autarky* (a typical Stalin approach), and the 'radial' trade links with Moscow were strengthened. There was no indication that it was intended as an embryo supra-national economic community – Monnet's influence did not extend beyond the 'Iron Curtain' – indeed, there was a built-in veto to secure national sovereignty (a recognition of national independence that does not fit the Western picture of a single Soviet-dominated system in the East). Its members produced their National Plans, strongly influenced by Soviet experience, but independently, and without coordination or even officially informing the newly formed COMECON. With the onset of the Korean War, Stalin's control increased and member countries complemented the Soviet economy and added to military production. The Soviet Union increased the spatial imbalance in her economy by absorbing surpluses arising from duplication and overproduction resulting from the failure to coordinate national economies, and her influence was augmented by the creation of joint soviet and national corporations for heavy industry: national *autarky* remained a major principle.

The death of Stalin (1953) and the ending of the Korean War produced a relaxation of tension and the Soviet controlled state corporations were returned to national control. Greater emphasis on consumer goods typified some member countries and bilateral trade developed particularly between the advanced industrial members, Poland, Hungary, Czechoslovakia and East Germany (a division between them and the strongly agricultural Romania and Bulgaria was appearing). In 1954 agreements on the conduct of intra-COMECON trade were made (balance of payments problems arose as trade links widened). The organisation was beginning to develop its potential for cooperation, if not for international specialisation. 1954–60 was a period of institutional reinforcement, and the coordination of national plans was discussed. A 'new course' was set at the Berlin meeting (May 1956) by the decision to seek the advantages of international specialisation through the coordination of national plans – a possible first step to an economic community. The negotiations leading to the creation of the EEC may have acted as a spur to action, (Gomulka, the Polish leader, is reported to have personally proposed to Khrushchev that COMECON be developed as a rival to the EEC) but the pattern of development was already appearing in 1954. It is ironic that the evidence suggests that the Soviet Union was seeking to extend potential areas for international cooperation – pushing, indeed, the principle of economic integration in COMECON – in the year of the Hungarian rising and invasion.

A series of meetings between 1957 and 1959 reached agreement for cooperation in a number of areas, especially in transport and the supplying of raw materials, but there was also begun a multilateral clearing scheme to facilitate payments between members, operating through a special account held by the State Bank of the USSR. Joint investment projects were signed between Poland and East Germany for coal mining; the Iron Gates hydro-electric project with related irrigation and agricultural improvement; the Halex project (Poland and Hungary) for processing coal slack and inter-governmental Commissions were set up for collaboration in economic and technical fields. Multilateral projects of considerable importance date from the late 1950s – the 'Mir' electric grid (approved 1959) with its central control office opened in Prague in 1962 and the grid extended throughout COMECON by 1967; or the 'Friendship' (*Druzhba*) pipeline (1958) for crude oil, operational by 1964. It is worth noting that by exporting crude oil instead of refined products, the Soviet Union gratuitously makes a substantial contribution to the importers' balance of payments and national refining industries, as well as allowing the DDR to export refined products in competition with the Soviet Union (times have changed since Stalin's reparations). In 1960 COMECON established a Commission for the peaceful uses of nuclear energy.

The creation of the Warsaw Pact (1955, see page 28) imposed defence expenditure on members, and there may well be more than the formal link (1957) of the COMECON Standing Commission on Defence with the Economic Committee of the Warsaw Treaty Organisation between the two organisations.

This adds military arguments to economic arguments for closer cooperation, if not integration.

The appointment of Fadayev as Secretary (1958) strengthened the administrative organisation of COMECON, and in 1960 a new Charter was signed establishing a formal organisation:

> Considering that the economic cooperation which is being successfully carried out between these countries is conducive to the most rational development of the national economy, to raising the standard of living of the population and to strengthening the unity and solidarity of these countries (Preamble)

The principal organ is the Council, which has powers of initiative and decision: it is composed of the premiers and chief planners of member states who attend as delegates and are allowed one vote per state, which is cast according to national instructions. Its annual Session is held in a member's capital, changing each year; it may meet more frequently if necessary. It can issue recommendations on economic, technical and scientific cooperation which it is up to member states to apply, and also decisions on questions of procedure and organisation which are normally enforced without further ado. It is supported by a Secretariat in Moscow. This is not to be compared to the EEC Commission, for its rôle is no more than that of coordination and liaison – though its Secretary has been accorded the dignity of representing COMECON diplomatically in negotiations with other non-member countries and the EEC. The officials are enjoined to act as 'international officials', and the working language is Russian. It is assisted by a Legal Department (1969) whose task is primarily that of drafting recommendations and decisions so that they do not conflict with the laws of member states (the absence of a court or a precise legal adjustment mechanism has proved a problem as COMECON agencies become multilateral as opposed to bilateral). The Secretariat is also assisted by a complex series of organisations; three Institutes, six Standing Conferences and twenty-three Permanent Commissions (twenty-one concerned with different specific sectors through which integrative policies might be carried out; and two general commissions, Foreign Trade Standardisation concerned with financial and monetary matters, meeting in East Berlin, and finance statistics, meeting in Moscow). These were created between 1956 and 1975 and are responsible to the Executive. Each meets in a specific city in a member country.

The Executive was established in 1962 as the chief organ of the Council, executing policy and directing the work of the Secretariat. It is composed of Deputy Party Leaders from member nations and also of permanent delegates who sit in Moscow maintaining the permanency of the Organisation. It is assisted by a Bureau for Integrated Planning Problems and a Standing Commission on the Coordination of Scientific and Technical Research (1962). Two Committees (which have a higher status than commissions) were added in 1971, that of the Planning and Economic Council, and that of the Science and Technical Cooperation Council. In addition there are international organisations for special functions, like the International Bank of Economic Cooperation (IBEC,

The structure of COMECON

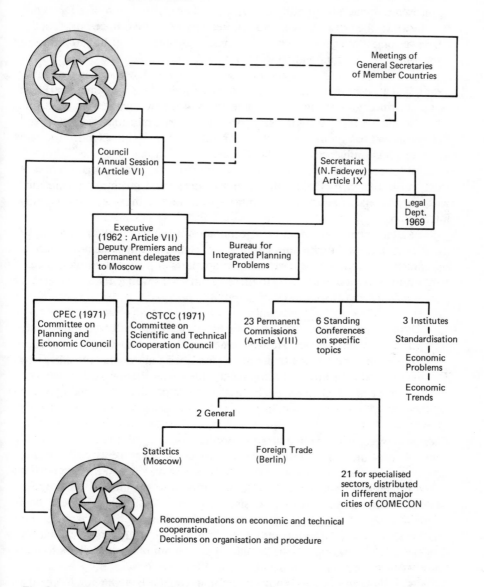

Meetings of General Secretaries of Member Countries

Council Annual Session (Article VI)

Secretariat (N. Fadeyev) Article IX

Legal Dept. 1969

Executive (1962 : Article VII) Deputy Premiers and permanent delegates to Moscow

Bureau for Integrated Planning Problems

CPEC (1971) Committee on Planning and Economic Council

CSTCC (1971) Committee on Scientific and Technical Cooperation Council

23 Permanent Commissions (Article VIII)

6 Standing Conferences on specific topics

3 Institutes
Standardisation
Economic Problems
Economic Trends

2 General

Statistics (Moscow)

Foreign Trade (Berlin)

21 for specialised sectors, distributed in different major cities of COMECON

Recommendations on economic and technical cooperation
Decisions on organisation and procedure

The Council initiates proposals. It meets once annually in different capitals and is composed of Premiers and chief planners who attend as delegates of their governments: each member country has one vote and may exercise a veto under Article IV (3). The Executive is the chief organ of the Council and coordinates policy and carries out recommendations. The Secretary is responsible to the Executive and is primarily an administrator. The 23 Permanent Commissions (some dating from 1956) are also responsible to the Executive, and integrative policies might be carried out by any one of them. They are technical working commissions.

The Legal Department is not a court, and the absence of an arbitrator may cause problems as agencies become more multilateral.

1963), or the Organisation for the Soviet Power Grid, and various common agencies on a bilateral or multilateral basis: trading organisations like Domkhim (chemicals in the Soviet Union and DDR), Assfoto (films), Inter port (docks). These become the agents or executive organs of integration or international cooperation, though individual states retain full powers.

Until 1960 COMECON rested on a series of agreements only; indeed, until 1953 it had little more than a formal existence. Under Khrushchev and Brezhnev, it has assumed greater significance and in 1974 a new revised version of the Charter was issued. During the seventies particularly, meetings of the General Secretaries of the Communist Parties of member countries have tended to wield an overriding influence over the Organisation – rather like the European Council. Superficially, there are points of comparison with the organisation of the EEC, but COMECON is altogether less formal and much more concerned with direct relations between member governments than with developing integration.

Since all members have 'command' economies, all cooperative and integrative agreements have to fit with national plans of members, and as each plan has its own system of costings, measures to integrate parts of plans will prove difficult. Partly for this reason, and partly to preserve national sovereignty, each member has an effective veto. Article IV(3) states:

> All recommendations and decisions by the Council shall be adopted only with the consent of the interested member countries of the Council, and each country shall be entitled to declare its interest in any matter considered by the Council. The effects of recommendations and decisions shall not extend to countries which have declared their lack of interest in the question concerned.

There is no need of a 'Luxembourg compromise' (see page 62) in COMECON – although pressure for majority decisions to be binding seems to be rising, especially from Czechoslovakia. The 1978 Session gave some indication of this.

The principle of *autarky*, when applied to the Soviet Union, is not without certain advantages; but if applied to smaller states it is unlikely to benefit them simply because of the supply of raw materials. Considerable advantages for smaller countries arise if their trade is linked with a larger country that can supply their basic needs, and this was the situation arising out of the 'radial' pattern of trade between the Soviet Union and her satellites after the war. But Khrushchev was especially keen to gain the advantages that would arise from developing the potential for integration between COMECON members, in order to achieve economies of scale and 'international socialist division of labour'. His proposal for a 'united planning organ' (1962), which would have fitted fairly closely the theoretical plans of some supporters of closer economic integration in the EEC, was rejected by Romania and not pursued (a further pointer to the absence of dictatorship in the relationship between the Soviet Union and her satellites).

Romania remains nervous of integration lest it interfere with political independence, and the development plans of a country less economically developed than her neighbours (except for Bulgaria): she has no wish to become a mere supplier of agricultural produce and raw materials and so takes her stand on national sovereignty. Romania has developed extensive trade links with the West. Her response over the Warsaw Treaty Organisation proposals of 1961 to share defence costs and integrate military forces (pressed especially by the DDR) was hostile, broadening into supporting the Chinese in the Sino-Soviet split of 1963 and in 1966 going so far as to demand the withdrawal of Soviet forces (see page 31) – the parallel with France's withdrawal from NATO has been widely drawn (although France's position in NATO was substantially more significant).

The treatment of Romania throughout the seventies, especially as she persists in following an independent line (the early resumption of normal relations with West Germany, for instance, or the official presidential visit to Britain in 1978), contrasts oddly with the Soviet reaction to the Czechoslovakian reforms in 1968. The explanation may lie partly in the fact that Romania offers neither a strategic nor a military threat, and partly in the unexceptionable 'directive' communism of the régime. The treatment confirms the impression of a Soviet control less than complete over the Communist bloc, and of an increasing confidence and sophistication in Soviet relations with her satellites.

Economic reforms in member nations

The Sino-Soviet dispute of the early sixties imposed severe strains on COMECON (Albania withdrew, taking China's side), but there were other strains closer at home, indicative of changing relationships in the Communist bloc. Among them was a shift in attitude from the bureaucratic central planning of the 1950s in favour of making use of the market mechanism to increase efficiency: pragmatism seemed to be replacing ideology. In place of detailed planning directives, came a degree of indicative planning with incentives for managers and profit as a criterion, allowing a flexible price system responsive to local conditions. Some have called this change 'socialism with a human face'.

Something of this nature had already appeared in Poland in 1956 where basic market conditions were permitted to influence the response of local managers. It was taken further in Hungary which was to be in the van of economic reforms in the fifties and sixties, despite the trauma of the invasion of 1956. All governments of advanced industrial countries exercise some control over investment and the conduct of the economy, either by directly influencing interest rates and major sectors of the economy (e.g. through the nationalised industries in Britain), or by detailed regulation of most aspects of the economy, as in the Soviet Union. Hungary has developed a compromise, leaning towards the Soviet practice: central planning remains, but at the micro level opportunities occur for local initiative. Economic reforms were one of the many factors involved in the 1956 invasion, but the presence of Soviet troops and the shock to the régime did not reverse the trend in economic policy. By the sixties Hungary's methods of economic management were attracting the interest of the West. They involved a degree of decentralisation which in some cases allowed an enterprise to control up to fifty-five per cent of investment funds. The system was known as the 'guided market'; the enterprise was allowed to operate within set limits and central control and directives were reduced, but not removed. Certainly 'guided market'

The planning structure of industrial management in a 'directive' economy

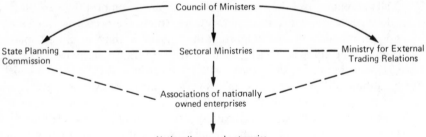

In this simplified diagram the chain of command is clear: the sectoral ministry exercises a general control. All activities must conform to the National Plan and the consent of the Ministry for External Trading relations is needed if export trading is contemplated (especially for foreign exchange arrangements).

conditions abandon universality of method, though not of centralism; they allow an interaction of the market and the current Economic Plan so that each may influence the other and induce a balance. Prices play an active rôle and influence the availability of raw materials and resources in a way that does not occur under a 'directive economy'.

The trend away from the centralist Soviet model was eventually systematised in what has been called the New Economic Mechanism (1968) which has had considerable influence beyond Hungary, both in the USSR and in the West. In this system, the State continues to own the means of production and to manage the economy in broad outline, but the local manager (appointed by the State) recruits his own staff and is responsible for the running of the enterprise (rather as in the case of the non-shareholding executive of a standard market economy). Attempts to match production targets with the supply of resources on a central basis have been abandoned in favour of the deliberate introduction of consumer attitudes and orientating management towards economic growth through incentives and bonuses for the work force. Within set limits (for the enterprise remains firmly under the appropriate ministry) the manager may reap the rewards of risk and innovation, and he may form subsidiaries in partnership with others (usually two or three persons), with the profits divided by agreement. The 1956 workers' councils, following the pattern of Yugoslav practice, were a victim of the 1956 invasion: they were replaced by factory councils having only consultative rôles and the right to allocate incentive funds. But it is important not to exaggerate the changes from the centralist system: the local manager is still circumscribed. For example, only in very unusual circumstances would he be permitted to switch from one sector to another and thus reap the benefits of diversification. The heavy concentration on horizontal industrial organisation results in industries becoming often 'conglomerates of small plants'. (It should be remembered that in Hungary, as elsewhere, the 'Black Economy' flourishes – and is not always rigorously checked by the authorities.)

Cooperation decision-making in Hungary

Level I: Final Decision powers rest with the Interministerial Cooperation Committee.

Level II: Ministries and other key state bodies are represented on the ICC and its secretariat.

Level III: Offices within these bodies vet the cooperation proposals and prepare the opinions presented at the ICC.

Level IV: The enterprises discuss their proposals with Level III but are in addition responsible to the ministries exercising ownership functions over them.

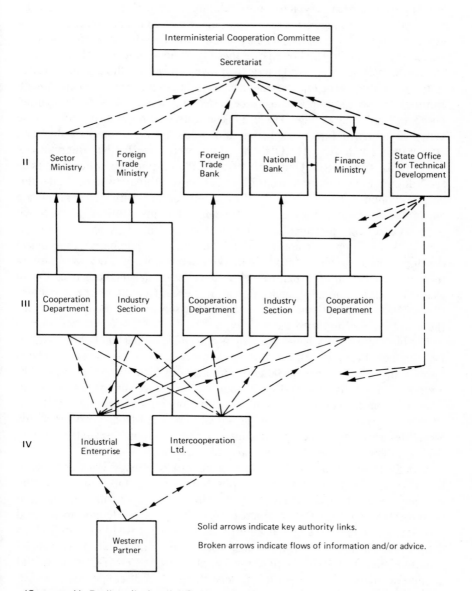

(Source: H. Radice, 'Industrial Cooperation between Hungary and the West', paper presented at University of Stirling, 1979)

The successive Plans have an overriding influence, although since 1968 they have been subject to annual review and modification. The New Economic Mechanism allows the local manager an autonomy that is more apparent than real – for example, the 1976–80 Plan promoted credit facilities by banks without their being pre-allocated by the appropriate planning ministry, but such credits first required consultation with and the approval of the responsible branch ministries. Projected reforms for the early eighties, however, suggest managers will gain the right of dismissal of workers.

Hungary has been very active in developing links with the West. These are principally for the engineering sector, particularly machines and machine tools – especially from West Germany which accounts for nearly fifty per cent of western agreements. Flexibility is allowed over these agreements, and by the late seventies enterprises were allowed to conclude their own contracts without going through state cooperative agencies or having to consult the state cooperative department. But the enterprise's proposal has to be vetted and approved by the Hungarian National Bank and Foreign Trade Bank and its sectoral ministry; after being vetted in terms of foreign exchange and industrial development policy and cooperation with COMECON, it is registered with the International Cooperation Committee. Under the 1976–80 Plan export promotion credits by the National Bank have risen from 10 per cent of total credit to 35 per cent – this despite economic depression in the West. Joint ventures with western firms are encouraged, provided they conform in general terms with the Plan. Much research and development is tied up in western agreements, since the common view is that it is cheaper and less time consuming to purchase technological developments available on the world markets and to concentrate upon adapting them to local conditions, than to seek to develop similar methods oneself – an example of international specialisation and a retreat from Stalinist *autarky* (see page 124). A variety of monitoring and incentive schemes are used to encourage the adaptation of imported technology.

The big success story is the Ikarus bus enterprise (under the Public Vehicles Development Programme), which is one of the largest producers of commercial buses in the world – some 15 000 units annually of which over sixty-six per cent are exported, largely to COMECON countries and especially the Soviet Union. There is a concentration on a few models and economies of scale are augmented by modern assembly-line technology, largely imported from West Germany. Many western parts are incorporated into the engine, but the front axle is a Soviet design – a fine example of international cooperation.

Initially it was hoped that western trade would provide Hungary with a technological base for winning a better position in COMECON trade by creating comparative advantages for Hungary, while, on the other hand, specialisation agreements in COMECON, by increasing the scale of production in selected products would make Hungarian enterprises more attractive to western firms as cooperative partners. This is now recognised as too simplistic: to have a really extensive impact, it would require specific planning at COMECON level and assume a more rapid growth of specialisation and cooperation within COMECON. However, Hungarian agreements with western firms will be likely to increase, although on a piecemeal basis, because of the price rise of Soviet oil and the need to increase western trade to earn hard currency to pay for additional imported raw materials.

East Germany has probably the most efficient industry in COMECON, despite chronic labour shortages and lack of domestically produced raw materials. 'Intensification' of industry to achieve higher output from the same materials, was one of the slogans of the 1976–80 Plan. But the response of the work force has not been as great as was hoped, and there has been resistance to new methods, especially to automation. As in other COMECON countries, including the USSR, the seventies saw an economic reform movement that seemed to imply a desire to modify the centralist system of central control through sectoral ministries, in favour of greater independence of local enterprises, perhaps in combination.

In Czechoslovakia economic reforms in the mid-sixties originated with academic economists helped by discussions with party officials. As in Hungary, the principal beneficiary was the manager – increasingly a professional. East Europe, indeed, witnessed a managerial revolution in the sixties with a transfer of decision making from the centre to local state-owned industry (as in East Germany, 1964–7 or Bulgaria, 1966–9) together with some relaxation in favour of private enterprise, especially in retailing, catering and local transport. The ordinary worker, however, did not benefit particularly. In Czechoslovakia the economic reforms took on a new intensity in the late sixties, covering a wide front and involving considerable imports of western technology to support a consumer-orientated programme. The pattern of reforms was not out of line with what was being contemplated in other COMECON countries, but their speed and breadth made their impact more dramatic. There was also serious difficulty between the Czechs and the Slovaks. The 1968 'Prague Spring' seemed less a change in emphasis than a new model of society. It was a model promoted by the professional and skilled technician in the interests of efficiency, with an eye to greater differentiation in terms of rewards for the quality of work performed (greater rewards for the manager than the worker), and a deliberate acceptance of the possibility of unemployment to induce greater effort from the worker, whose organised participation in decision-making would be at a rudimentary level only.

It was a challenge to established Soviet lines of economic structure, whilst the projected decentralising reforms would lead to the dismemberment of existing enterprises to introduce diversity and competition within the broad context of a free market. There were also daring financial relations with western banks that were likely to spread and to increase the already serious indebtedness of COMECON. In addition there was some possibility of Czechoslovakia making an *entente* with Yugoslavia and Romania. The Soviet leadership seems to have been as divided over what action to take as it had been over Hungary in 1956: clearly, intervention was the weapon of last resort. In the event, though troops were posted on the Romanian frontier ready to intervene if necessary, the Czech invasion was a complete success (see page 31): NATO issued a severe warning but did not intervene – and *détente* survived the international repercussions of the invasion. The rapid social changes were stopped, but it did not halt economic reforms in Czechoslovakia or elsewhere. Kadar in Hungary did not reverse the

New Economic Mechanism; in Poland, Gomulka (who had come to power in 1956 through workers' riots) was replaced by Gierek after the riots of 1970, and in the 1976 riots Giereck was helped not with tanks but by bank credits to allay popular discontent. Despite the less favourable economic situation, reforming tendencies pointing to a form of pluralism have continued throughout the seventies.

Moves towards integration within COMECON

In 1962 Khrushchev proposed a 'united planning organ' for COMECON in order to achieve some of the advantages of integration, or at least far closer cooperation. It was promoted by Gomulka who urged a New Programme rationalising resources and investment policies with capital projects for the entire area, since this would ultimately benefit members more than limited national schemes; economies of scale and maximisation of markets would arise from integrated policies. In addition to economic benefits, Khrushchev had other motives for pressing integration, notably a wish to strengthen COMECON against the successful EEC, particularly as Britain was at that time negotiating for membership, and also the hope of coordinating the foreign policies of the Soviet satellites (although this was unstated). But forced integration failed. Romania headed the resistance – from fear of its consequences, for it would be likely that international specialisation arising from integration would reduce Romania to the position of supplying raw materials and food to her industrialised neighbours. Romania took her stand on national sovereignty, and the other members sidestepped the issue by making extensive bilateral agreements, and avoiding the problem of the veto by substituting 'voluntaryism' for the original principle of 'interestedness'.

Institutional reforms pointing towards policies of integration followed this check to Khrushchev's wishes. In order to assist East-West trade and intra-COMECON trade, a modest step towards an international clearing house was taken in 1963 by the establishment of the International Bank of Economic Cooperation (IBEC) on which each member has drawing rights to cover the cost of foreign trade during each year, using the rouble as a transferable currency and also settling accounts in foreign currencies. As compared with the European Payments Union (see page 53) it was modest, but it was a pointer towards later developments and by 1968 proposals to stimulate trade were far advanced – particularly as it was openly admitted that COMECON needed technological and economic help from the West if it were to make an economic leap forward.

The Czech crisis (1968) did not stop the proposals, rather it served to concentrate efforts to achieve greater cohesion; indeed, from 1962 to 1971 there was a proliferation of Permanent Commissions and economic organisations. Measures for economic integration were openly discussed at the twentieth annual Session of the Council (1969), and a new COMECON Centre for Scientific and Technical Information, especially that gained from the West, was opened in 1970. There was talk of a common data system (COMECON lags badly behind the West in computer sciences), and the Soviet Union was actively encouraging closer economic ties, despite Romania's opposition. An

International Investment Bank (IIB) was launched in 1970 to help finance different schemes in member countries and to improve capital flow. Multilateral cooperation and joint agreements in a number of fields were already well developed, the need for increased trade with the West providing an added spur. The projects cover a range from the Ust'-Ilimsk cellulose complex and the sulphate pulp plant (in which nearly all COMECON members are concerned) to nuclear research. But integration is more than an economic policy: it has political and diplomatic implications. This was the time of *Ostpolitik* success in the treaties normalising relations between East and West Germany (see page 115) and also the enlargement of the EEC from Six to Nine – the emergence of two strong and cohesive economic blocs would affect the balance of Europe: integration is to be viewed in a wider context than economic affairs.

Active discussions from 1969 came to fruition at the Bucharest meeting of the twenty-fifth Session of COMECON in July 1971, which produced the 'Complex Programme' for attaining complete planning and economic integration by 1980. It was launched with a flourish with proposals to coordinate national plans and harmonise costing and pricing systems with the aim of using the transferable rouble as a collective COMECON currency to facilitate multilateral clearing arrangements – there was even the suggestion of Pan-European Payments Union combining the EPU and IBEC. But the Programme was really a compromise, revealing uncertainties among the membership, demonstrating that COMECON was not a Soviet poodle. There was also a military aspect, linking it to the Warsaw Treaty Organisation – 'a strengthening of the ability of the member countries to defend themselves' as it was phrased. The Complex Programme was an ambitious scheme, indicative of the very different atmosphere current in communist circles from that of the previous generation: but, like similar and less ambitious proposals in the EEC, it has not worked out. Members were not uniformly enthusiastic, each saw particular advantages, but none was prepared to admit the predominance of a supra-national authority which integration implied. Nationalism is not the monopoly of the West.

Integration policies were limited during the seventies to a few major sectors with a longer time span than was originally intended. As a short-term measure, there has been considerable importation of Western technology, which greatly increases the already sizeable COMECON debt (by the later seventies, perhaps twenty-five per cent of total Polish exports to the West were earmarked for debt redemption). Inflation and bad harvests have interrupted economic growth – crop failures in the Soviet Union in 1972, 1975 and 1979 have involved massive purchase of grain on the world market (in defending these purchases, Brezhnev urged integration as a defence against world inflation). The good Soviet harvest of 1974 and 1976 were offset by poor ones in Hungary, Czechoslovakia and East Germany in 1974, 1975 and 1976. Hungarian farmers, free to respond to market conditions without having to meet compulsory procurements, have adjusted to these set-backs more quickly than their neighbours. Another factor has been the world recession after 1973 which has affected the performance of all economies throughout the world. Polish riots in 1976 and grumblings about 'meatless Thursdays' in Soviet restaurants were merely signs of a renewed tension in the economic field. Retrenchment has followed reform, and at the Thirtieth Session of Council in East Berlin (1976) the 'Complex Programme' was modified by the Long Term Target Programme for Improved Planning Activity, with the accent being on cooperation in the fields of energy, machine production, agriculture and consumer goods; the time scale has been extended well beyond 1980.

The Berlin decisions illustrated a revision of the Bucharest proposals in the light of experience and changing economic conditions. A limiting factor is the relatively low level of intra-COMECON trade reflecting the parallel nature of members' economies and confirming the 'radial' nature of their trade with the Soviet Union (Bulgaria is particularly dependent on Soviet trade). It is not surprising that Gosplan economists should propose (1978) the extension of joint planning activity to projected single plans for entire industrial branches throughout COMECON. The Soviet orientation of trade could promote integration: after all, the Soviet Union has little need for this trade, but encourages it particularly for political reasons and for future trade expansion. Far more important is the steeply rising debt of Soviet and COMECON trade with the West which gives rise to concern, although credit remains high. The use of the rouble in COMECON trade produced effectively a second hard currency Euromarket system throughout member countries, using Western banking methods which give greater flexibility than a centrally planned system. Attempts to coordinate COMECON energy policies has helped this development, as has progress towards an integrated transport policy. Finally, it is worth remembering that invisible earnings, especially on tourism and transport, help member nations to manage their own foreign debt. Should a member get into serious difficulty, there is the 'umbrella theory' by which individual members (notably the Soviet Union) will come to the aid of a member in danger of financial collapse. This does not mean the Soviet Union would necessarily adopt this theory to prevent Poland or Romania negotiating covering loans with Eurobank, or even the IMF (which would involve discussion of economic plans with the West).

Energy policy

For entirely political reasons, the development of nuclear power played a part in the launching of the EEC (see page 59). But by the late seventies, a world shortage of energy, especially oil, altered many of the political calculations of East and West and deepened the world slump of these years. At the same time energy supplies have played a substantial rôle in strengthening the bonds that tie COMECON members. The Soviet Union has immense reserves of fossil fuels which become increasingly valuable as world prices soar. The principal problems associated with the reserves are the difficulties of extraction and transportation across difficult and marshy terrain affected by a harsh climate (see page 156). Energy supplies, however, make it possible for the Soviet Union to underwrite the Long Term Target Programme (1976) – though there are difficulties over price and quantities.

The principle of the 'compensatory contract' permits the Soviet Union to transfer a proportion of the cost of extraction and transportation to consumer nations. The compensatory contract is a joint cooperative venture that allows the purchasing country to provide credits towards the cost of extraction and transportation of a particular fuel and receive in return quantities of the fuel to the value of the credits. Once the credits are exhausted, the fuel has to be purchased at market rates (although for COMECON members these have been below world market prices). The advantage to importing countries is that the fuel is actually made available at minimum cost and remains available thereafter – and if the credits are in the form of manufactured goods rather than cash this benefits the purchaser and effectively transfers the credits into exports. The advantage to the Soviet Union is threefold – the fuel is extracted and transported at minimum cost to the producer; the installations, once 'paid for' in terms of fuel, become the sole property of the Soviet Union; and the consumer nation is effectively tied to Soviet trade first by the need to redeem the credits and then by the relative cheapness of the fuel (assuming the continuance of, favourable prices). The system does not necessarily ensure the integration of socialist economies, but it offers evident advantages to both sides.

It has been used in the development of three major energy projects; the extensions to the supra-national COMECON electricity grid called the 'Mir', with its control centre in Prague and with power stations feeding into it from the Ukraine to East Germany; the *Druzhba* oil pipeline; and in particular, the major undertaking of the Orenburg natural gas pipeline (the agreement signed in 1974, commissioned in 1978 and on line ahead of schedule), which has been constructed by all members of COMECON (save the Soviet Union), Romania contributing to machinery in the fields. As world prices for oil and natural gas escalate, these fuels play an increasingly important rôle: they are supplied on set contracts so that COMECON does not suffer the same energy crises as the West, and they can be traded (at western prices) for western technology. It has been estimated that access to western technology will increase Soviet national production by one per cent annually – hence they become an important source of foreign exchange to pay for much-needed imports. But there is only a limited supply of fuel that can be exported at any one time, so the Soviet Union must choose between reducing supplies to COMECON neighbours (and suffering whatever consequences follow) so that more may be exported to the West to earn hard currency, or increasing the supply by further installations for extraction, and extensions to pipelines (which has its problems). Either way, the Soviet Union remains in control of production and supply, which adds to the economic advantage a political dimension, since the threat to cut off fuel supplies would become a very powerful card to play. Control of fuel supply, therefore, underwrites Soviet control over COMECON. What Stalin and the leadership in the fifties found necessary to achieve by armed force, the present leadership may do more effectively by simple economic pressure.

But the argument is not so simple. To supply COMECON with oil and gas at low rates represents a considerable financial loss, especially in hard currency, to the Soviet Union, and in 1975 a COMECON price review changed the relationship between raw materials and machinery, making the former more expensive. Oil and gas prices were to be based for the period 1975–80 on a 'rolling basis' taking the average world prices of the previous five years: this meant a price increase, but one that lagged behind the escalating prices in the West, so that COMECON countries continued to be subsidised (in return they contributed to

COMECON joint energy supplies

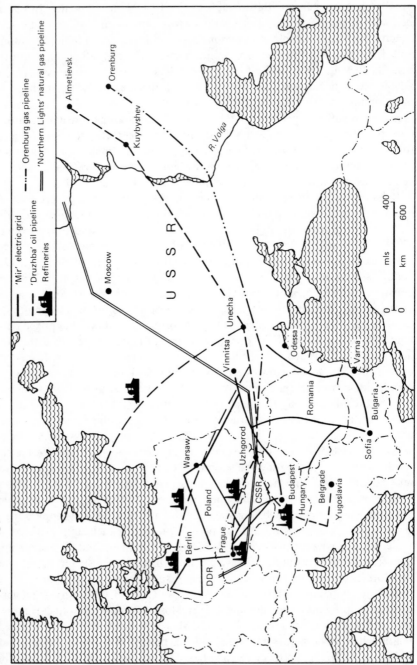

The growth of East-West European trade

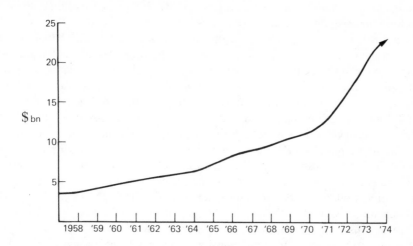

East European dependence on USSR trade: the percentage of COMECON trade with the USSR, 1960–75

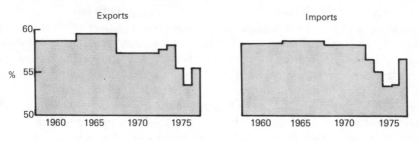

joint investment projects). If the Soviet Union continued to suffer a potential economic loss, and so indicated that it was less willing to increase oil supplies to COMECON in the eighties (preferring to benefit from high world prices), her satellites would face serious problems – some COMECON countries were badly hit by the moderately rising price after 1975, East Germany particularly. For this reason East Germany put up its internal prices for oil and gas to industry (not to domestic users) by 30 per cent from January 1980 – a use of the price mechanism that is the first recourse of the West 'free market' economies. The energy crisis has had a severe impact on western economies: for communist economies it appears to be a major factor in a replacement of traditional Marxist economic theories by a return to the use of capitalist price mechanism techniques. Eastern Europe is expected in the eighties to seek some 33 per cent of its energy needs in the West (at western prices): this appears to be a determined change in Soviet trade policy, at the expense of 'socialist solidarity', and may be partly due to the difficulties and cost of extraction (see page 161). But the majority of COMECON energy needs continue to come from the Soviet Union; and it is worth recalling that she sustains high technology industries within COMECON by delivering crude oil which is then refined in national refineries.

Socialist solidarity appears to weigh more heavily with Soviet Russia than short-term financial gain, for in 1978, although world prices were high, oil exports to the West fell by twenty per cent so that COMECON members might be supplied. The Iranian crisis in the winter of 1978, which led to a further rise in the world price for oil, also had its impact on Soviet Russia for the closure of the IGAT I gas pipeline between Iran and the Soviet transcaucasian republics had severe effects in Georgia, while the projected IGAT II pipeline, by which Iranian gas was to be piped to Russia so that more Russian gas could be piped to COMECON neighbours and to Western Europe, was abandoned. The energy crisis even affected Romania's position: she (being herself a producer) does not import Soviet oil, but at the Moscow meeting of COMECON (1979) she called for coordinated COMECON efforts to cope with the fuel crisis. By the end of 1979, vigorous efforts were made to curb Romanian oil imports from the West and plans were launched for an expansion of energy from nuclear power, the specialist reactor machinery coming from Canada, not the USSR.

Nuclear energy has once more become important. Declaring that there was no significant risk, either in the manufacture or in the storage of spent fuels, the thirty-first session of COMECON (Warsaw, 1977) projected a major increase in nuclear energy beyond the existing four per cent of total energy production to a target of twenty-five per cent by the 1990s. It was confirmed at the Moscow meeting in 1979. Significantly enough, West Germany was interested in importing Soviet nuclear-generated electricity in exchange for participation in the Soviet peaceful nuclear programme: an indicator of growing East/West interest in energy cooperation. The Soviet Union has a monopoly of supplying nuclear reactors to COMECON (a 'fast breeder' model is expected to be in use by 1985). It is likely that COMECON will remain in a stronger position than the West so far as energy is concerned, particularly if nuclear energy can be developed sufficiently rapidly to allow for the export of more oil at favourably high prices.

COMECON and the EEC

The Soviet Union does not recognise the EEC and only occasionally has there been direct negotiation between them (normally, relations are conducted through a 'neutral' host). Even so, a trade agreement was suggested as early as 1962, and repeated by Brezhnev in 1972; a draft treaty was presented in 1976. One of the problems for the EEC remains that of Berlin – despite the success of the *Ostpolitik* treaties – for if closer integration were to develop in the EEC, with West Berlin taking a full part, a diplomatic crisis could well arise. Furthermore, except in energy matters, any agreement between the two blocks would be likely to result in COMECON reaping most of the benefits through most-favoured-nation status (as East Germany has done for two decades). The two organisations are not strictly comparable: for example, COMECON lacks an equivalent of the EEC Commission and so may not make treaties as the

Commission may do under Article 113 of the Treaty of Rome. A revised version of the COMECON Charter (1974) empowers the General Secretary to make specific treaties, but he must first obtain a mandate from member countries. A full diplomatic treaty between the two organisations would introduce a new perspective well beyond matters of trade. Not only would it push the EEC into adopting an actual foreign policy, but it would be an all-Europe treaty, settling affairs without reference necessarily to NATO or the USA (one of the traditional Soviet proposals). Nevertheless, negotiations for closer links between the two economic blocs formally began in 1978. They proceeded in a desultory way, and it was one of the results of the energy crisis that the Moscow Session of COMECON (1979) should request an urgent meeting with EEC authorities to try to speed up the negotiations.

It may be false to view European diplomacy of the eighties from the standpoint of the sixties, yet the West remains suspicious of the intentions of the communists (that there was no prospect of her slipping away from communist orthodoxy is part of the explanation for Romania being able to assert so independent a line). Two decades of *détente* and one of mutual disarmament negotiations (SALT I and II) have only partially altered the situation. It is apparent that Soviet influence in Eastern Europe in the seventies was not as pervasive as was once thought, and that, far from being a unity, COMECON remains a grouping of separate centrally planned economies sheltering behind national frontiers – and still nursing boundary disputes that go back at least a couple of generations. If living standards have increased to something near to comparability with the West, there is still a wide gap between richer and poorer member countries. Bilateral agreements remain the norm and progress towards economic integration seems no faster than in the EEC. The various types of planned economies (for COMECON presents no simple model) have neither ironed out the fluctuations that are so common a feature of the less regulated economies of the West, nor established a satisfactory basis for economic unity that might displace the national state. What can be stated with confidence is that, given the starting point of 1945, Eastern Europe has experienced a veritable 'economic miracle' and by the seventies accounted for some thirty per cent world industrial output as opposed to only eighteen per cent in the fifties. There has also been a surprisingly large number of western firms investing in COMECON countries providing sorely needed specialist technology – Poland began reorientating her farm tractor industry through cooperation with Massey Ferguson, and Hungary did the same with International Harvesters, and preferred to use US combine harvesters manufactured under licence in East Germany to those offered by Soviet Russia.

Members have a significant dynamic relation with each other, which is not always typical of the EEC. The explosion of trade with the West that has occurred in the seventies has had a profound impact on intra-COMECON trade (which still dominates the trade pattern). Integrated transport policies are further advanced than in the EEC – particularly in standardisation (following the Soviet GOST institution) and in long-distance route networks. The plan is to switch the balance of transport from rail to road in the 1990s and to make far greater use of pipelines.

Superficially, there are points of convergence between the EEC and COMECON, but the latter remains a collection of countries with centrally planned economies and most of the industry in state hands. The political philosophy of the EEC stands at a different pole. The likely future for Europe is of two loosely combined economic groups with considerable diversity within each, and with strongly developed mutual trade links. In terms of defence and foreign policy, should either of these areas become a practical proposition, neither bloc can think merely in terms of Europe.

7

The USSR since Stalin

Russia spreads across Asia and into Europe. Her traditions are not those of the West, although Western ideas and culture have had great impact over the last three centuries. European Russia is traditionally the developed region of this huge country, and it is still fashionable to look beyond the Urals as though to 'new lands' yet to be colonised. Though her technology and administrative systems derive from the West, there is an 'otherness' about Russia that makes for something of a cultural divide which it is easy to overlook when called upon to make quick judgments of particular situations.

In the chaos of 1917, Lenin seized the main chance and carried through the first successful communist revolution, modifying Marxist theory to suit Russian conditions. Despite incredible difficulties, foreign intervention, civil war and famine, the Bolsheviks survived to create the USSR and to build a new and different society – and to hold the torch of the communist revolution as an example to the world. Stalin, who eventually succeeded Lenin, cut the USSR off from the rest of the world, calling for the creation of 'socialism in one country' and achieving massive industrial progress at an incalculable cost in human terms. The West feared that his ultimate purpose was the overthrow of capitalism and the establishment across the world of the rival value system of communism. A tradition of distrust, suspicion and fear, that even the popular enthusiasm engendered by the Great Patriotic War against Nazi Germany could not assuage, dominated East/West relations. So strong was hostility to communism in the West that some revisionist historians have pointed to the period of the Cold War (see page 21) as one extreme example of the western intolerance that dates from the Bolshevik Revolution. Today, we have come to realise that the Communist system is neither as simple nor as monolithic as was once popularly supposed, and that there is more to the politics of Soviet Russia than quarrels of Byzantine proportions among rivals for leadership, or for the favours of the leader.

The Soviet Union is a federation of fifteen Socialist Republics. These vary in size and ten of them are subdivided into *oblasts* (regions) and *krays* (territories). Massiveness is the feature of the Soviet Union, for it covers a sixth of the earth's land surface and stretches over eleven time zones; its contrasting climatic conditions range from permanent ice to hot desert; its huge store of mineral wealth (much of it difficult to exploit) permits a policy of *autarky* to be contemplated. Its rivalry with the West leads to comparisons of a propaganda nature with the USA – frequently to the Soviet Union's disadvantage, because transport and climatic conditions are by no means comparable. Canada presents some fairly similar conditions, and would be a more suitable area of comparison, although comparative figures of total production etc. are not particularly helpful when so many differences and imponderables are involved. Its population contains at least twenty-four different ethnic groups although the traditional emphasis has been on European Russia, where there is less diversity.

Political structure

The Supreme Soviet is the parliament of the Soviet Union, elected by adult suffrage but in practice nominated by the Communist Party machine, since there is only one list of candidates. In principle, laws may only be adopted by the Supreme Soviet, but as its sessions are infrequent, it elects a Praesidium which exercises its legislative powers between sessions. The Council of Ministers is elected by, and responsible to, the Supreme Soviet. This pattern is effectively mirrored in each of the fifteen federal republics. Throughout, the Communist Party of the Soviet Union (CPSU) duplicates and controls the government structure. At its head is the Politburo, elected by the Central Committee, and the chain of command downwards through federal and local party bodies severely restricts freedom of action: efforts begun by Khrushchev to devolve more power to local party bodies were ended in 1968.

Since 1917 the communists have transformed the life and wealth of Soviet Russia, building a new society ostensibly based on Marxist principles. This was achieved at tremendous cost in human terms, and it is now popular to lay the principal blame for this on Stalin (although his successors rose to power under him). By the late twenties, Stalin had established a dictatorship, but his position was not always secure – there was talk at the Seventeenth Congress (1934) of transferring him 'to other work'. But his dictatorship was consolidated by a series of purges during the 1930s that left him in complete control, with power greater than had been wielded by the Tsars. The Great Patriotic War was a tribute to Soviet achievement and Stalin proved worthy of his great office. Official propaganda heaped fulsome praise upon the Leader, but the terror through which he controlled the Soviet Union (well documented in Solzhenitsyn's *The Gulag Archipelago*) continued until his death. It is partly because of the tight personal control wielded by 'the new Tsar' (as Stalin has been called), and the evident struggles among his followers to achieve power at his death, that many have interpreted Soviet politics in terms of in-fighting in the Kremlin (the Kremlinology school, as it has been termed). But later scholars have rejected this view, both because it is inspired by too narrow a concept of politics and because it ignores the many different pressures within the political structure, from the grass roots upwards, to which any government, however despotic, must be responsive. Nevertheless, because of the concentration of power to which the Soviet system gives rise, the political leadership will always assert primacy. When, at the famous Twentieth Party Congress (1956), Khrushchev delivered his well publicised 'secret speech' denouncing the crimes of his former leader and launching an almost hysterical wave of de-Stalinisation (a truly momentous change in Soviet political life), he was doing more than claiming for himself a new basis of political power; he was declaring that the nature of the political leadership itself had changed.

Once Khrushchev had established his personal ascendancy, (partly maintained by securing to himself the principal administrative government posts), he launched upon a widely ranging series of organisational reforms, substituting reconciliation for the previous policy of coercion, ending mass terror, reducing censorship, relaxing control over the Soviet republics and improving living standards (this latter point may help to explain why there has been no Russian equivalent of the Polish riots of 1970 and 1976). But by 1964, partly because of the failure of many of the reforms to produce their desired effect, partly because of failures in foreign policy (especially over the Cuban missile crisis and the Chinese Republic), but particularly because of growing fears that he was consolidating a personal dictatorship, Khrushchev was ousted in the name of the 'collective leadership' of the Party. No purge followed his fall (he was allowed to retire), but a formal decision was taken 'not to permit the concentration of excessive power in the hands of one person', and was strengthened by preventing any future leader combining the offices of First (General) Secretary of the Party and Chairman of the Council of Ministers.

Khrushchev's overthrow was a victory for the forces of stability and conservatism, and there was some attempt to rehabilitate the reputation of Stalin (the use of the phrase 'period of the cult of personality' with reference to Stalin was forbidden, and a statue showing Stalin in pensive stance was erected behind the Kremlin). Significantly enough, it seems that it was pressure from the leaders of foreign Communist Parties that prevented a more complete rehabilitation on the occasion of the ninetieth anniversary of his birth in 1969. Brezhnev emerged as leader and First Secretary, but with less power than Khrushchev. The Party organisation had reasserted its control. However, Brezhnev's ascendancy over his colleagues has grown and in 1977, Podgorny, who had played a significant part in Khrushchev's overthrow, was unceremoniously dismissed as Head of State. He was succeeded by Brezhnev, who had already (1976) been accorded the title *vozhd'*, a title closely associated with Stalin's personality cult. Yet, although attention necessarily is focused upon the persons of the leader and his colleagues, more depends upon the structure of the political edifice: in this respect there is a comparison with Britain and the USA, where the character of the prime minister or president does not explain the politics of either country.

1977 was the sixtieth anniversary of the Communist Revolution, and the occasion was marked by the ratification of the New Constitution. It had been a long time coming – Khrushchev had promised it in 1961 – and to a degree it reflects the conservativism of the ageing leadership, although it contains a completely new section on foreign policy

> aimed at ensuring international conditions favourable for building communism in the USSR . . . and consistently implementing the principle of the peaceful coexistence of states with different social systems.

In home affairs, the principle of democratic centralism (Article 3) is officially recognised, and the structure of government organisation clearly defined.

Federalism is retained, but the Politburo, through the authoritative principle of democratic centralism, retains full control. The Party, of course, remains the rock core; Article 6 puts it straightforwardly:

> The leading and guiding force of Soviet Society and the nucleus of its political system, of all state organisations and public organisations . . . . The CPSU exists for the people and serves the people . . . (it) determines the general perspectives of the development of society and the course of the home and foreign policy of the USSR.

The Constitution is authoritarian, though it may not be out of line with the long tradition of Russian political life extending far into Tsarist times, where the concept *zakreposhchenie* (the individual submitting to the authority of the state) presents a basic difference from the liberal West. It has been criticised as showing signs of totalitarianism, indeed Bukovsky has described it as a *coup* against the people – but Western ideas are not necessarily applicable to all political situations.

The CPSU

The Communist Party of the Soviet Union is the heart of the system. Its function goes far beyond that of western political parties for it is an institution that both effects and symbolises the unity of the nation in the cause of Marxism-Leninism. The 'Leninist path' to the creation of a communist society assumes the character of dogma, and from this stems the obligation to a wholehearted commitment to the cause as expounded by the leadership. This means that membership of the Party is a thing not idly offered or accepted, and involves political activism at whatever level one is working. The Party permeates the political and social life of the community and provides for participation at all levels through the Leninist-Stalinist doctrine of democratic centralism, by which the lowest level in the party structure elects delegates to the executive committee of the level above, and so on throughout the structure at local, regional and national levels, to the leadership itself. Each level is subordinate to the one above and strict party discipline, enjoining implicit obedience, applies. Within the hierarchy thus created each party body is responsible for (and receives reports from) any lower party organisations. The election of officers is subject to the same procedure and the vetting of candidates or appointment of officials is a major task, so that each secretariat, from district level upwards, maintains official lists of political candidates. Effectively, election becomes a matter of appointment of the appropriate individual and for all posts of political and economic importance, requiring party recommendation, only those on the *nomenklatura* list will be considered. The Party, therefore, exercises an imminent control over careers and appointments and to 'get on' one needs to be a full party member.

Membership has trebled since the war – over sixty per cent have joined since the Twentieth Party Congress, reflecting Khrushchev's big drive to increase membership (although it seems the increase will probably not be continued at the same rate). A significant change in the social structure of the Party is reflected in

Membership of the CPSU

	1971	1976
Full members	13810089	15058017
Candidate members	645232	636170
Total	14455321	15694187

(Source: A. Brown and M. Kaser, *The Soviet Union since the Fall of Khrushchev*, p. 314)

The stability of Party membership since Khrushchev

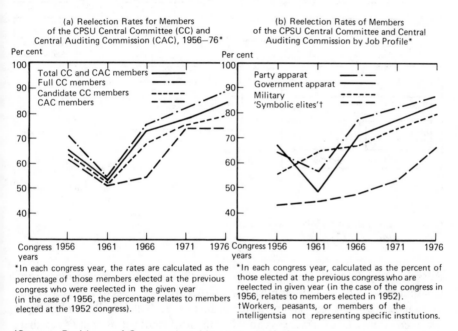

(a) Reelection Rates for Members of the CPSU Central Committee (CC) and Central Auditing Commission (CAC), 1956–76*

(b) Reelection Rates of Members of the CPSU Central Committee and Central Auditing Commission by Job Profile*

*In each congress year, the rates are calculated as the percentage of those members elected at the previous congress who were reelected in the given year (in the case of 1956, the percentage relates to members elected at the 1952 congress).

*In each congress year, calculated as the percent of those elected at the previous congress who are reelected in given year (in the case of the congress in 1956, relates to members elected in 1952).
†Workers, peasants, or members of the intelligentsia not representing specific institutions.

(Source: *Problems of Communism*, March/April 1979)

the increased number of working class members (at the expense largely of the peasantry and less educated white collar workers), of the trained specialist and the gradual increase in women members (sex equality is established with access to all the prestigious professions, like doctors, lawyers, engineers; yet women play only a minor part in the higher party organisation). There is considerable variation in membership between nationalities, with a huge membership among the Russians (60 per cent in 1976) and Ukrainians (16 per cent) – European Russia accounts for 81.86 per cent. This reflects the traditional pattern of

The structure and size of the CPSU, 1973

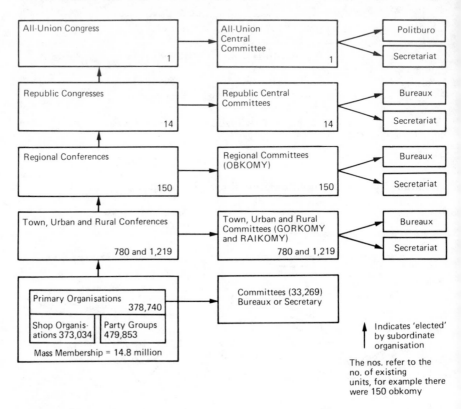

(Source: M. McAuley, *Politics and the Soviet Union*, p. 273)

Russian development, but it is a pattern that is under increasing strain. Compared with other Communist Parties (notably the Czech) it has a young average age, though this is rising as recruitment is curtailed. Full membership is achieved after years of service as candidate members and before that as members of the *Komsomol* covering the age group 14–28 (there are Pioneers, aged 10–13 and Octobrists 7–9, for the school population, for there is strong emphasis on the social implications of education).

As contact with the West increases and living standards rise, there have been repeated complaints from the conservative leadership about the evident lack of idealism and self-sacrifice among the younger generation: this has more significance than similar complaints in the West, since it has implications for the self-discipline and dedication that service with the Party involves. As an earnest of their concern, the leadership has strengthened its guardianship over the *Komsomol* – which had pursued a vigorous campaign to get the young and active to volunteer for settling the virgin lands of Kazakhstan and the Siberian Republics and to form student construction detachments: such work ranks highly in the Soviet scale of values. An important new town on the Amur river in

Khabarovsk, Eastern Siberia, is named Komsomolsk. Yet, despite huge efforts by Party institutions and especially the schools, modernisation and industrialis-ation tend to produce much the same attitudes among the young as in the West, ideological differences notwithstanding. Opinion surveys do not support the view that a new socialist generation different from previous generations is appearing.

Central government

The soviet government system has two pillars, elected at each stage, the Party and the government structure, reflecting the unified structure of the régime. The organs of each pillar are not composed of two separate sets of officials or delegates: particularly at the top of the hierarchy, cohesion is increased by members occupying posts in both pillars – members of the Politburo being on both the Praesidium of the Supreme Soviet and the Central Committee of the Party, for example (but no minister sits in the Praesidium). This interlocking creates an authoritative inner core that welds together Party and Soviet institutions. An enormously complex and bureaucratic structure, well placed to resist fundamental change, results.

Only a tiny group of leading politicians actually participate in making national policy and for this the Politburo is the principal agency. This is a small body of leading party and Soviet officials under the General Secretary of the Party. The latter (Brezhnev) is strengthened by his command over the Party machine and his right to make appointments to a wide range of senior posts. Though he held this position as well as Chairman of the Council of Ministers, it did not save Khrushchev from being ousted in 1964 – leaders have no guarantee of security, they must take pains to maintain support among their colleagues – since 1964 the Soviet Union has had a 'collective leadership' within which Brezhnev has emerged as something more than *primus inter pares*. The leadership would not survive against serious disagreements among the Politburo, or if it were directly associated with a major policy failure. Like the rest of the political structure, the top leadership does not present that monolithic structure of popular western legend. Since 1973 the Politburo has tended to become an institution similar to a 'national government', composed of leading Party and ministerial politicians including leading central officials; those from the republics and the two major cities, Moscow and Leningrad; ministers responsible for the most important branches of government policy and chairmen of a few key institutions like the KGB and the Party Control Commission. This enlarges the Politburo, and may inhibit strong and vigorous action.

Two other bodies closely concerned with decision-making and carrying out those decisions, are the Council and the Secretariat. The Council of Ministers is a large body appointed by the Supreme Soviet to carry out its orders. It meets as a body perhaps twice a year and so is more of a collection of competing ministers than a council – it leaves to an inner core the task of issuing decrees. The Secretariat of the Central Committee of the Party provides the Party's civil service and wields considerable political influence assisting the individual ministers in the Council to take decisions and to formulate policy. Beyond the

The Party/Soviet governing structure

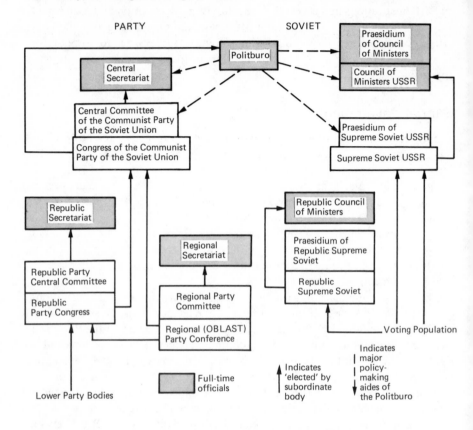

(Source: M. McAuley, *Politics and the Soviet Union*, p. 199)

centre of political power its influence is augmented by the right to appoint general secretaries to the republics' and *oblasts*' party organisations.

The Supreme Soviet is a two chamber assembly elected every four years with delegates from the fifteen Soviet Republics. It meets infrequently to pass important legislation, but not to debate it. Clearly, political power does not reside here. The Central Committee of the Party provides a forum where many delegates from different institutions discuss policy. It no longer contains Party men of great standing, but is theoretically the highest consultative body in the land and no major decision on party matters may be taken without consulting it. The Party Congress ceased to be a decision maker in the 1920s and is little more than a gathering of the faithful elected from republic and regional party levels every five years. Its meetings are huge propaganda affairs of some five thousand delegates, but it has not influenced decision making since the 1961 Congress refused Khrushchev permission for more de-Stalinisation measures.

Economic policy

Traditionally, the Soviet Union has a centrally planned economy. The basic economic model for such an economy replaced the normal market mechanisms and variable prices with an artificial set of arbitrary prices and ideal production targets determined by government agencies with little regard to consumer demand in order that priority economic needs might be achieved. Producers are required to fulfil their targets which may take local conditions into account, if the model is sufficiently sophisticated. The enterprise belongs to the State and its manager is a state servant. Both agriculture and industry are controlled by the State and the economic conditions prearranged so that a balance is maintained between the exploiting of resources and the production of goods. Gosplan, the government agency for economic planning since 1921, endeavoured throughout the Stalin period to manage the economy upon these relatively arbitrary lines; and from the late twenties a series of Five Year Plans served to force forward agricultural reorganisation and heavy industrial production. This was a 'command economy' (Kosygin called it 'directive planning') in contrast to Western techniques of 'indicative planning'. Although Stalin's policy of 'socialism in one country' served to insulate the Soviet Union from economic variations suffered in the West, the planning mechanism was neither sufficiently sophisticated, nor in possession of enough data to operate the ideal system with maximum efficiency.

The planned economy has had notable successes, particularly where it has proved possible to divert immense resources to achieve particular ends (as, for example, over armaments in the 1960s); but it suffers from rigidity and it inhibits spontaneous response to local conditions. In addition, the practice of concentrating upon specific sectors has resulted in severe shortages elsewhere, especially of consumer goods. By the 1970s, with foreign trade beginning to feature increasingly in the Soviet economy, and thereby introducing extraneous factors beyond the control of the planning mechanism, the whole approach to Soviet economic planning was being seriously modified – with experiences of the smaller COMECON countries serving as different models. The evident success of the 'socialist market' in Hungary was an obvious pointer: however, there has been no attempt fundamentally to change the Soviet planning system since the ill-fated measures of 1965. The Tenth Plan (1976–80), for example, threw a renewed emphasis on consumer goods, partly in an effort to meet the rising expectations of workers and forestall discontent (the Polish riots of 1976 were a serious warning). But it was also committed heavily to energy creation schemes in response to the world energy crisis (as much to ensure self-sufficiency in energy for herself and COMECON, as to respond to world conditions and to take advantage of opportunities of earning hard currency for further foreign trade). It also introduced, for the first time, major schemes of environmental protection and conservation (re-cycling of water, for example, is expected to lead to a marginal increase only in water consumption despite a projected sixty per cent industrial expansion in some sectors). In contrast with their predecessors, later Plans have not achieved their targets. The Ninth Plan suffered badly from the impact of poor harvests in 1972, '75 and '77, and it fell seriously short of its targets. The Tenth Plan has suffered even more so, and a significant drop in growth rate was openly admitted by the end of 1979. As with the development of heavy industry and the extraction of raw materials, herculean efforts have been put into the development of agriculture.

Agriculture

The bulk of Russia's agricultural land lies in what has been called the 'fertile triangle' covering the southern part of European Russia and tapering off at the Urals: it is a fertile area where agricultural land is beginning to be threatened by expanding urbanisation. Most of the rest of the huge land area of Russia is not suited to cultivation, and here lies the problem of Soviet agriculture. The aim of Soviet policy is to be self-sufficient (if not an exporter) – an aim increasingly difficult to achieve when rising standards of living are allied with a rising population over all. Stalin, for all his concentration on collectivisation, allowed agriculture a low priority: Khrushchev and Brezhnev have both made agriculture a major development industry which has made surprising strides under them, despite severe disappointments resulting from climatic and other factors. There is a surprisingly low total acreage suited to intensive agriculture – twenty per cent – and in Central Asia, the growth region of Soviet agriculture, the severe climate, with a combination of severe frosts and light summer rain, together with the *sukhove* (hot dry wind), makes farming very uncertain. Furthermore, even in the prosperous Black Earth Ukraine grain lands, Soviet agriculture is surprisingly backward by Western standards (and after some forty years it is difficult to account for this in terms of enforced collectivisation, the destruction of the *Kulak* class of wealthy farmers, and the deprivations of the Great Patriotic War).

From the outset of the enforced collectivisation (which led to the man-made famine of 1931) two types of state-controlled farms emerged: the *kolkhoz* (collective farm) was a producer cooperative not unlike the *mir* of late Tsarist days, where the land was given by the State in perpetuity to the families originally living on the collective. It was a useful half-way house to socialised agriculture, because it assumed almost complete responsibility for its families, thus relieving the State of the cost of supplying social services, education and pensions to the rural community – each family received a small private plot to serve both for additional personal food supply and provision for old age (they were, after all, effectively tied to their *kolkhoz*). By the 1970s a typical *kolkhoz* had about 400 families farming some 3000 hectares. The manager was a Party nominee and from the outset was required to deliver crops according to his quota to the local town at nominal prices (which remained stable throughout the 1930s). Farm machinery and ploughing was generally in the hands of the Motor Tractor Stations (MTS) staffed by Party members who provided an additional control over the *kolkhoz*. By and large, the performance of these collective farms was very poor in terms of agricultural production: they would not meet the needs of the rising standard of living in European Russia, quite apart from the growing population of the Siberian Republics. In a major effort to make the *kolkhoz* more efficient, Khrushchev dissolved the MTS (1958) thus releasing machinery for the collectives. Delivery quotas were replaced by contracts to supply the State at reasonable market prices, and Khrushchev's reforms were carried further by

Brezhnev: old age pensions (although at a lower level than for industrial and white-collar workers) were provided from 1965 and in 1966 *kolkhoz* workers were allowed to earn minimum wages. In 1968 a long-delayed *Kolkhoz* Congress adopted a new Statute setting up a Kolkhoz Council and permitting some degree of local control over crops and farm management. In 1974 the Kolkhozniki were permitted passports allowing the possibility of movement from the collective – though they still needed the police regulation *propiska* to travel. Price levels were raised in the seventies and a fifty per cent bonus paid for deliveries of crops in excess of quotas – an astronomical subsidy was offered in 1977 for dairy and meat produce. But despite the reforms, the collective farm remains an inefficient instrument, characterised by a labour force that is ageing and increasingly female.

Types of Soviet farms (total areas in million hectares)

	1954	1963	1970
Collectives (Kolkhoz)	389.7	241.9	204.5
Household Plot (on Kolkhoz)	6.9	5.0	4.8
State Farms (Sovkhoz)	88.7	283.1	333.1
Personal Plots	1.1	2.5	3.4
Total for farming	486.4	532.5	545.8

The second form of large farm, dating from 1929, is the State Farm (*Sovkhoz*) larger, more efficient, owned by the State and with families occupying a more independent status (comparable with the industrial worker). The number of *Sovkhoz* is increasing and Brezhnev has outlined a policy moving towards a union of the two forms of collectives. The *Sovkhoz* has been the usual form of agricultural settlement in the Virgin Lands. In both cases, the importance of the private plot has increased: to meet pressure on production, especially meat, there has been increased reliance on them during the seventies and private livestock farming has been permitted on a small scale to meet local demands in some areas.

But differences of farm organisation do not answer the major agricultural problems of the Soviet Union. Agriculture accounts for a huge proportion of total investment – perhaps as high as twenty per cent (five times that of the USA). Huge advances in rural electrification and mechanisation have been made and scientific methods have improved insecticides, fertilisers and seeds. The farm manager has gained the right to make use of local market conditions, and incentives have been introduced both to diversify crop produce (the Ukraine is moving towards mixed farming instead of almost exclusive reliance on grain and hay) and to encourage production in marginal lands – a differential price for sugar beet allows 210 roubles per center (100 tonnes) in the Ukraine, but 320 in the marginal Volga-Urals lands (the USSR is the world's largest producer of sugar beet, refining some ten million tons of sugar in 1971). Yet agricultural yields remain low and with poor protein quality – which makes for low quality animal feeds (much grain is needed for fodder and animal feeds and low quality affects the meat yield). There is very little acreage available for grain, and the marginal increases resulting from irrigation and heavy fertilising (at huge cost) only keeps pace with what is lost to non-agricultural use. Other problems lie in transport – the climate makes field transport in spring and autumn very difficult, and the lack of adequate railways, roads and of sufficient lorries, together with the inadequate storage facilities leads to crop wastage especially in bumper years like 1973. Farm storage space for fertilisers is often inadequate, and there is too great a delay in large farms adopting new seed types.

Khrushchev's dream was to make Kazakhstan a grain republic to rival the Ukraine. Vast sums were expended on his Virgin Lands scheme in the mid-fifties and the Irtysh-Karaganda canal was constructed for transport and irrigation. But the uncertainty of climate and the over-ploughing of new lands has led to disappointing results, and, especially in the Tselinograd Oblast, to 'dust-bowl' conditions. However, the economy of Turkmenia and other Central Asian republics began to be transformed in the seventies by the audacious Kara-Kum canal, for transport and irrigation in desert areas, and the extensive planting of trees to check soil erosion, and of cash crops like cotton, rice and winter wheat as well as stock breeding.

Variations in Soviet grain harvests, 1960–76 (million tonnes)

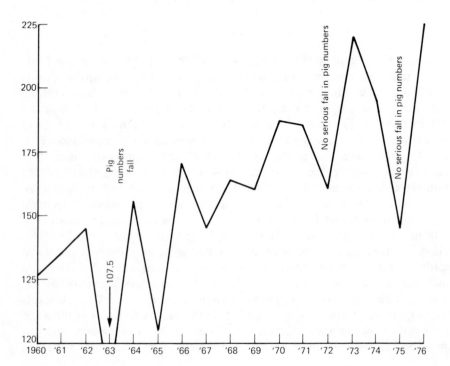

Climate remains a determining factor and limits agricultural expansion. When it affects grain production, livestock are in danger for lack of fodder means a substantial proportion of grain goes for animal feed. A bad harvest, or the drought of 1963, may decimate livestock: thus, following that 1963 drought the pig population dropped thirty per cent. It says a great deal for agricultural advance since then that the bad harvests of 1972, 1975, 1977 and 1979 did not seriously affect the livestock population. However, the serious shortfall in grain production in these years meant that the Soviet Union had to buy heavily on the world market, with serious consequences both for balance of payments and the level of world grain prices: in 1977 ten million tonnes of US grain was purchased and an agreement made to import between seven and ten million tonnes annually until 1985. Agricultural experts in the West, who warned against some of the disasters that have struck Central Asian developments, tend to blame the excessively centralised bureaucracy of the Soviet system. Yet clear evidence of progress in output, yields, diversity of crops, availability of equipment and improvement in rural living conditions – albeit at a heavy cost in terms of investment and current production expenses – indicate that Khrushchev and Brezhnev were not mistaken in giving so much prominence to Soviet agri-culture.

Industry

Tsarist Russia did not end its days as an underdeveloped country; indeed, much of the justifiably vaunted achievements of the first five-year plans rests on work first begun, or projected at the beginning of the century. The exploitation of the mineral wealth of the Siberian Republics is nothing new – only the scale of that exploitation is new. Climatic difficulties, the absence of adequate geological surveys, 'empty' inhospitable lands without proper transport, all add to the very heavy cost of opening up the mineral resources.

Stalin's policy was simple and direct – a controlled economy unaffected by the vicissitudes of international trade could achieve wonders. His ideal was to achieve as equal as possible a level of economic activity throughout each region of the Soviet Union but with priority given to selected sectors, beginning with extractive and heavy industry. Gosplan controlled the allocation of resources and hence the system of supply (*naryady*) – the consumer interest would take second place. Where there were labour shortages, as in the Siberian Republics, wholesale shifting of population to create new centres of human activity was carried out, and forced labour ensured the basic necessities for existence.

Since Stalin's day, if central control is still in evidence, two of the major bases of the Stalin tradition have been rejected; first, there is now greater flexibility allowing for regional specialisation, rather than seeking to create a balanced development between all Republics. Various factors have combined to change Eastern Siberia from a region to be settled (despite the inhospitable countryside and climate) to a purveyor of raw materials for Western Russia; and because much of Siberian iron ore is low grade, the richer ores from European Russia are transported east. But regional specialisation does not mean that regions are not expected to provide for their own needs, particularly in foodstuffs. Secondly,

The transportation of freight in the USSR

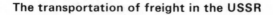

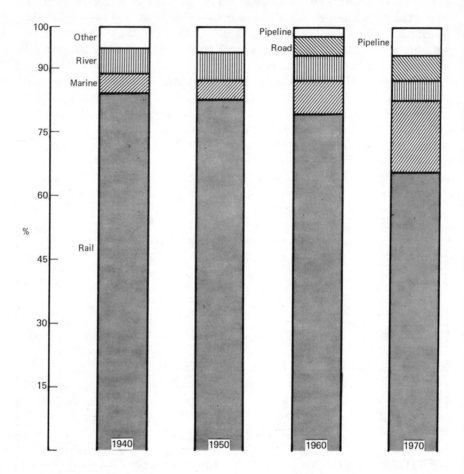

wholesale direction of population to new areas has ceased and migration controls have been relaxed. There is now much more attention paid to personal preference and the need to provide amenities in order to attract workers. But Eastern Siberia, especially, does not attract workers except on a temporary basis, and the cost of providing social amenities is so great that there appears to be developing the policy of maintaining only so many workers in inhospitable areas as is consistent with efficient extraction of raw materials and transport of commodities. Regional specialisation may increase as the Soviet Union becomes more integrated in the world economy: the Stalin tradition is being eroded fast. Nevertheless, despite the manifold difficulties, the Tenth Plan envisaged a global industrial output for the Siberian Republics of nearly fifty per cent above 1975 levels.

Transport is the key to both agricultural and industrial development, and in a country of such a vast size, with a climate that renders much of the countryside a sea of mud twice a year, a highly developed transport system has yet to be

Resource development in the Soviet Far East

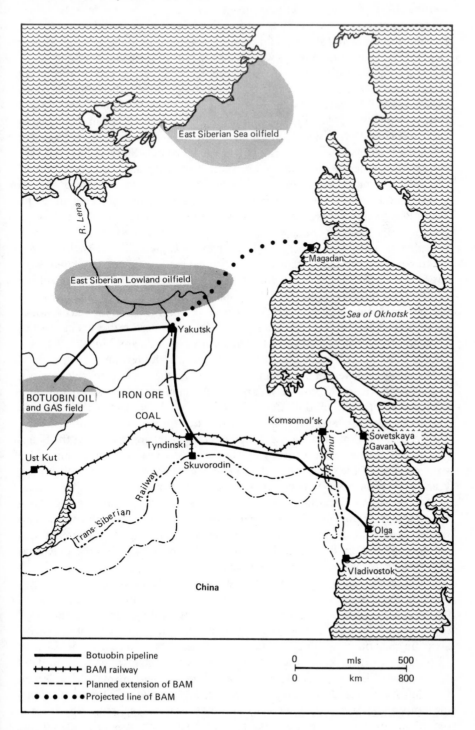

East Siberian Sea oilfield

R. Lena

East Siberian Lowland oilfield

Magadan

Sea of Okhotsk

Yakutsk

BOTUOBIN OIL and GAS field

IRON ORE

COAL

Komsomol'sk

Sovetskaya Gavan

Ust Kut

Tyndinski

Skuvorodin

R. Amur

Trans-Siberian Railway

Olga

Vladivostok

China

——— Botuobin pipeline
+++++ BAM railway
– – – – Planned extension of BAM
••••• Projected line of BAM

0   mls   500
0   km   800

devised. But already in south Central Asia the road construction programme is shifting from major inter-city routes to providing feeder roads for rural communities. Further west 'motor-trams' have been organised for the efficient transport of grain and sugar beet during harvest time. In Stalin's day great projects for roadways and railways were begun as part of the equal development of regions, sometimes without regard to economic need, so that some of them were abandoned. One such scheme, begun with forced labour and then abandoned for twenty years, is BAM, the Baikal-Amur Magistral single track line from Ust Kut to Komsomolsk – 2000 miles through inhospitable virgin Siberian *taiga*, begun again in 1974 with volunteer Komsomol labour and scheduled to be completed in 1982. It has clear strategic importance (the existing Trans-Siberian line runs very close to the Chinese border) and will serve to open up gigantic reserves of timber, iron ore, coking coal and other minerals. A major branch, from Tynde to Yaktusk and beyond, has also begun and is scheduled to be completed under the Tenth Plan. This will open up huge reserves of timber, metals, oil and iron ore in North Eastern Siberia. Japanese finance is involved in the line and there is a prospect of a Russo-Japanese steel complex to exploit the newly discovered Yakutian ores (though Japan is hesitant, having considerable surplus steel capacity herself). However, a major Soviet, Japanese and US co-operative project for a pipeline bigger, and three times as long as, the Alaskan pipeline, is under negotiation to carry natural gas from Yakutia to Olga on the Sea of Japan, where it will be liquefied for transport 4200 miles across the Pacific to the USA. Another major south-north rail project is the ambitious Tyumen – Urengry line in central Siberia, across difficult, marshy terrain.

Major canals have a similar effect to railways and there is an extensive network in European Russia (Moscow is an important inland port). The Karaganda and the Kara-Kum canals in south Central Asia have a great impact on the economic life of Kazakshtan and Turkmenia. Water transport is important in Soviet Russia, and the Tenth Plan lays an emphasiş on coastal areas, whether the Black Sea, with the new rail ferry from Ilyichevsk to Varna in Bulgaria (important strategically), or the great northern sea route, kept open for five months of the year by the atomic-powered ice-breaker, *Lenin*: the Soviet merchant marine fleet is of international importance. Pipelines for oil and natural gas (see page 137) have featured prominently in the seventies; and air routes (including a supersonic service from Alma Ata to Moscow) for both passenger and freight are developing. But in Russia, rail is king, and electrification of the extensive European Russian network is well advanced.

The succession of Five Year Plans have made Soviet Russia a major producer, rivalling the USA in coal, steel, oil, nuclear energy and electricity generation (there is a proposal to link together the existing grid systems into one huge supranational grid from the Oder to Vladivostok). Many of the great industrial areas in Siberia were begun under the Tsars – the Kuzbas complex, the Cheremkhovo-Irkutsk and the Krasnoyarsk complex. Others like the Bratsk-Llim and the Lower Angarsk project are Soviet developments, examples of Gosplan's vision of large Territorial Production Complexes (TPK) developing the industry of a region through diversified industrial enterprises grouped round central energy sources and using the raw materials of the area. Despite all the accent on exploiting the potential wealth of the Siberian Republics, however, the old heartland of European Russia and the Urals region remain predominant.

A very significant development, beginning with the Eighth Plan (1966–70) was the open acceptance of direct manufacturing agreements with the West – for example, the gigantic Togliatti car plant on the Volga, linked with Fiat, or the Kama River Truck plant, or 'North Star', the West Siberian natural gas pipeline built with US technical aid. The agreements are frequently in the form of compensation agreements, paying in goods rather than hard currency, and they have been frequent with France in the seventies, and to a lesser extent with the USA, Japan and West Germany. Such agreements are likely to increase in the eighties, although the advantage lies heavily with the Soviet Union and possibly to the disadvantage of the West – for example, cheap Soviet chemicals flooded on to the world market in return for high technology: a new and ironic version of the old 'dumping' theory.

Soviet oil exports, 1973–76

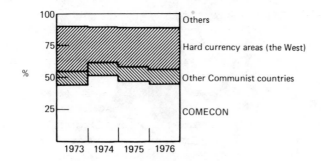

Soviet domestic consumption of energy (estimates), 1976–90

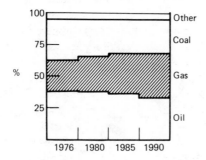

Soviet sources project a possible larger percentage of nuclear energy usage by 1990, which would correspondingly reduce oil and gas consumption.

Soviet natural energy resources

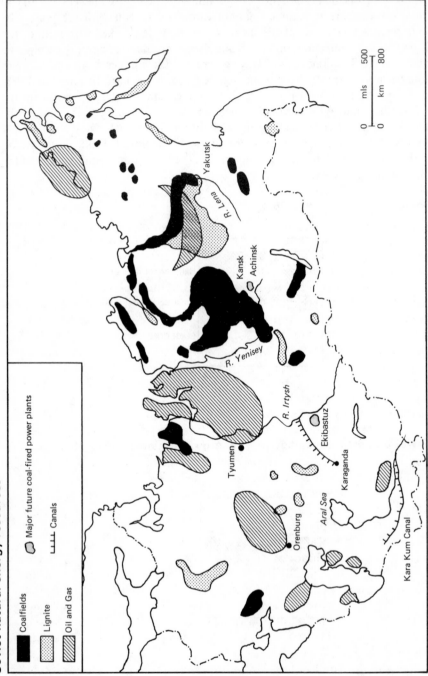

Legend:

Coalfields

Lignite

Oil and Gas

Major future coal-fired power plants

Canals

Yakutsk

R. Lena

Kansk

Achinsk

R. Yenisey

R. Irtysh

Ekibastuz

Tyumen

Karaganda

Orenburg

Aral Sea

Kara Kum Canal

mls 0   500

km 0   800

Energy resources are not a great problem for the Soviet Union – she is the world's largest producer of oil with 546 million tons in 1977 – it is a matter of extraction costs, climatic problems, and transport (the lignite fields of the Kansk-Achinsk Basin are likely to be converted into electrical energy on site during the eighties because of transport difficulties). Planned energy consumption will increase at around three per cent annually and this will still allow for export at favourably high prices in order to earn hard currency. Energy exports may, indeed, prove the key to the future development of *détente*, although the Soviet union has to balance the advantages of trade with the West with the need to supply her COMECON associates (see page 137). The problem will be the rate of extraction, because the new fields are difficult of access and in areas not easy to exploit. Since 1975 the Soviet Union has been charging its COMECON partners a price for natural gas and oil close to world prices, an interesting development, since it implies a greater faith in the price mechanism than in traditional Marxist economic theory. The need for US and Japanese technical and financial help in exploiting oil fields has led to complex negotiations – but the Japanese, concerned for the low returns, have shown signs of preferring cooperation with China in order to get cheaper energy more conveniently. Another development is the West German interest in importing Soviet nuclear-generated electricity in exchange for participation in the Soviet nuclear programme.

The development of extensive trade links with the West, despite the impact of the world slump in the seventies, presents another indication of a major shift in emphasis in the Soviet position. Under Stalin, it is customary to observe that a policy of *autarky* was pursued. This may be a little simplistic. There seem to have been three factors at issue; first, the natural Soviet desire for strategic independence (an unwillingness to rely upon imports from a potentially hostile country), which was most marked in the thirties, when the doctrine of 'capitalist encirclement' was most forcibly presented. Then there was economic nationalism that caused the production of a range of items at uneconomic cost and against any principle of rational specialisation. There was also the Marxist heritage of rendering as small a tribute as possible to Caesar – an aversion to the exploitative nature of trading policies. Hence, Stalin permitted a limited rôle for foreign trade, importing only essentials or to relieve a sudden bottleneck in supply, and paying either in gold or with whatever products would find a ready market abroad. After Stalin, a quite different attitude developed, recognising that trade and aid had a direct bearing on diplomatic influence, particularly with the Third World. There was also the influence of COMECON economists advocating the advantages of specialisation through trade; it was preferable to export in order to be able to buy a commodity that it was too costly or inconvenient to produce at home. Hence the new concentration on export industries and the export of raw material and energy resources. There was also, of course, the need to gain hard currency to purchase both Western technology and the large quantities of grain that were imported in the late seventies: the balance of payments was as sensitive an issue as in the West.

The pattern of trade seems to be an exporting of Soviet high-cost raw materials and an importing of machinery and goods to meet shortages (including grain) and promote economic growth. Compensation Agreements work to the Soviet

Soviet GNP growth rates

	Per cent
1950s	5.8
1960s	5.1
1971–5	3.7
1976–80	3.3

advantage, especially if they are continued after the credit has been repaid – exports from the Togliatti plant are said to have already earned in foreign currency the cost of the imported equipment (although this success has not been repeated with the Kama Truck Plant). Clearly, the Soviet Union is becoming increasingly linked with international trade patterns, which must introduce a new element of uncertainty into her directed economy. There has been a notable improvement in her balance of trade with the West since 1976, although this to a large extent depends upon the level of grain imports, which in turn depends upon the Soviet harvest. West Germany continues to lead the West in trade with the

Soviet energy consumption in the Ninth and Tenth Five-Year Plans

	Coal *(M. tons)*	*Oil* *(M. tons)*	*Natural gas* *(Th. m. cu. m)*	*Electric power* *(M. MWh)*
Soviet production				
1975: Plan directives	685–695	480–500	300–320	1,030–1,070
Plan law	695	496	320	1,065
Actual	701	491	289	1,038
1980: Plan directives	790–810	620–640	400–435	1,340–1,380
Plan law	805	640	435	1,380
Soviet deliveries to other COMECON members				
1966–70	6	138	8	14
1971–75	5	250	30	40
1976–80	..	364	90	67
– percentage of quinquennial production				
1966–70	–	9	1	–
1971–75	–	12	3	1
1976–80	–	13	5	1

(Source: A. Brown and M. Kaser, *The Soviet Union since the Fall of Khrushchev*, p. 285)

Soviet Union, and foreign trade is expected to increase by ten per cent with many joint projects coordinated by COMECON.

However, a serious problem remains the slow growth rate and low productivity in both agriculture and industry. Khrushchev's boast of 1961, that the Soviet Union would overtake the West within a generation rings hollow. Defence spending (including the navy) swallows a significant proportion of GNP, and considerable investment in heavy industry continues: but there is a rising demand for consumer goods, to which the leadership is particularly sensitive, the more so as resources have been switched to energy and raw material extraction thus making improvements in the supply of consumer goods a slow process. The consumer demands are low in Western terms – and much lower in the Siberian and southern republics (where the biggest population increase occurs) than in European Russia. A concentration on European Russia results – Asiatic Russia will benefit in the next generation. This makes nonsense of the traditional Marxist-Leninist principle of 'evening-out' levels of development between republics (although it may only be temporary). The principle has been breached by the Tenth Plan's concentration on about a dozen large regional complexes (TPKs), mostly in the Eastern regions.

Labour shortages are beginning to affect the economy and an open debate (itself a sign of relaxed political life) is taking place over the question of whether mothers should go out to work or remain at home with their children. Factories tend to keep labour unnecessarily, partly because of the obligation in some areas to send out workers to help with the harvest, partly to cope with any sudden increased production target, partly because official policy allocates additional funds to factories for overheads according to the size of their pay roll (a staff cut might mean no swimming bath). Over-employment (92.4 per cent of able-bodied adults are employed) is preferred to unemployment on ideological grounds. In Central Asia the low technical aptitude and immobility of the indigenous population does not help the labour situation. Meanwhile, increasing consumer demand is complicated by a new feature in Soviet life – the rapid rise in real incomes in the sixties and seventies has led to a levelling-up of previously underprivileged groups, so that previously high-status groups – teachers, technicians, engineers, doctors – are beginning to suffer relative deprivation. Overall, Soviet society is decidedly more egalitarian than it was in Khrushchev's day, and the narrowing differential between occupation groups is causing some concern. Inflation, too, although distinctly modest by Western standards, is a factor – disguised partly by a product being withdrawn and then issued under a different label at a higher price (e.g. vodka in 1970). In July 1979, price increases of eighteen per cent on luxuries were imposed: the Soviet news agency, Tass, explained the increases by blaming a short-fall in supply which caused the decision 'to use the price mechanism to adjust trade' – a remarkably Western reaction for a controlled economy! The slowdown in Soviet growth continues and the targets of the Tenth Plan will not be achieved. The loss of momentum in the seventies may partly be explained by the difficulty of managing a 'command economy' at a time of world depression, without the aid of large-scale computerisation.

Clearly, the Soviet economy is vulnerable to the movement of world prices and

Declining economic growth rates in the USSR

(a) GNP	1950s	1960s			1971–5		1976–80
%	5.8	5.1			3.7		3.3
(b)	1976^1	1976^2	1977^1	1977^2	1978^1	1978^2
%						
National income	5.6	4.8	4.2	3.1	4.5	3.9
Industrial production	4.3	4.8	6.3	5.8	6.0	4.5
Producer goods	4.9	5.3	6.5	n.a.	6.4	4.7
Consumer goods	2.7	3.0	5.7	n.a.	5.1	3.7

[1] Estimated   [2] Actual

(Source: *The Times*, 26 January 1978)

no longer conceives of itself as independent of economic events elsewhere; the need to import grain, both for human consumption and to help with animal feed, and the desire for sophisticated technical equipment are obvious examples. But the political implications of 'creeping stagnation' (1979 was a particularly bad year for the economy as well as for the harvest) in a society where central control has been relaxing, give rise to grave concern. Agriculture, for example, absorbs twenty-five per cent of the total investment (double what it was under Stalin) and yet imports are vital, not only of essential grains, but also of semi-luxuries. Russian standards of living have risen and there is an increasing demand to eat better – especially meat, which continues to be in short supply (meatless Thursdays are a standing joke in city restaurants). There seems to be more actual cash available and there is the possibility of the emergence of some sort of consumer society as understood in the West. In such circumstances, popular demand must be satisfied – and with a food shortage and a short-fall in production of factory goods, the pressure for a reduction in defence expenditure must be considerable.

The nationalities

Demographic problems face the Soviet Union in the eighties and nineties. The catastrophes of the century – wars, famines, purges – have left a population considerably lower than would be the case in the West, although it had reached 255.5 million in 1976. The workforce in European Russia will be in short supply, and this will have serious effects on industrial production; since the Seventh Plan (1961–5) there has been no significant expansion in industrial labour productivity. Social factors, like rising standards of living and widespread use of birth control, also seem to be important in European Russia. But the most significant change has been in the distribution of population: there has been a decided switch to the periphery in terms of population growth. The Baltic States, Moldavia and the southern Ukraine have grown at a faster rate than the European Russian heartlands, and more significantly there has been a big increase in the Asiatic Republics. The age distribution also presents problems,

Population changes in the USSR, 1950–2000

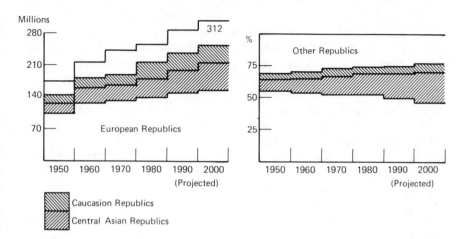

Millions

312

280 · 210 · 140 · 70

European Republics

1950 1960 1970 1980 1990 2000
(Projected)

%

Other Republics

75 · 50 · 25

1950 1960 1970 1980 1990 2000
(Projected)

Caucasion Republics
Central Asian Republics

The increasing proportion of Russians living away from the traditional Slav heartlands is apparent. This underlines the shift in the ethnic balance of the population. (Figures from NATO Colloquium, 1979).

The Soviet population, by ethnic group

Births in the USSR, by ethnic group

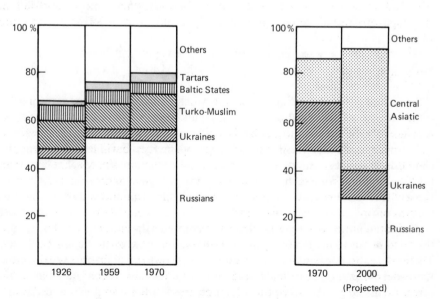

100 % · 80 · 60 · 40 · 20

Others
Tartars
Baltic States
Turko-Muslim
Ukraines
Russians

1926 1959 1970

100 % · 80 · 60 · 40 · 20

Others
Central Asiatic
Ukraines
Russians

1970 2000
(Projected)

for whereas European Russia has an ageing population, the non-Slavs of Eastern Russia have a young population with all the ensuing problems of educational and social provision, of a likely further increase in population, and of employment. Employment is a particular problem for Central Asia, for cultural reasons; the required leap from a background of nomadic society into an advanced industrial factory-based society has inhibited many young people in Central Asia from moving to towns, even though there are inadequate employment opportunities at home – they show an unwillingness to move to urban centres in their own Republic and few venture as far as European Russia. By the end of the century, the Slav population will compose only twenty-five per cent of the Russian peoples: some Soviet demographers, alarmed at this prospect, have even proposed a differential system of social benefits to encourage Slav families to have more children, as opposed to the non-Slavs.

There are implications for the Party, too, in the relatively rapid growth of non-Slav peoples: hitherto the Party has been very heavily Russian and the organisation in Eastern Republics has been frequently relatively rudimentary. This will have to change to take account of a new balance in society, and the rapidly expanding young non-Slav generation has grown up with a political sense under a leadership that has renounced terror as an instrument of policy. Muslim influence is very strong among the Asian Republics, and this raises the problem of religious policy. The active repression of religion that featured under Stalin has been replaced by a more gentle, psychological pressure against strong public expression of religious belief, whether Christian (notably the Baptists), Jew or Muslim; Khrushchev's anti-religious policy was ended after 1964 as being counter-productive. The 1977 Constitution is notably open on religious toleration – Article 52 states:

> Freedom of conscience, that is the right to profess any religion and perform religious rites, or not profess any religion, and to conduct atheistic propaganda, shall be recognised for all citizens of the USSR.

The possible link between religious observance and political dissent is not lost on Soviet authorities, the more so as with the Muslims it can have decided nationalist overtones.

Stalin had adopted a policy of crushing Muslim nationalism, even resorting to genocide against some nationalities (Muslims were active in the labour camp revolts after Stalin's death). Official policy in the sixties and seventies has encouraged a docile Muslim leadership to emerge, but there is extensive clandestine activity, with many unofficial mosques and secret Muslim brotherhoods (*tariqa*). From such activity dissident groups can grow into an overt threat – already there is some evidence that Muslim groups are threatening the pattern of official secular education.

The nationalities' demographic increase represents the possibility of a threat to the unity of the Soviet Union and to the survival of the Marxist-Leninist system. There have been examples of overt national dissidence in the years since Khrushchev, especially in the extensive private dissident literature (*samizdat*) often circulated in manuscript in urban centres. In Estonia (1967) and Latvia

(1971) and the Ukraine (1972) there has been extensive police action against dissidents (Shelet, the Ukraine First Secretary, was dismissed for not being hard enough on nationalists), and in Kaunas, Lithuania's second city, there were nationalist riots after a student had burned himself to death (1972). In Georgia, specially favoured under Stalin, nationalist dissent appeared in 1973, following a purge of party officials on charges of gross corruption: there was arson in Tbilisi and assassination attempts. Bombs exploded in the Ukraine, and in both Georgia and the Ukraine there was some fear that the Russian Orthodox Church had become a local vehicle for dissent.

The Jews have a very high membership of the Party. But they also have been very successful in bringing pressure to bear on the authorities through violence and open agitation, and through gaining the public sympathy of strong political voices in other countries, especially in the West. Over 100 000 Jews were allowed to emigrate during the seventies (there are about two million Jews in Russia); the hollow mockery of granting a special Jewish area at Birodidzhan, Manchuria (1927), is a precedent that has not been followed since Stalin. The success of Jewish militancy seems to have encouraged other dissident groups. So far as the Central Asian Republics are concerned, an increasing threat of dissidence arises both from clandestine Muslim activity and the development of an urban intelligentsia. But there are particular groups whom Stalin moved, who present particular problems. The Volga Germans were exiled after the war on a collective charge of having collaborated with the Nazis. They were officially exculpated of their crime in 1964, but hopes of a return to their former homeland (now occupied by others) have faded. Militancy among them, together with the normalising of relations with West Germany following the success of the *Ostpolitik*, has led to the permitted emigration of large numbers to West Germany (few appear to have chosen East Germany).

The Meskhetians, a small Turkish community of probably less than 200 000, were deported to Central Asia in 1944 from the border of Georgia as a military measure in preparation for a possible invasion of Turkey: they are there still. Similarly, the Crimean Tartars, some 500 000 strong, transported in 1943 for collaboration but rehabilitated in 1965, remain dispersed. The Crimea is the Riviera of Soviet Russia, and their land has been settled by Russians: they have little hope of being allowed to return. Both these communities are Muslim and both have very little cultural contact or inter-marriage with other groups in their vicinity.

The growth of Muslim political dissent is worrying to the authorities, since the new militants regard Communism not as a political doctrine, but as a technique for preserving the political power of the Russians – a modern version of Tsarist repression. It is no wonder that the Soviet government is sensitive on matters of Human Rights: the potential connection between political and religious dissent and nationalist activity gives cause for concern, especially when the demographic perspective is considered. Alexis de Tocqueville correctly observed that the most dangerous moment for an arbitrary government was when it had begun to reform.

The 1977 Constitution reiterates the federal structure of the Soviet Union, but the imminence of the CPSU renders the opportunity for local self-government of individual republics relatively small – in reality the leaders of constituent republics are dominated by the Party and their republics are little more than sub-divisions of a highly centralised system. Any relaxation of central political control would undermine the official political doctrine of democratic centralism. A policy of assimilation, hastened by social and economic change, is the most likely one to be adopted by the Soviet leadership. It is significant that an increasing number of the minority national groups are joining the Party, and this may well have an impact in areas where party organisation has formerly been weak. Current moves to diversify regional economies and decentralise planning may also break down national resistance. Russian will clearly remain the official language: surveys show that seventy-six per cent of the population are able to communicate in it, but that ninety-three per cent of non-Russian speakers continue to regard their native tongue as their first language. However, the assumption that modernisation will sap the roots of local nationalism has been disproved by experience throughout Europe since the war. Nationalist activity is particularly acute in the Baltic States; but it is also present in the Asiatic Republics, and there it is promoted by the indigenous intelligentsia, the very product of modernisation – nor is it confined to intellectual circles. Nationalism and the problem of the nationalities could have a devastating effect on the future of the Soviet Union.

Education

The Soviet system puts great store by education: its primary task is a social one, to produce the 'new communist man' to build a new society: Khrushchev put it to the Twenty-first Party Congress, 'To arrive at communism, that most fair and perfect society . . . we must start right now educating the man of the future'. But mere acquiescence is not enough: the schools must instil patriotism, loyalty and commitment to Soviet society arising from knowledge and understanding. Beyond this lies the need for a literate and numerate and well trained population, if rapid progress from traditional agricultural to urban factory life is to be made.

Different races and languages add a complication. Russian is the official language (and most of the mass media is in Russian) but it is the mother tongue of only fifty-eight per cent of the population, so it becomes the first foreign langauge for many children; the native language is used in schools and some colleges as appropriate, but all the pressures are towards using Russian. The education system is rigidly centralised with a common curriculum and teaching methods; higher education is available at Vocational Technical Schools, specialised schools and colleges and universities, where a grant is available to meet expenses. The schools are co-educational and comprehensive, although special schools for more able mathematicians and scientists and linguists, as well as theatre schools, have been opened, some of them boarding schools. Recent documents suggest that the Russians have had a 'great educational debate' and are not persuaded of the absolute value of the few selective schools. Streaming is ideologically unacceptable, but extra and more demanding work is provided for the more able in mixed ability classes, and this is supplemented through optional subjects at age fourteen, and through highly organised out-of-school activities. The curriculum

The Soviet educational system

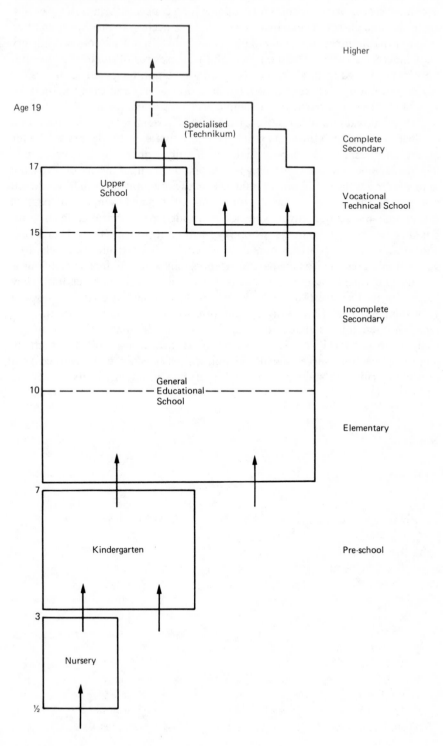

is heavily academic (there is provision for repeating a year's work if standards are not satisfactory). In big schools it is possible for a concealed selection process to occur through passing a child to another school (especially to one whose children tend to leave at fifteen and go on to blind alley jobs). In pre-school years nursery and kindergarten schools exist on a local basis; these are not run by the state, but are often provided by large factories or big farm complexes. Some are boarding. All help mothers to go out to work (a common feature) and even to go off for several months on a particular assignment or on seasonal work.

The social training programme of the school system receives attention in a number of ways, often through extra-curricula activities; attitudes of concern for others and respect for parents and the family appear to be successfully inculcated. Since full-time schooling is not compulsory until the age of seven, the family exercises the predominant influence on the bringing up of children. Much is made of the family as an institution, and the active support of parents throughout the school career is achieved through pedagogical councils composed of teachers and parents (who may sit-in on lessons): its members secure cooperation and liaison with parents and may interview troublesome children with parents present – for the parents' responsibility for children's behaviour is heavily underlined. Youth movements are closely linked with schools. They begin with the Octobrists up to the age of ten, which is largely an informal social group activity. The Pioneers (aged ten to fifteen) have considerable prestige and most children join: activities are varied and include summer camps in the Caucuses or on the Black Sea coast. At fifteen the Komsomol, an essentially adult organisation, serves social and political ends, since it is regarded as a possible recruitment stage to membership of the Communist Party.

8

Cold War to Détente: the developing pattern of Western diplomacy

In the forty years since the Second World War three new factors have dominated diplomacy, altering its perspective fundamentally from that of the pre-war world. The first is the appearance of Super-Powers – the USA, then the USSR and by the sixties the Republic of China – and its corollary, the progressively diminishing importance of the former great powers of Europe, in particular Britain and France. Secondly, there is the possession of atomic and subsequently nuclear weapons, together with the development of orbital communications satellites and of sophisticated missiles capable of delivering a war-head with great speed and accuracy over vast distances: this has introduced a new concept into diplomacy, that of deliberately avoiding major war because of the possible destruction of huge numbers of the human race, and also changed strategic thinking completely since the sixties. Finally, there has been the emergence of the Third World at first from colonial status and then from political and economic dependence upon the West to a position, by the end of sixties, of diplomatic and economic significance capable of influencing directly the pattern of world events. All these things point to the late sixties as a turning point of great significance to world diplomacy. It was also the time when the EEC felt sufficiently confident to move towards its first enlargement (1972) and when the US had begun to seek a means of disengagement from the Vietnam War and thus profoundly to modify its rôle as anti-communist policeman for the world.

It is difficult to recapture the idealism and confidence that characterised public attitudes in 1945. War would be outlawed through the United Nations, an international body that would avoid the mistakes of the League, and would go beyond diplomacy to bring relief to stricken areas and aid to the poorer regions so that the world could march towards prosperity in peace and security. But the UN was dominated by its Security Council and the veto. As the world slipped into the hardening attitudes of the Cold War, it rapidly became clear that it would be controlled by great power diplomacy. It took a little while for diplomats to realise that three of these great powers were not capable of playing this rôle. France first, and later Britain, recognised their former status had changed; it was partly a function of their economic problems, partly because their empires would soon shrink and their global political influence (but not their commercial influence) would diminish. Europe, though its problems dominated the post-war world, was no longer the centre of that world.

The third of the great powers, Nationalist China, under Roosevelt's protégé, Chiang Kai-Shek, from the outset was not considered seriously by informed opinion. As early as 1944, US advisers in China were underlining this. General Stilwell (a prejudiced witness) recorded in his diary:

> The cure for China's trouble is the elimination of Chiang Kai-Shek. The only thing that keeps the country split is his fear of losing control. . . . If we do not take action our prestige in China will suffer seriously . . . and the seeds will be planted for chaos in China after the war.

In September 1944, Roosevelt demanded reforms in the Chinese government and Stilwell, who delivered the demand, recorded:

> At very long last FDR has finally spoken plain words . . . at last FDR's eyes have been opened . . .. It has taken two and a half years for the Big Boys to see the light . . .. I handed this bundle of paprika [the demand] to the Peanut [Chiang] and then sank back with a sigh.

But this was a well kept secret from US public opinion. However, the White House was not surprised when the communists secured control (1949) of mainland China. Dean Acheson, US Secretary of State, explained the communist success to an amazed American public:

> Nothing that this country did or could have done within the reasonable limits of its capabilities could have changed that result . . .. It was the product of internal Chinese forces, forces which this country tried to influence but could not.

When the US China White Paper appeared (January 1950), proposing 'limited commitment' in Asia, it was greeted with a howl of protest that strengthened McCartheyism and made the Cold War a global thing. World diplomacy was fast becoming a matter of the relationship between the two Super-Powers: for this reason, it was the US army that was the principal UN force in the Korean War (1950–3), and a coherent Western defence policy soon emerged. The Truman Doctrine (see page 25), though centred on Europe, nevertheless had a global implication and by the fifties, Soviet Russia was ringed by 'free world' defensive pacts (see map) which sometimes required direct US involvement far from home. In 1953, for example, the Shah was imposed on Iran, anti-Russian bases secured, and US oil companies received a forty per cent interest in Iranian oil (the reckoning was to come in 1978 with the expulsion of the Shah by the Ayatollah Khomeini's anti-US régime); and in Indo-China, there were even suggestions that US aid to French forces should extend to using the atom bomb against the Vietminh investing Dien Bien Phu (which fell to them in July 1954). US policy was typified by the vigorous anti-communist Dulles: 'For us there are two sorts of people in the world: there are those who are Christian and support free enterprise, and there are the others.'

But the policy involved a heavy commitment to the armed forces (some ten per cent of the US workforce in the fifties) and for a generation much of US industry was tied to defence spending. It was partly to relieve this burden that President Eisenhower was anxious to promote European union and to stop Britain interrupting the negotiations for the EEC. For the same reason he supported the rearming of West Germany and the inclusion of her forces in an integrated European Army under the Pleven Plan (1950). With France embroiled in Indo-China and Britain in Malaya, West German industry and manpower were needed to supplement NATO defence. Eventually, West Germany was rearmed (without nuclear, biological or chemical weapons) and joined NATO (see page 28). The Soviet reaction was predictable and immediate, the formation of the Warsaw Treaty Organisation, but Khrushchev also proposed a European Security Treaty, which was eventually achieved in principle at Helsinki in 1975. Some commentators blame US policy for this delay. Others lay the blame on provocative Soviet action.

Under Dulles's direction, US foreign policy was characterised by a confident assertiveness that earned the name of 'brinkmanship'. With it went the idea of 'roll-back' (1953) – the assumption that communism was so unwelcome to the peoples of Eastern Europe that they would rise up to help throw off its yoke at the first American trumpet call. Yet no US troops moved to help the East Berlin rioters in 1953, or the Hungarian 'freedom fighters' in 1956, for all the public outcry. But by 1954 a formal policy of 'massive retaliation' had been adopted (the threat of the simultaneous release of sufficient atomic bombs to destroy the Soviet Union militarily and politically). It was a policy that was already out of date, for after Stalin's death (1953) there was an evident relaxation in Soviet attitudes towards the West. It was also misconceived. In 1945 only the US had the atom bomb: the Soviet Union exploded its first nuclear device in 1949. In 1952 the US tested its more powerful H-bomb: the Soviet Union tested theirs in 1953 – their technology was fast overtaking that of the West. 'Massive retaliation' was a realistic policy only so long as it was accompanied by massive superiority in nuclear weapons – otherwise, what was intended as the means to keep the peace for the West, became no more than one side of the 'balance of terror' that held back statesmen and generals alike from launching into a nuclear war. In 1957 Sputnik demonstrated the Soviet Union's capacity to deliver missiles on the US – distance had ceased to count in strategic terms. Is it to be wondered at that the sixties were concerned to limit the spread of nuclear weapons and their testing in the atmosphere, and the seventies with balancing, if not actually reducing, the nuclear arsenals of the two Super-Powers?

In retrospect, 1956 seems to have marked a major change in world diplomacy. In the Soviet Union, Khrushchev's famous speech to the Twentieth Party Congress admitted the fallibility of the Party Leadership and ushered in 'de-Stalinisation': but he also proposed 'peaceful coexistence' as the basis of relations with the Capitalist West – peaceful economic competition, not war and revolution, would demonstrate the superiority of Socialism. It was a major step from traditional communist ideology. In due course, the idea was to be transposed to become the basis of *détente* in the seventies, but for the moment the suppression of the Hungarian rising (1956) prevented any progress: co-existence did not mean

US alliances in the 1950s and the US under pressure in the 1970s

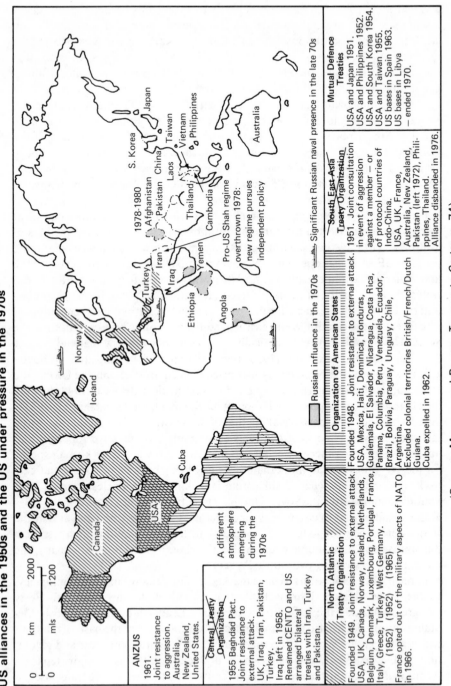

(Source: Mooney and Brown, *Truman to Carter*, p. 74)

surrendering any satellite state. In the West, unity was shattered by the Anglo-French intervention in Suez (1956) and the refusal of the US to support it. Britain's 'special relationship' with the USA was never fully repaired and it was assumed that not only had NATO been fundamentally weakened by the whole enterprise, but that the US was turning to West Germany as her major European ally. In the Middle East the influence of Britain and France was temporarily eclipsed and this was to produce what some have called the Eisenhower Doctrine (September 1957) of giving economic and military aid to the Middle East in order to overcome communist influence: 'The existing vacuum in the Middle East must be filled by the United States before it is filled by Russia'.

Dulles's policy had proved altogether a failure. The threat of 'massive retaliation' had not prevented the Soviet Union seeking to enlarge its influence and it was evident that there was to be no 'roll-back'. Apart from the Middle East, in Cuba, Castro overthrew Batista in 1959, and in 1960 a group of Soviet advisers were in the Congo to begin Soviet penetration into the Third World. The check to Soviet advance came in the celebrated Cuban missile crisis of 1962 which brought the US to the verge of nuclear war. That both sides were prepared to back down was a tribute to their good sense – President Kennedy even sanctioned a $250m surplus wheat sale to the USSR in 1963.

But the Cuban missile crisis had been handled without consultation with NATO, and this caused much concern among US allies (Cuba was within the NATO 'area' and the crisis could have been interpreted as a threatened attack on one of the members of the Alliance under Article 5 of the Washington Treaty). The very real threat of a nuclear war was patently a matter of concern to US allies. Macmillan, the British Prime Minister, echoing a catchphrase of the American Revolution, spoke of 'annihilation without representation'. If Britain's 'special relationship' still existed, it amounted to very little and the Nassau Agreement (December 1962) replaced Britain's independent deterrent with US Polaris submarines. De Gaulle rejected the same offer, preferring his own '*force de frappe*' and subsequently withdrew from NATO (1966). Ironically, de Gaulle rejected Britain's first application to join the EEC (1963) partly on the grounds that Britain's 'special relationship' with the USA would be damaging – 'In the end there would be a colossal Atlantic Community under American dependence and leadership which would completely swallow up the European Community'. President Johnson had no easy inheritance in Europe. In the Americas his position was quite clear: the speedy intervention against the democratic revolution in the Dominican Republic (1965) prevented 'another Cuba' and was, in effect, an early version of the Brezhnev Doctrine (see page 32).

The Middle East continued to present a serious problem, for in the Six Days' War (1967) Israel achieved a staggering victory over Egypt. The US was worried at Soviet aid to the Arabs, the implicit threat on NATO's southern flank, and the possible interruption of oil supplies; the Soviet Union was worried over US support for Israel and at the position of her Sixth Fleet in the Eastern Mediterranean. Fortunately, both sides were anxious for an accommodation – the Soviet Union, particularly, for since the mid-sixties a positive rift had opened in Soviet relations with China and she was obliged to keep an army on the Sino-Soviet frontier. There were tentative moves towards what was to become détente in the next decade. A Nuclear Non-Proliferation Treaty (1968) sought to check the spread of nuclear arms and, since parity of nuclear missiles between the two Super Powers was in sight, Dobrynin, Soviet Ambassador in Washington, suggested SALT talks might open. But the Czech crisis (1968) prevented their beginning and put the West on the alert. Nevertheless, Ambassador Dobrynin called at the White House to inform the President of the intended invasion before even the CIA; and in the next couple of years President Johnson gave quiet support to the policy of *Ostpolitik* (see page 115).

It was Vietnam that ruined Johnson and destroyed his dream of a 'Great Society'. The policy of intervention had already been determined under Kennedy, if not before, and the 'domino theory' gave support for action in pursuit of 'containment' policies. Boldly, Johnson went for a quick victory (1965) telling Henry Cabot Lodge (ambassador to South Vietnam), 'I am not going to lose Vietnam. I am not going to be the President who saw South East Asia go the way China went'. But there was no UN backing for the US war in Vietnam and he got little support from his European allies: indeed, Britain's withdrawal from 'East of Suez' (1967) in consequence of her serious economic difficulties and the devaluation of the pound, finally ended the pretence of an Anglo-US global defence 'special relationship'. By 1968 it was already privately admitted that the Vietnam War could not be won, and a peace offer was made to Hanoi in March of that year.

President Nixon entered office when US foreign policy was on the point of changing. The decisions of the sixties had been based on the prosperity and nuclear predominance of the fifties. He recognised that an 'era of negotiation' would have to displace the 'era of confrontation' – and he, of all presidents, could escape the charge of being 'soft' on communists. The success of his foreign policy, directed by Dr Kissinger, was to blossom by 1974 in the establishment of *détente*. But throughout, he spoke as President of the United States, not as proclaimed spokesman of the 'Free World', and this strained relations with his European allies. The pressing need was to find an avenue that would bring 'peace with honour' in Vietnam, for by 1970 US public opinion, overborne by direct TV pictures of the horrors in Vietnam, had begun to turn against the war. His immediate policy was the 'doctrine of Asianisation' by which some of his Asian allies were required to look to their own defence (with US help), thus permitting a major US withdrawal (some have called this the Nixon Doctrine): but the fact of a US retreat could not be concealed, and it was confirmed by the collapse of the Saigon régime in 1975.

Already by the late sixties the Atlantic Alliance was under strain, although Nixon approved both the *Ostpolitik* policy (which was no doubt helped forward by the development of détente) and the enlargement of the EEC. There had been no serious consultation with West Europe over the Non-Proliferation Treaty, and doubts were being expressed among NATO allies as to the effectiveness of trusting to the US deterrent for the defence of Europe. The possibility of the EEC emerging as a 'Third Force' was given some serious consideration in 1970, and Dr Kissinger's call for a 'New Atlantic Charter' (1973) with its clear implication of US primacy over the EEC, was not well received and collapsed in the crisis of the Yom Kippur War (1973).

The Middle East, indeed, put the two Super Powers under considerable strain: the cease-fire in that war was agreed between them and imposed on the belligerents by them – one factor was the supposition that Israel had produced an atomic bomb from peaceful nuclear energy supplies; of this some observers were convinced, and the vital need was to avoid pushing Israel to the point of having to reveal her hand. The Arab oil boycott and the huge increase in price for crude oil determined upon by OPEC (see page 181) merely underlined the inter-relatedness of diplomacy and commerce. What also disturbed other NATO members was US action during the war. Fearful of the intentions of Soviet naval concentration in the Eastern Mediterranean, Nixon ordered a scale-three nuclear alert (some cynics suggested it had more to do with diverting public attention from Watergate than with diplomacy) – and Europe heard of it *after* it had been implemented. That so grave an action should have been taken without prior consultation or warning, an action in its implications directly bearing upon the security of Western Europe, seemed to impugn the unity of the NATO Alliance on that most sensitive of issues, the control of nuclear weapons. Would the electronic locks on 'theatre' warheads in Europe be a sufficient guarantee? And the 'two-key' system did not extend to strategic weapons. Would Western Europe suffer a nuclear attack because of military insecurity elsewhere in the world? That the US had been using her West German air bases for ferrying arms to Israel added to the discontent. Was NATO to be subsumed in some new version of the Brezhnev Doctrine dictated by the USA? There was a good deal of strain within NATO in the seventies. But the US did not surrender the initiative over the Middle East, and it was at Camp David (1978) that President Carter was to secure the basis of a peace agreement between Israel and Egypt, designed in hopes of restoring security in the area and leading to lasting peace.

The achievement of détente was a personal triumph for both President Nixon and Dr Kissinger. In effect it was two parallel *détentes*, one with the Soviet Union and the other with China, since the two Communist powers had become mutually hostile – the former had apparently contemplated a 'surgical strike' against China's nuclear installations (1969) and the latter by 1970 was looking to the US as a bulwark against her erstwhile friend. This double *détente* did not conceal ideological conflicts nor impede the Super-Powers in their habit of enforcing an acceptable tolerance of their ideas within their spheres of interest; but it did make possible strategic arms limitation talks – SALT I was signed in 1972 between the USA and the Soviet Union (the British and French deterrents, small but significant, were not included). But *détente* depends upon stability and security and implies a willingness between the Super-Powers not to alter the existing balance: US 'total security' depended on the Soviet Union feeling totally secure – which would mean accepting nuclear parity. A *détente* that depended on the hostility of a third Super Power (China) lacked that essential factor of security and stability: but Nixon's resignation (1974) prevented his reconciling this seeming contradiction, for at the moment of his triumph abroad, his position at home had been destroyed by Watergate. Dr Kissinger viewed *détente* as a tripolar stability in which the basic interests of the three Super Powers were not challenged, and peripheral wars kept both isolated and at a minimum: it had also a further perspective, that of extending it to a penta-polarity in which the EEC and Japan joined the Super-Powers to ensure greater stability.

SALT I was welcomed in Europe, but China denounced it as 'nuclear collusion'. In fact, it reflected the reality of the situation: in 1967 the US had over twice as many inter-continental ballistic missiles (ICBM) than the Soviet Union; in 1972 the Soviet Union had half as many more than the US – the nuclear *pax Americana* was over.

ICBM totals

	1962	1967	1972
US	294	1054	1054
USSR	75	460	1528

Détente continued under President Carter, but there was a different atmosphere. On the one hand, increasing NATO concern at the evident growing strength of WTO nuclear and conventional weapons led in 1979 to a modernisation programme of NATO 'theatre' weapons (see page 46) after SALT II had been signed by Carter and Brezhnev. On the other, there was especial emphasis laid on Human Rights as the corner-stone of American moral leadership (the Helsinki Final Act was signed in 1975). Confidently, President Carter announced a new chapter in American foreign policy: 'We are now free of that inordinate fear of communism which once led us to embrace any dictator who joined us in our fear'.

The Human Rights issue proved disruptive: not only was the Soviet Union antagonised (Giscard d'Estaing publicly complained in July 1977 that it was damaging *détente*) but it was resented also among the Third World. Many blamed the failure of the Belgrade Review Conference of the Helsinki Agreement (1978) on this issue. By 1979 the issue was less often aired. The strained relations with the European Allies of NATO were not entirely repaired. The indefinite postponing of the Enhanced Radiation Weapon (neutron bomb, 1978) in the face of vigorous Soviet propaganda, was not well received in all West European capitals – it would have been ideal to use against the fast mobile armour of a Soviet *Blitzkrieg* without inflicting 'unacceptable loss' of civilian life. In 1978, the Senate Foreign Relations Committee rejected President Carter's plan to appease Turkey in her continuing quarrel with Greece over Cyprus. When Turkey hinted at quitting NATO, it was West Germany that moved to offer aid and to mollify the discontented ally – it seemed a reversal of the Truman Doctrine and added weight to the gloomy talk about the state of NATO. There were even doubts expressed about SALT II, on the grounds that NATO was not involved in the talks, and that Congress might be dilatory in approving military action to ensure the defence of Europe. It could be argued that the 1979 modernisation programme of 'theatre' weapons was as much to restore confidence within NATO as to regain the advantage in Central Europe.

The uncertainty of US policy in the later seventies partly reflected the economic recession and the new weakness of the dollar – by 1977 it was becoming clear that the US considered Japan should rearm herself to take full responsibility for her defence, a move that would reduce US foreign expenditure. Partly, also, it was because communist pressure was appearing in unfamiliar areas – particularly in Africa, where Soviet advisers and Cuban volunteers were successful in Angola and Ethiopia and also in the Yemen, thus controlling the entry to the Red Sea. In Central Africa, from Zaire in the South to Chad in the North and Gabon in the West, French troops had created by 1979 a positive buffer zone against further Soviet influence: it looked as though America's allies were beginning to take the sort of initiative that the US had claimed as its own since Suez. Even the Middle East did not hold – perhaps because of the success of the Camp David agreement between Israel and Egypt, and of the new militancy that characterised the recrudescence of Islam in these years. In 1978 the Shah was overthrown and the Ayatollah Khomeini's régime adopted a particularly anti-American stance, rising to a climax in a student attack on the US embassy in Teheran (1979) resulting in the taking of fifty embassy staff as 'hostages' against the return of the Shah from US protection to be tried in Iran for the alleged crimes with which his régime was associated. There was much international sympathy for the US and as much condemnation of this breach of diplomatic custom, but there was no great international action (although US aircraft carriers were sent to the Persian Gulf area in December 1979) even in terms of economic sanctions through the United Nations. Significantly, Russia did not intervene – even to help the Kurds in north Iran. In April 1980 EEC countries agreed to apply economic sanctions against Iran; but an unsuccessful US attempt to rescue the hostages caused considerable strain among US allies.

Afghanistan provided a testing crisis for the West in January 1980, when a pro-Soviet régime was replaced by means of a Soviet invasion imposing a new government. The reaction in the rest of the world was hostile, culminating in a condemnatory resolution by the United Nations. Diplomatically, the area is sensitive because of the proximity of Pakistan, China, India and Iran and there was some recrudescence of fears arising from the old 'domino' theory (Soviet desire to push towards an ice-free port on the Indian Ocean, a favourite interpretation of nineteenth-century diplomacy, may be discounted in view of the distances involved and the difficulties of the terrain between Russia and the sea): economically, the area is sensitive because of its proximity to Middle East oil supplies. President Carter was especially vigorous in his condemnation and ordered economic sanctions including the withholding of extra grain supplies for the Soviet Union (a strong card, since the grain was needed for bread and animal feed and its absence would mean significant shortages in a country hard-put to meet normal demand and which was also the host country for the 1980 Olympic games). Cynics argued that the President was as much concerned for opinion polls in election year, but the economic measures represented a courageous move – no sanctions had been taken after Hungary (1956) or Czechoslovakia (1968). Some observers suggested a new Carter Doctrine was emerging, shifting US foreign policy towards a greater emphasis on Asia and the Middle East than on Europe – a shift that would mean a greater US presence in the Indian Ocean, with consequent need for naval and air bases; a shift that could affect the defence position in West Europe very shrewdly; and a shift that would result in a policy combining the old Monroe 'sphere of interest' principle with the Dulles 'containment' principle.

President Carter received, among major powers, active support only from Britain; both France and West Germany were too anxious about the effect on *détente* and consequently upon their position in Europe. West Germany had most to fear from a war and most to gain from *détente*. Both Chancellor Schmidt and President Giscard d'Estaing implicitly raised the old banner of a clearly defined and separate *European* foreign policy, not tied to the USA. This had implications for NATO unity. Certainly the NATO Council failed to agree on any positive help to be rendered to support the US stand requiring Soviet withdrawal by March 1980. The EEC Commission and the Council of Ministers similarly failed to agree, and the European Parliament was no more helpful. It was not enough to argue that Afghanistan lay both beyond the NATO area and the bounds of Europe: it was clear that there was a rift in Western unity. The old anti-Soviet unity of the Truman Doctrine had given way to accommodation under *détente*: President Carter's problem was forging a basis of firmness within the limits of *détente*. He was also in danger of aiding with arms, régimes which had been denied arms earlier (Pakistan showed no inclination to give up the determination to build her own nuclear weapon).

For the Soviet Union, the biggest danger was not a hostile world press, but the possibility of closer Sino-American relations resulting from the crisis. Defence Secretary Brown toured China and Japan in January 1980, where he was well received and the US demand for Soviet withdrawal from Afghanistan supported. It looked as though it was a return to Dr Kissinger's penta-polar diplomacy, with diplomatic use of China and pressure on Japan for greater expenditure on defence. But even in this area, support was less than forthright, for the suggestion of greater defence expenditure was not popular with the Japanese. The fundamental difficulty presented by the Afghanistan crisis was achieving the delicate balance between registering sufficient displeasure to discourage Soviet Russia from further action, and yet retaining an overall basis of *détente*. Neither side wished to see the stability upon which *détente* depended irremediably upset, the more so as SALT II had yet to be confirmed by the US Congress and the anticipated SALT III begun.

Clearly, certain of his allies felt that President Carter had gone too far in treating the Afghanistan crisis as an issue of East-West confrontation, rather than a hardening of a local situation. A far greater threat to world peace in the eighties lay in the complexity and instability of the Third World, where West Europe's interests are predominantly commercial, not military. The reaction to the Afghanistan crisis suggests the West might not hold together in a united front to contain and settle a major dispute affecting them arising in the Third World.

9

Unity or Fragmentation?

The world of the 1980s is infinitely more complex than that of the 1940s. It was then possible to think predominantly in terms of Europe – for the pattern of trade was still directed by Europe, even allowing for variations in harvests in different parts of the world. Since the 1940s the concept of a 'developing Third World' has become not only a commonplace, but it has assumed a political reality that affects trade, defence and economic policy throughout the 'developed world'. Europe has become one of a number of different factors affecting the relationship between the two Super-Powers that had emerged in the 1940s; and its influence, if still considerable, is at least balanced by the emergence of a third Super-Power, the Chinese Republic. Within Europe, two economic communities, the EEC and COMECON, have established themselves and affect the balance of world power and economic relationships. To view the world as divided into East and West is to persist in the simple model of the Cold War period and to overlook the major changes wrought within the last generation.

Planning and the State

Among the most pronounced of the trends over the last forty years has been an acceleration of world trade that has resulted in a close inter-dependence between nations. Today only the Super-Powers retain limited possibilities for independent economic initiatives, and even they can be particularly affected by sudden shortages, price rises or political changes in quite minor countries. The impact of OPEC's control over the price of crude oil is a case in point. It is possible to simulate conditions akin to those of a Super-Power, with its capacity for economies of scale and rationalisation, by effecting closer economic cooperation between different countries. This would allow a degree of independent action, even in times of world shortage or depression. Of itself, this is a powerful argument for carrying the EEC beyond the initial stage of a customs union having internal free trade, towards fuller economic integration. Proposals to integrate economic policies at national level involve the increasing importance of the State, if only as an instrument of administration. But if several governments adopt policies of closer cooperation or even integration between their respective economies and certain of their industries, then the importance of the State both as an instigator and as an instrument of policy becomes vital.

Any State, whether regarded as a means of effecting a policy or of merely determining it in principle, has to overcome a number of barriers, even when there is no disagreement over the end in view. Economic growth is recognised as the consistent aim of all advanced countries, but there are immediate constraints on even so unexceptional a policy – for example, a hostile climate, the lack of raw materials, the upward movement of commodity and energy prices, and inflationary spirals. Extraordinary measures, beyond the control of a single industry within a country, are necessary to overcome these constraints and thus industries must look to the State, if only for regulating acceptable conditions of trade whatever emphasis is placed upon the existence of a free market economy. Some degree of planning becomes a requirement of each advanced country. No one sector of a country's economy can have an overall command of its own development. A national economy is an inter-weaving of different facets, not a collection of distinct sectors and this demands a sophistication of analysis for any particular problem, which may become highly complex and quite beyond the scope of any single industry or sector. Hence the importance of the State. Hence also the widespread recourse to a measure of 'indicative' planning, even in the free market economies of the West.

Yet government machinery (particularly in the West) is organised upon a sectoral basis so that attempts at overviews of the economic life of the community become increasingly remote, and the task of even a modicum of national economic re-adjustment assumes major proportions. Various attempts to achieve a broader perspective for 'indicative' planning, for example through the creation of 'super-departments' of State, have generally proved unsuccessful – witness the British experience in the late sixties. Even within the EEC itself, the Commission is organised on a sectoral basis, and only since 1975 have serious efforts been made to coordinate research projects between Commissioners' departments. Western democratic traditions also inhibit long-term planning (elections can result in a change of government and a switch of policy) so that government plans tend to concentrate on immediate problems rather than on underlying structural faults to the possible detriment of the ultimate best interests of the nation. It is partly because of this unwillingness to be constrained by a single central plan that Western countries have developed so great a confidence in what has been called the 'technological fix' – the assumption that science will somehow always come up with the innovation that will permit continued expansion. This is particularly dangerous for Western Europe with its shortage of raw materials. The energy crisis of the seventies is an object lesson not only in the overdependence on one form of energy (oil) but in the capacity for organised suppliers to hold the West to ransom – a lesson that cannot be lost upon the political leaders of the Third World. In economic planning one cannot simply think in terms of the nation state: the concept of the world as a 'global village' becomes increasingly relevant. The achievement of integral policies within the EEC, or the integration of energy supplies in COMECON, arises as much from this consideration as from the search for continued economic growth.

These developments argue the case for longitudinal forecasting (despite the manifold problems involved) as a basis for planning, rather than short-term plans on the basis of past experience. Structural changes may result more easily from it and more attention may be given to the disequilibria that arise from extra-

European factors – terms of trade, supply of raw materials, population growth and its consequences (in 1920 the countries forming the EEC constituted about ten per cent of world population: by 1970 it was about seven per cent – by 2000 it is estimated to be four per cent!). Yet, despite the pressures for more precise planning to smooth the path of economic growth, the seventies have seen a growing reaction against central planning techniques and a rising demand both for a devolution of central powers and a greater participation in decision making, whether in central administration, local government, industry or even in schools. Some have seen Schumacher's *Small is Beautiful* as a tract for the times, attacking the overwhelming super-human scale of large organisations. The growing demand for regionalising administration may be seen as partly a desire to achieve greater personal identity within administrative processes. The gathering force of nationalist movements is a further indication, perhaps, of popular dissatisfaction with the remoteness of central government decisions, the more so as many peripheral areas have not shared in general prosperity, despite government efforts to relieve regional decline.

Much more obvious reasons for public dissatisfaction are to be found in disillusionment with the failures of planning and the evident inability of the developed world to break out of the world depression of the later seventies. National Plans have completely failed (like the British 1965 Plan) or failed to approach the original targets (like the Sixth or Seventh French Plans) or failed to sustain earlier growth rates (like the Soviet Ninth and Tenth Plans). Even institutions with high prestige have not escaped the same shadow. The ECSC, for all its initial success, patently failed to adjust coal and steel supplies to world demand, and it has not been able to prevent national cartelisation of firms, whilst an intra-Community solution to the problems of the steel industry has not been achieved. Similarly, EURATOM has not developed into a major supplier of energy – even with the incentive of the oil crisis only seven of the projected twenty-three nuclear reactors in France were in service by 1980 – and in-novations in nuclear energy since 1958 have frequently been at national rather than Community level. Policy integration (agriculture apart) has been a conspicuous failure of the EEC – and COMECON can offer no better record. Meanwhile member governments continue with national planning arrangements that sometimes lead to unnecessary and uneconomic duplication or hinder industrial rationalisation. Both Communities, East and West, lack internal coordination, which seems to arise from an absence of political will on the part of member governments.

It would be too simplistic to argue that in planning the choice lay between authoritative politics and democratic practice. Indeed, there has been a curious convergence upon an intermediate mixed type of planning in which the operation of market influences are apparent, in both East and West. Ideally, economic planning ought to be neutral and 'de-politicised', but experience has proved this an impossibility – even within the Soviet Union, where central planning and the elimination of the market mechanism was an ideological requirement from the first. The trouble with a 'command economy' is that it works as a theoretical model, and when applied with vigour to a particular sector (at the expense of others) can achieve remarkable success – witness the huge strides since 1962 in the Soviet Union's sophisticated defence industries and the heavy industry and energy resources needed to support them: but it is far less successful when applied on a broad front, especially where undirected consumer demand is a factor (for, despite all the choice-direction supplied by mass advertising, the consumer market remains unpredictable beyond set limits).

In the West, 'indicative planning' has developed different patterns: in France, *concertation à la Monnet* has degenerated into routine consultation and the original concept of a 'national' plan has been replaced by that of the 'government' plan, more in the French *étatiste* tradition but far removed from East European 'command' methods. In Britain, traditional pragmatism and institutional inertia has acted as a strong curb on planning. In Italy, the use of public corporations having a large measure of managerial autonomy has not been successful – but the British version of this approach in the National Enterprise Board has been blocked by political factors. West Germany (reluctantly drawn into some effort at federal planning since the late sixties, despite the influence of the *Länder*) seeks to preserve as much independence as possible for the individual firm – although the banking system fulfils some of the functions of state planners elsewhere. But indicative planning has not worked well in unfavourable economic conditions, either as a determiner of economic growth or as a 'fine tuner' of a national economy.

In advanced societies, developments in one sector of the economy tend to influence, and are influenced in their turn, by many other sectors. If the rôle of government were minimal, it would no doubt be enough to leave things to the natural processes of the market, as nineteenth-century Free Traders would have argued: but the rôle of government has increased throughout the present century and shows no sign of diminishing. It is not merely expected to take the responsibility for maintaining economic growth (even in West Germany), but it must find the means to administer and finance a range of welfare services that were not available before the Second World War: and the pressure for greater social and economic equality exerts a strain on the economy, so that even governments committed to traditional liberal ideology indulge in some degree of economic planning and direction if only to preserve stability and encourage economic growth.

'Social relevance' has been the popular phrase in the seventies, and policies also have been successfully developed to check and correct problems of environmental pollution arising from industrial practices and other sources. All this results in an increase in centralisation and the emergence of the State as a huge employer especially within the vastly increasing tertiary sector, with its influence extending throughout the community. The close relationship of economic and political power – of industrial management, public authorities and civil servants – is a fact of political life that commits the West to a degree of planning whatever political attitude is taken. The State has gone beyond the provision of welfare services and now actively promotes particular enterprises, both directly and through investment in high technology industries (the defence industries particularly exercise a pervading influence here in which, of course, the government is the prime consumer). Beyond this, larger industrial units resulting from rationalisation can develop a special relationship with relevant government departments – sometimes with government and industrial bureaucracies working extremely closely together. More than this, the conspicuous presence of pressure groups with direct access to the seat of political power, shrewdly alters the traditional forms of popular representation in the decision making processes of Western democracies – a process compounded by the increasing presence of the State within the economy. At the very least this involves increased centralisation, an expanding tertiary sector and extensive consultation so that major interest groups may be satisfied on major policy matters before they become contentious issues. It seems that there is an inevitable tendency of advanced industrial communities to move towards a sort of corporate state (on the Swedish model, perhaps rather than the inter-war Italian one).

In Eastern Europe the political structure is neither so monolithic nor the ranges of choice available to individuals so restricted as might be supposed from the traditional picture portrayed in the West. The State is subordinated to the Party, which controls the administration: but terror and dictatorship have given way to 'collective leadership' by the senior party oligarchy (except in Romania and perhaps Bulgaria). The style of leadership has changed from Stalin's day, for the accent now is towards observing legal forms with greater emphasis on persuasion – particularly in Hungary and Poland (where workers discontent remains a sensitive point) and in Yugoslavia (where national differences are a complicating factor). The Party has surrendered none of its control but in a number of COMECON countries it has loosened its authority over some aspects of business and daily life and allowed a new pluralist-style diversity in economic, cultural and political affairs. In some cases centralist management has given way to state-owned enterprises having responsibility for their own profitability and productivity and permitting a local response to market conditions – the New Economic Mechanism in Hungary is a good example (although the degree of independent responsibility should not be exaggerated). The Kadaresque 'social compromise' (allowing local initiative within limits closely established by the strong state-directed system) has had considerable influence in other COMECON countries, and considerations of relative standards of living – not unconnected with the need for popular support – have played a new and important rôle in deciding policy. This has involved greater civil liberties, in the Western sense, and a new 'apparatus pluralism' (especially with trade unions), but wholly political factors continue to be of importance in the taking of economic decisions. A new stability and prosperity has emerged, permitting a merging of economic and political power and allowing for the expression of disagreement or discontent before it reaches explosion point (the lesson of the Polish riots has been well learnt). Polycentralism within the Communist bloc, and pluralism within some of its members suggest a limited measure of convergence (despite basic ideological barriers) in the administrative methods of East and West. Pluralist politics may give rise to a degree of consensus in which the choices are between different emphases of similar policies rather than fundamental choice between types of society.

The multinational corporation

Generally, multinational corporations are parent holding companies that control clusters of firms of various types run by various nationalities in different parts of the world. They are not new; but since the Second World War there has been a large expansion of them in the manufacturing sector – so large that by 1971 their aggregate value, excluding socialist economies, was some twenty per cent of the world GNP. Their rapid growth has been made possible because of major developments in communications, transport and computerisation. They are not by any means all USA dominated, but during the sixties increasing concern was expressed about a few of the largest that were American and which were condemned by Soviet propaganda as yet one further proof of American economic imperialism, and by some groups in Western Europe as constituting a threat to the continued independence of major industries – Servan-Schreiber's *Le Défi Americain* (1969) was merely the most popular of a number of diatribes against the American challenge. By the mid-seventies their presence was so much in evidence that the OECD actually drew up a code of conduct for multinationals in Europe. But these OECD 'guidelines' are effective only if taken up, so countries, and especially the EEC, must adopt a common policy and enforce it. Occasional cases brought before the EEC Court of Justice are no substitute for a determined policy, even when multinational corporations are fined heavily for contravening regulations. The technique of transfer-pricing, for example, is almost impossible to control without an effective common policy.

Multinationals may be welcome in developing countries, or for the establishing of new industries in other countries, but they tend also to produce a good deal of ill-feeling and the belief that by means of their size they can divert resources and exert unfair competition is widespread. It is perhaps not surprising that international corporations were increasingly a target for terrorist attacks (including ransom kidnappings) during the late seventies. The development of new national industries may well be impeded by the presence of multinationals. By transferring raw materials and products between member companies, they may by-pass normal patterns of trade and operate at prices below those prevailing in local markets. Concern has been expressed over taxation policy and the advantages multinationals may obtain by routing orders through particular well-placed offices; the suspicion that they escape a full and fair share of national taxation is common. Other fears have been expressed over the effect of their operations upon a host country's balance of payments and over their effect on employment policies. But the main fear centres on their potential corporate power against competitors and even against host governments; the charge has been made that the US in particular utilises multinationals for penetrating the economies of other countries, and to capture prestigious industries especially in the high-technology market – they have had considerable success in computers, rather less with nuclear technology, and the Anglo-French aerospace industry manages to compete well enough.

So far as COMECON countries are concerned, an amazing reversal of attitudes has taken place during the seventies. Whatever propaganda points are made against them, there are now some 140 Western multinational concerns operating in COMECON countries – reflecting the expansion of East-West trade and the heavy purchases of Western technology both for research and development of national industries and for the exploitation of national resources. The ideological gulf continues to divide, but developments in trade and high technology provide increasingly strong links between East and West and point towards the emergence of a modified social order in the emergent 'post-industrial' state.

Eurocommunism

In the mid-seventies it became popular among some political leaders of NATO and the EEC to talk of an old spectre in a new guise haunting the freedom of the West: it was a reformed 'new look' communism anxious to accept, and to be accepted by, the democratic institutions of the West – in order to continue the Marxist revolutionary struggle from within the capitalist citadel. It earned the name Eurocommunism, but it has proved difficult to define what is meant by the term and who, indeed, are the Eurocommunists. The Portuguese under Cunhal are not; nor are the Yugoslavs nor the Romanians. The name has been generally applied to communist parties in France, Italy and Spain with their respective leaders Marchais, Berlinguer and Carrillo. But even with this regional definition, it has not been possible to determine a common policy beyond a wish to pursue methods that may differ from those currently administered in the Soviet Union. Yet the idea that the whole phenomenon is a matter of tactics in an ideological struggle –'*le communisme à la Roumanie*' – seems both naive and inadequate: a more reasonable judgment would be that it reflects a developing political realism among communists in the West and a recognition that there are different roads to communism than violent revolution.

There are so many strands in Eurocommunism that it may be regarded more as a political movement than a philosophy – thus, there is an evident independence of Soviet control; a rejection of Marxist-Leninism as the only model for a communist state; an abandonment of democratic centralism in favour of democratised internal party organisation; a presentation of 'socialism with a human face' and an acceptance of western democratic forms of election (democratic pluralism) including the acceptance of an unfavourable popular vote. The French have even renounced (1976) the dictatorship of the proletariat as a dogma, and preach instead cooperation with bourgeois parties and respect for the Atlantic Pact. In seeking to distinguish itself from Soviet policies, Eurocommunism treats the CPSU as merely a large and important party, not the central motor of an international communist movement – thus shrewdly altering the balance of world power by disrupting the cohesion of the Soviet bloc. Between the wars a slavish subjection to Moscow had been the norm – resulting in the internecine strife of the Spanish Civil War, or the incredible switch in the Communist propaganda effort following the 1939 Nazi-Soviet Pact; but in July 1977, in an interview on French television, Snr Santiago Carrillo spoke of the 'redirection of socialism through democracy, pluralism and universal suffrage . . . Communist states no longer obey an international discipline' – and he added, significantly, 'We want the communist movement to cease to be a church'.

But it would be too simplistic to seek an explanation of Eurocommunism in terms of anti-Soviet attitudes. Its roots lie deep. One can trace through the nineteenth century a tradition of individual response to local conditions in order to advance the communist cause, reaching a peak in the controversy surrounding Bernstein's views at the end of the century. At a less fundamental level, one can perceive a wish to break down the fifty year Stalinist monopoly of the revolutionary tradition – an open recognition of other ways to socialism. Already, in 1955, Khrushchev had tacitly renounced the inevitability of war by propounding the doctrine of peaceful coexistence: then, in February, 1956, came the epoch-making 'secret speech' at the Twentieth Congress of the CPSU denouncing Stalinist dictatorship, implicitly admitting the fallibility of Soviet leadership. Stalinist dominance of the revolutionary tradition was at an end – symbolised by the formal dissolution of Cominform (April 1956) and the acceptance of the poly-centrist view of 'other roads to Socialism' by a form of reconciliation with Tito at Belgrade. Significantly enough, however, the crushing of the Hungarian reforms in November 1956, although it raised protests in the West, especially from the Italian communists, was accepted throughout the Soviet bloc.

The formation of the EEC obliged communist parties in the West to assess their position: so did the gradual emergence of the Sino-Soviet rift – loyalty to world communism became an impossibility when there were two different versions. When peaceful coexistence grew into *détente* there was a further relaxation of tension between East and West which seemed to have a destabilising impact on the unity of the communist world. By 1968 the atmosphere was different, and it may be gauged by the psychological impact of the invasion of Czechoslovakia. Spanish and French communists were especially vocal in denouncing the Soviet action. Yet even here there was no common response: Carrillo was in exile in Prague and experienced the 'Prague Spring' – but so was Cunhal, who remained unaffected by it. But 1968 saw disruption in the West, too, with serious disturbances in France leading to what in effect was a military *coup* by de Gaulle to maintain order and control of the country. The stable pattern of political relationships that had developed since the war was in disarray. In the seventies came the deepening economic crisis, and the evident increase (at least until the mid-seventies) of support for left-wing parties. By 1973 there had been the experience of the communist President Allende of Chile, whose overthrow demonstrated that a narrow electoral victory was no secure basis for political power. But the argument that society could be reformed through existing institutions by cooperation with strong socialist parties was a telling one and Berlinguer for the Italians first (1973) publicly accepted the idea of an 'historic compromise' between the Italian Communist Party (CPI) and the socialists and the Christian Democrats. Marchais, for the French communists, developed the same principle between 1971 and 1975. The seventies saw, therefore, a rising acceptance of cooperation with left-wing parties and working within parliamentary institutions – especially among the young communists, whose experience had not included the Stalinism of twenty years before. Furthermore, a new sense of security had been brought to East-West relations by *détente*, symbolised by the success of *Ostpolitik* (see page 115) and the Helsinki discussions, 1973–5. The death of Franco (20 November 1975) opened opportunities for the communist party in Spain. The new atmosphere was further promoted by Brezhnev's calling of a Pan-European conference of Communist Parties in East Berlin in June 1976.

The preparatory meetings for that conference revealed a significant degree of agreement between the Italian, Spanish and French communist parties upon tactics; the pluralist idea that other socialist parties might also represent the real interests of the working class was openly accepted. Under the leadership of Berlinguer, Carrillo and Marchais no longer looking to Moscow for direction, the three parties issued a statement (1975), agreed between the Italian and Spanish, and the French and Spanish parties, that socialism, freedom and democracy were mutually dependent: the new 'parliamentary and electoral roads to socialism' permitted electoral alliances with bourgeois parties and even respect for the Atlantic Pact if returned to power (Marchais even endorsed the French *force de frappe* in 1977). If no coherent body of political philosophy was appearing, at least there was agreement on political tactics – the parliamentary majority now displaced revolution as the means to the communist end. The 1976 East Berlin conference was intended to be an important occasion – even President Tito had been persuaded to attend – and it was the first public confrontation between Eurocommunism and the Soviet Union. The disappointing results, for the Soviet Union, were underlined by the demotion of Katushev from his position in the Central Committee with special responsibilities for relations with other Communist Parties, to the position of Soviet representative to COMECON (1977). The conference repudiated the hegemony of one national party over others in favour of a recognition of different 'paths to socialism'. It was said that Stalin died a third time at Berlin. That Moscow no longer expected to direct the Communist movement throughout the world was underlined by Brezhnev's substitution of 'international solidarity' for the familiar traditional doctrine of 'proletarian internationalism'. The responses of other Communist Parties varied: Portugal did not go with the Eurocommunists, Poland was silent, Hungary offered a cautious welcome and only Romania defended them. It would seem that Eurocommunism was more than a disagreement over tactics; and its electoral success by the mid-seventies was causing Western governments enough concern for them to reiterate the point that the leopard does not change his spots and that it was all an attempt by communists to seize power through the ballot box rather than by revolution.

But the 1976 conference was probably the high water mark of Eurocommunism in the seventies. There was no follow-up. Clearly concentrated in the communist parties of France, Spain and Italy, no formal organisational link was forged – not even when the three leaders met at Madrid in March 1977. There was no common policy beyond accepting flexibility in response to the realities of national politics, and when it was overtaken by electoral defeat (Spain 1977, France 1978, Italy 1979) the excitement engendered by the name faded away. But it would be wrong to dismiss the phenomenon as no more than a bid for power by alternative means. It demonstrated changing attitudes within communist parties, and the persistence of a strong national response within even so international a movement as the 'proletarian revolution'. Eurocommunism is not a coherent body of doctrine, but primarily a grouping of three national responses to the changing political realities of the later twentieth century.

Of the three, perhaps the Italian had the strongest roots in tradition – it also came nearest to controlling the national government, both in the 1940s and the 1970s. Between the wars, Antonio Gramsci had urged a modification of tactics in the class war from the orthodox Marxist-Leninist line to a 'war of position' implying a gradualist rather than a dramatic revolutionary (Leninist) approach – a modification taken further after the war by Togliatti, whose *Testament of Yalta* (1964) criticising the lack of freedom within the Soviet Union was a remarkable document, urging a 'unity in diversity' within the Communist movement: a polycentrist argument for different (national) roads to socialism – which could include China – rather than a continued imposition of direction and doctrinal orthodoxy from Moscow. From such roots grew Enrico Berlinguer's idea of 'hegemony in pluralism', gaining power through accepting democratic parliamentary institutions and working in coalition with other parties – eschewing revolution.

The Spanish communists, emerging from the shattering experiences of the Civil War and Franco's long dictatorship, might be expected to produce their own version and Santiago Carrillo's *Eurocommunism and the State* (1977) has received much publicity. It urges different national ways to socialism – in effect, a mirror of Stalin's 'socialism in one country' – because there exist between countries different national traditions and current economic conditions. Hence a policy founded on Russian experience need not be relevant in other countries. His critique of 'Stalinist degeneration' went as far as suggesting similarities between it and fascist totalitarianism and doubting whether the Soviet State would ever become a 'workers' democracy': capitalism, replaced by the 'organised irresponsibility' of a new bureaucracy obstructing the road to socialism was not the way forward; that way was by gradualism through changing administrative structures within the advanced industrial state leading to progressive socialism and centrism. Furthermore, the organisational differences (whatever the *political* ones) between advanced capitalist states and communist ones are more apparent than real, since the tendency of the latter is towards the acceptance of strong central government influence and controls through economic and administrative policies; hence there was no clear contradiction in working alongside capitalist policies pointing to a similar organisational end. (He also proposed a European power bloc standing between the Soviet Union and the United States.) Communism, he was arguing, should be less of a religion and more of a realistic political programme – small wonder the book was viewed in Moscow as the beginnings of a new schism in communist ranks; hence the celebrated attack in *New Times* (July 1977). The immediate reaction was so hostile that Moscow rapidly adopted a more conciliatory attitude: the Spanish reaffirmed their own 'road to socialism' and Italy and France supported them, as did Romania, whilst Bulgaria and East Germany were for Moscow. Clearly the international communist movement, even in Europe, was not monolithic, and the Soviet leadership was aware of the need for conciliation. If Eurocommunism did not exist, Brezhnev took good care to ensure it was not conjured up.

Eurocommunism is a portmanteau term without internal cohesion (but it need not be rejected for that reason: much the same could be said by a hostile critic of the British Labour Party). Clearly it elicited a response in each Western country with a strong communist party, and found an echo in Eastern Europe, too. Even in Portugal, where Alvaro Cunhal, returning from exile (1974) and retaining his faith in Stalinism, did not go with the three other parties, there remained enough of a national flavour for Zarodov to denounce the Portuguese party (1975) for seeking parliamentary majorities in preference to the revolutionary tradition, once the Portuguese dictatorship had ended. But Eurocommunism is more than a debate over tactics; it reflects the general uncertainty of response to the changing conditions of the later twentieth century – raising standards of living, shorter working hours, greater social security, greater choice, as well as an increasing distance between the individual and the decision making organs of the bureaucratic structure of the modern advanced industrial state. It is part of the problem of adjustment experienced as much in democratic parties, as in communist countries. Eurocommunism has an international perspective as well and has a place among a number of western political groupings that argue for a Western European bloc to stand between the two Super Powers of the Soviet Union and the United States: such a bloc would be destructive of NATO and might lead to the 'finlandisation' of Western Europe. It is partly for this reason that NATO regards Eurocommunism with extreme suspicion, believing it to be a further manifestation of the traditional communist aim of destroying capitalism. Such a view may be too extreme, for the Portuguese communist party does not seek to withdraw from NATO, and is not numbered among the Euro-communists, whilst the communist parties in France and Italy both affirm support for NATO and the Atlantic Pact. It is always possible that the West is being hoodwinked and it is all a deep-laid plot, but this seems a little unlikely.

Eurocommunism appears to reflect a division within the communist ranks and to underline a rejection of Soviet policies and leadership. It is not simply a rejection of Stalinism, nor simply an alternative method of achieving an ultimate goal; it does seem to link with unease felt more generally about current administrative practices in advanced industrial societies, and it is rooted in national aspirations, attempting to reach out to the future rather than looking back to the past. Its accent upon national responses to current situations seems also to worry the Kremlin because of its potential attractiveness to Eastern European countries. The poor showing in the elections of the later seventies may reduce the urgency of discussion about Eurocommunism, and certainly there is a long way to go before communist parties become generally committed to pluralist democracy as opposed to a tactical coalition with all progressive parties to achieve the initial stages of socialism in Western Europe. But it is wise to concentrate upon the essential, not on the election results which are in any case transitory: if there is no identifiable dogma, Eurocommunism seems to reflect underlying forces of change, and the proof of the seventies is that the communist parties do not represent a monolithic organism, but rather a group in loose association with continually adjusting relationships.

By early 1980, Eurocommunism appeared to have subsided: but it would be idle to dismiss the movement as a mere passing phenomenon. Its impact in the seventies indicated that entrenched Western attitudes towards the Communist bloc needed to be reviewed, the more so when there is a question of impending changes in Soviet leadership. The acid test for Eurocommunism is the degree to which a national communist party is prepared to criticise the Soviet Union – in this respect, it is not confined to Europe, but serves to emphasise the differences within world communism. Indeed, it may not be inappropriate to point to the Spanish Eurocommunist argument that the post-war pattern of a Soviet bloc has now become an anachronism – witness the independent (if not downright hostile) stand of the Republic of China, and the various alignments of Third World countries with communist-style leadership. The logic of this view is to substitute for an East-West hegemony the concept of a multi-polar world – a view not wholly removed from Dr Kissinger's analysis (see page 177). Neither Washington nor Moscow can welcome the emergence of communist governments pursuing divergent aims in foreign policy, since this would prove to be a major destabilising agent within the diplomatic balance among Super Powers. Ultimately, from the Soviet point of view, the knowledge that in the last resort all Eurocommunist parties would side with Moscow in any direct East-West conflict must be the vital consideration. If the Soviet Union can guarantee this principle, it has been argued that in the conditions of *détente*, open debate and even direct criticism might actually advance the cause of communism outside the Soviet block: no doubt Soviet subsidies to national communist parties will continue on this understanding!

Human Rights

That Human Rights should have assumed the place of a shuttlecock in the relations between East and West indicates a lowering of tension, although the West's concentration on this issue has at times disturbed the pattern of diplomacy, and was instrumental in causing the failure of the Belgrade Conference (1978). Major developments in the field of Human Rights have taken place in the Soviet Union in the sixties and seventies – they add a deeper perspective to the divergence among Communist Parties illustrated by the acceptance of 'different roads to Communism' with Togliatti's advocacy of polycentrism; the French denunciation of the doctrine of the dictatorship of the proletariat and the Spanish denouncing Leninism. Many of the prison camps of the Gulag Archipelago have been disbanded, and the release into exile of Solzhenitsyn (1973) and the widespread publication of his works in the West is itself a comment on the changing attitudes of the Kremlin. So, of course, was the signing of the Helsinki Final Act (1975) with its Human Rights 'basket'.

The place of the individual and his relationship with the State differs greatly between western democracies and the Soviet Union. The Russian tradition is authoritative and collectivist, with the individual perceiving his social rights in terms of relationships and specific status, not as abstract concepts; his subjection to the overriding importance of the state – *zakreposchenie* – has no parallel in the West. Attitudes differ, and comparisons of social and political conditions are not altogether helpful. A pointer to these differences may be the disagreements between exiles in the West which sometimes are as vigorous as those with their former opponents the Soviet authorities. Human Rights protesters fail to attract extensive support within the Soviet Union, and it would be too simplistic to explain this in terms of the ordinary Russian's fear of the KGB. Nor have the protesters formulated an alternative programme.

There would seem to be some uncertainty in the Kremlin as to the most suitable policy to follow in order to liberalise the régime – and persistent Western pressure may not be the best method of aiding the process. Dissidents have been variously dealt with; for example, Aleksander Ginzburg and Yuri Orlov received harsh sentences in 1977 for agitation on behalf of the group to Promote the Implementation of the Helsinki Accord, whilst Bukovsky was released (1976) in exchange for Luis Corvalan, General Secretary of the Chilean Communist Party. Supporters of the Campaign Against Psychiatric Abuse (imprisonment in mental hospitals) are often harrassed, whilst other distinguished dissidents continue to live in their Moscow flats. In other Communist countries, political censorship and imprisonment of dissenters continues: Czech leaders of the Charter 77 movement appealed to the United Nations against the conditions of their imprisonment in the summer of 1979.

A rather more serious problem for the Soviet government is posed by the minority nationalities (see page 166), but Western insistence on keeping the Human Rights issue to the fore has clearly caused some embarrassment in the Kremlin. It may have played a part in the failure of the Belgrade discussions (1977–8), although a further conference was arranged for Madrid (1980). Meanwhile, active signs of liberalisation continue; first, that there is dissent openly expressed; secondly, that prosecutions seem to be brought only when dissent has been accompanied by some other action regarded as provocative. Even prominent dissenters are not deprived of access to privileges, which is a significant point when there continues to exist a positive stratification of an *élite* above the proletariat. Public debate (of a sort) is allowed on the mass media, and emigration is permitted, if in a seemingly arbitrary manner. Organised religion (despite its potential for polarising dissent) is permitted – and specified in the 1977 Constitution (see page 166) – whilst in Poland, for example, it is a positive rival to the Party. A degree of pragmatism and tolerance has characterised the Brezhnev era, which is an advance upon the Khrushchev eta, although the increasing importance of consumer demand dates from that time.

Détente does not preclude 'human rights diplomacy' but it is scarcely compatible with a political crusade against Moscow under the banner of Human Rights. The West, with its avowed pluralism, can easily accommodate itself to dissent: the East regards dissent with suspicion and as a potential threat to stability. As yet, no clear policy appears to have emerged from the Kremlin to meet the different manifestations of political dissent.

National minorities in the West

A different sort of nationalist problem threatens the stability of the West from that which threatens the Soviet Union. It comes from the regions, often on the periphery, where local culture has retained a certain vitality, or been revived during this century, regions that are generally less prosperous than the main centres of population and which are not experiencing a population explosion. It takes the form of demonstrations, sometimes of a violent nature, and the major examples also have terrorist organisations which resort to bombings and in some cases assassinations.

Two broad causes of opposition to the nation state may be suggested: the first is a linguistic and cultural difference. In some cases this arises from the establishment of artificial political frontiers which divide a particular racial group from their original area, as, for example, the Slovenes of Carinthia (Austria) or of Friuli (Italy), or the Germans in the Italian (South) Tyrol, or the Basques across the Pyrenees; in others, there are ancient historical roots, like the Bretons, the Occitans (from Languedoc across to Dauphiné), the Alsacians, the Corsicans in France; the Basques in Spain; the Flemish and the Walloons in Belgium; the Welsh and the Scots in the United Kingdom. It must be admitted that with some of the cases the claim to a cultural identity has a certain artificiality, and does not always carry widespread popular support. The second cause is economic, arising from the particular area being relatively poor and feeling economically neglected, or suffering from declining heavy industry. But, the Basque area of Spain is the principal industrial area of the country, and the hope of gaining substantial regional advantages from North Sea Oil has helped the Scottish nationalists. Conversely, the Mezzogiorno, despite its rural poverty and slow industrial growth, shows no great enthusiasm to leap at the opportunity to run its own affairs; nor does the prosperous German community in Danish North Schlesvig – the economic explanation is much less convincing. Other, less identifiable causes have been suggested, such as an ultra-conservative resistance to the pressures for change in modern society, or hostility to increasing centralisation in national administration.

Division in Belgium

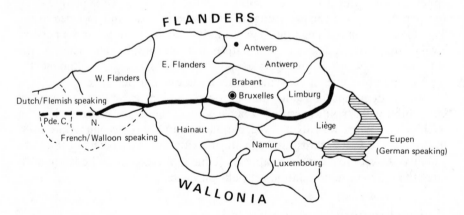

The political frontier does not separate Flemish speakers: Flemish is spoken among working-class French nationals in the *départements* of Pas de Calais and Nord. Brussels is a special region in its own right.

The seventies have seen some determined government action in several countries to counter and reverse economic decline in the regions, and, indeed, to decentralise administration through regional devolution of various types. This has tended to check excessive migration from declining regions – but it has not stopped nationalist agitation.

Belgium is something of an exception, since the entire country is divided into Dutch-speaking Flanders and French-speaking Wallonia (the south), a division that spills over into neighbouring France among working class communities. The linguistic division is deep-seated and seriously threatens the unity of the State: the 1968 election, following the Louvain University crisis, was widely regarded as a referendum on whether Belgium should remain a unitary state. The new constitution of 1971 transformed Belgium into a community state with parity between the two communities in the composition of the government, and the establishment of Cultural Councils for both communities and for the German community in the Eastern Cantons. Elected regional institutions received wide local government powers, and Brussels was recognised as a special region in its own right. Yet this major change has brought no solution, and several leading Belgian politicians now look to the directly elected European Parliament as a possible means of reconciling the two communities (the twenty-four Belgian MEPs were divided into fourteen Flemish and ten Walloon).

The Basque area is of ancient foundation. It extends over four northern Spanish provinces and into three others in France, giving the slogan '3 + 4 = 1'. A revival of nationalist sentiment occurred at the beginning of the century, and the Basque area suffered particularly during the Civil War and under the Franco régime. Violence, assassination and bomb outrages – some of them very dramatic – have been frequent since the sixties, and even the granting of effective Home Rule under the 1978 constitution has not quietened Basque opposition to Madrid – indeed, there was a series of bomb outrages in Spanish coastal resorts in the summer of 1979 directed against one of Spain's lucrative sources of foreign exchange, the tourist industry. Also in the summer of 1979 a referendum accepted with a significant majority the substantial measures of Home Rule offered by the government to the four Basque provinces: but this has not brought an end to terrorism and bombings. Nationalist movements do not often claim to have a majority of the population as committed members, but they can generally rely upon a considerable degree of passive support from the community as a whole.

In France, the Basque autonomous movement *Eubata* (1961) was banned, along with three other nationalist movements, after the Lyons bomb outrage of 1974. Other linguistic minority movements are the Occitans, the Catalans of Roussillon, the Flemings of Westhoek (North East France), the Alsacians and the two nationalist groups which have gained most publicity by bombings (that in Versailles in June 1978, was among the most provocative, though others have involved loss of life), the Bretons and the Corsicans. Much of the support for the nationalist movements comes from resentment at the over-centralised French state – but sometimes more than the desire for regional devolution is involved, as with the left-wing *autogestion* movement for an alternative society of self-management and self-government. The Bretons – who have links with the Irish

Basque areas

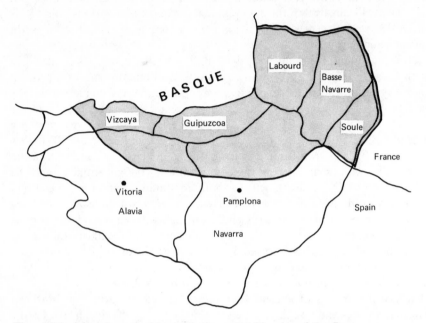

The political frontier coincides with the natural barrier of the Pyrenees.

Republican Army – have proved the most serious threat to the government with their orchestrated campaign of violence. But the various nationalist movements do not seem to carry great popular support, although in both Britanny and Corsica they clearly have considerable latent passive support: but they do not – as yet – constitute a threat to the unity of France. However, their continued agitation remains a constant reminder that regional devolution is a political movement that must by some means be satisfied. It is altogether too fanciful to talk of a crisis of identity within West European political society, linking nationalist bomb outrages with kidnappings, assassinations and other outrages (like the unsuccessful mining of General Haigh's car shortly before his retirement as NATO Supreme Commander in June 1979) by extremist organisations like the Red Brigade; but it is well to remember the incidents when criticising political conditions in Eastern Europe.

By far the longest period of civil disruption, violence and assasination in the West is associated with Northern Ireland where a seemingly intractable problem of reconciling opposed communities has evidently defeated the British genius for compromise. Nationalist movements in Wales and Scotland have further disturbed the political stability of the United Kingdom – despite their very poor showing in the 1979 devolution referenda and general election. Leading Belgian politicians look to the European Parliament as a possible means of reconciling their opposed communities within a wider unity of the EEC. There is no prospect of such an attitude gaining ground in the United Kingdom, with a 32.4 per cent turn-out for the direct elections! Furthermore, the prospect of an enlargement of the Community to Twelve before the next European parliament elections, does not serve to strengthen bonds of unity within the Community.

For all the idealist search for a broader, European, basis of unity in the latter half of the twentieth century, the nation state survives as the only effective form of government – whether in the West or the East. Even the nation state does not guarantee national unity and cohesion. The stability of established political régimes – quite as much as the re-establishment of economic growth – will be a major task of the eighties. Without this stability, the peace and security of Europe could be at risk.

List of Abbreviations

ACP	Africa, Caribbean and the Pacific
CAP	Common Agricultural Policy
CDU	Christian Democratic Union
CET	Common External Tariff
CFP	Common Fisheries Policy
CODER	Comités de Développement Economique Régional
COMECON	Council for Mutual Economic Assistance
COREPER	Committee of Permanent Representatives
CPI	Italian Communist Party
CPSU	Communist Party of the Soviet Union
CSU	Christian Social Union
DATAR	Délégation à l'Aménagement du Territoire et à l'Action Régionale
ECE	Economic Commission for Europe
ECSC	European Coal and Steel Community
ECU	European Currency Unit
EDC	European Defence Community
EDF	European Development Fund
EEC	European Economic Community
EFTA	European Free Trade Association
EIB	European Investment Bank
EMS	European Monetary System
EMU	European Monetary Union
ENA	Ecole National d'Administration
EPC	European Political Community
EPU	European Payments Union
ERDF	European Regional Development Fund
ERP	European Recovery Programme
ERW	Enhanced radiation weapon
EUA	European Unit of Account
EURATOM	European Atomic Energy Community
FDP	Free Democratic Party
FEOGA	European Agricultural Guidance and Guarantee Fund
GATT	General Agreement on Tariffs and Trade
GDP	Gross Domestic Product
GNP	Gross National Product
IBEC	International Bank of Economic Cooperation
ICBM	Intercontinental ballistic missiles
IDI	Institut du développement industriel
IIB	International Investment Bank
IMF	International Monetary Fund
IRA	Irish Republican Army
JET	Joint European Torus

MBFR	Mutual and Balanced Force Reductions
MCA	Monetary compensation amount
MEP	Member of European Parliament
MTS	Motor Tractor Station
NATO	North Atlantic Treaty Organisation
NEDC	National Economic Development Council
NTB	Non-tariff barrier
OECD	Organisation for Economic Cooperation and Development
OEEC	Organisation for European Economic Cooperation
OPEC	Organisation of Petroleum Exporting Countries
PAP	Priority Action Programme
SALT	Strategic Arms Limitation Treaty
SLBM	Submarine Launched Ballistic Missiles
SPD	Social Democratic Party of Germany
STABEX	System for Stabilisation of Export Earnings
SYSMIN	System for safeguarding and developing mineral production
TPK	Territorial Production Complexes
TUC	Trades Union Congress
UN	United Nations
UNCTAD	United Nations Conference on Trade and Development
UNRRA	United Nations Relief and Rehabilitation Administration
WEU	Western European Union
WTO	Warsaw Treaty Organisation

Bibliography

(All published in London unless otherwise stated)

A great many specialist journals are available for the areas covered by this volume; only a few are specifically noted here. Government and EEC publications and official statistics are also available and not recorded here. So are newspapers and political journals.

1. The Background to Contemporary Europe

There is a vast store of secondary sources available; among those that may be useful for reference are Barber and Reed, *The European Community: Vision and Reality* (1973); Gladwyn, *The Memoirs of Lord Gladwyn* (1972); Ghita Ionescu (ed.), *The New Politics of European Integration* (1972), which contains an excellent bibliography; Uwe Kitzinger, *Diplomacy and Persuasion (How Britain joined the Common Market)* (1973); W. Laqueur, *Europe since Hitler* (1970); A. Shlaim, *Britain and the Origins of European Unity, 1940–51* (Reading, 1978); P. H. Spaak, *The Continuing Battle* (trans. 1970); D. Thomson, *Europe since Napoleon* (1965); D. W. Urwin, *Western Europe since 1945* (1972); R. Vaughan, *Post-war Integration in Europe* (selected documents) (1976).

2. The Cold War and the Defence of the West

The following periodicals are particularly useful: *NATO Review*; *New Europe*; *Security*; *The World Today*; *Soviet Threat* (New York, especially volume 33, no. 1, 1978). The IISS publications must be studied, especially *The Military Balance*, 1978/9, and the various numbers of the *Adelphi Papers*. Many other periodicals will be useful for this section.

E. Barker, *Britain in a Divided Europe, 1945–70* (1971); C. E. Black (ed.), *Challenge in Eastern Europe* (New York, 1954); S. Breyer, *Guide to the Soviet Navy* (1977); N. Brown, *The Future Global Challenge, A predictive study, 1977–90* (1977); J. I. Coffey, *Arms Control and European Security* (1977); N. Dixon, *On the Psychology of Military Incompetence* (1976); Herz, *The Beginnings of the Cold War* (Indiana U.P., 1966); Hill-Norton, *No Soft Option (The Politics and Military Realities of NATO)* (1978); K. Kaiser and R. Morgan, *Britain and West Germany* (1971); R. L. Garthoff, *Soviet Military Policy* (1966); J. P. Jain, *Documentary Study of the Warsaw Pact* (New York, 1973); W. Kintener and W. Klaiber, *Eastern Europe and European Security* (New York, 1971); K. London (ed.), *Eastern Europe in Transition* (Baltimore, 1966); R. Mayne (ed.), *The New Atlantic Challenge* (1975); J. Steele, *Eastern Europe since Stalin* (Documents) (1974); N. Tolstoy, *Victims of Yalta* (1978); F. R. Willis, *France, Germany and the New Europe, 1945–67* (Stamford, Calif., 1968).

3. The Creation of the EEC

D. H. Aldcroft, *The European Economy, 1914–70* (1978) (contains an important bibliography for the period after 1950); M. Blacksell, *Post-War Europe, a Political Geography* (1977); Bougmans, *L'idée européenne* (Bruges, 1970); A. Buchan, *The End of the Postwar Era* (1974); D. Butler and U. Kitzunger, *The 1975 Referendum* (1976); M. Camps, *Britain and the European Community, 1955–63* (1965); C. M. Cipolla, *Fontana Economic History of Europe, Vols. 6 (1&2)*; P. Einzig, *The Case Against Joining the Common Market* (1971);

200

H. Fukuda, *Britain in Europe: Impact on the Third World* (1973); S. Holt, *The Common Market: How Institutions Work* (1974); S. I. Katy (ed.), *U.S./European Monetary Relations* (New York, 1979); A. K. Kerr, *The Common Market and How it Works* (1977); Uwe Kitzinger, *Diplomacy and Persuasion* (1973); J. and P. Kolko, *Limits of Power; The World and U.S. Foreign Policy 1945–54* (New York, 1973); W. Laqueur, *Rebirth of Europe* (1970); C. S. Maier, *The Origins of the Cold War and Contemporary Europe* (New York, 1978); Gerherd Mally, *European Community in Perspective* (Lexington, 1973); R. Mayne, *The Recovery of Europe; From Devastation to Unity* (1970); R. Mayne (ed.), *Europe Tomorrow* (1972); J. Monnet, *Memoirs* (trans. Mayne, 1978); J. Paxton, *The Developing Common Market* (Colorado, 1976); M. Palmer (ed.), *European Unity, a Survey of European Organisations* (1968); A. H. Robertson, *European Institutions* (1959); Roskamp, *Capital Formation in West Germany* (Michigan, 1965); P. Seabury, *The Rise and Decline of the U.S.* (New York, 1967).

4. The Institutions of the EEC

Among other journals, some useful articles will be found for the area of this chapter in *Journal of Common Market Studies*; *New Europe*; *The World Today*. The European Parliament publishes working documents.

D. Bell and M. Kolinsky, *Divided Loyalties, British regional assertion and European integration* (Manchester U.P., 1978); F. Bloch-Lainé, *A la recherche d'une économie concertée* (Editions de L'Epargne); D. Coomes, *Politics and Bureaucracy in the European economy* (1970); G. Denton, *Economic and Monetary Union in Europe* (1974); W. Dumas and W. B. Lee, *Social Studies in West German Schools* (Univ. Missouri Press); M. Fratianni and T. Peeters, *One Money for Europe* (1978); J. Hayward and Watson, *Planning, Politics and Public Policy* (Cambridge, 1975); V. Herman and J. Lodge, *The European Parliament and the European Community* (1978); J. Fitzmaurice, *The Party Groups in the European Parliament* (1975); J. Fitzmaurice, *The European Parliament* (1978); S. Holt, *The Common Market, How Institutions Work* (1967); House of Lords, Select Committee, *Enlargement of the Community* (1977); J. van Langendonck, *Prelude to Harmony on a Community theme (Health care)* (1975); N. J. D. Lucas, *Energy and the European Communities*; M. Niblock, *The EEC National Parliaments in Community Decision-making* (PEP, 1971); J. Paxton, *The Developing Common Market* (Colorado, 1976); G. and P. Pridham, *Trans-national Party Co-operation and Direct Elections to the European Parliament* (1980); M. Sant (ed.), *Regional Policy and Planning for Europe* (1974); C. Saunders, *From Free Trade to Integration in Western Europe* (PEP, 1975); G. Smith, *Politics in Western Europe* (1976); D. Swann, *The Economics of the Common Market* (fourth edition, 1978); R. Vaubel, *Strategies for Currency Unification* (Tuebingen, 1978); R. Vaubel, *Choice in EMU* (Wincott Lecture, 1979); R. Vernon, *Big Business and the State* (Harvard, 1974); R. Vernon, *Sovereignty at Bay*; H. Wallace and C. Webþ, *Policy-Making in the European Communities* (1977); S. J. Warneke and E. N. Suleimen, *Industrial Politics in Western Europe* (Prega, 1975); R. Williams, *European Technology* (1973); D. and A. Wood, *The Times Guide to the European Parliament* (1980); D. Yuill (ed.), *Regional Policy in EEC* (1979).

5. France and West Germany

A new journal, *West European Politics* (1978), contains some interesting articles for this chapter.

K. E. Birnbaum, *East and West Germany, a modus vivendi* (Lexington, 1973); F. Bloch-Lainé, *A la recherche d'une économie concertée* (Editions de l'Epargne, 1964); J. Blindel, *The Government of France* (1974); M. Crozier, *La société bloquée* (Paris, 1970); R. Dahrendorff, *Society and Democracy in Germany* (1968); G. Hallet, *Social Economy of West Germany* (1973); J. E. S. Hayward and R. N. Berki, *State and Society in Contemporary Europe* (1979); J. E. S. Hayward and O. A. Narkiewicz, *Planning in Europe* (1978); D. Pickles, *The Fifth French Republic* (2 vols, 1963); P. M. Williams and M. Harrison, *Politics and Society in de Gaulle's Republic* (New York, 1972).

6. COMECON

The study papers of a conference on economic reform in Hungary held at Stirling in 1979 throw a fresh light on the area of this chapter.

H. Brook (ed.), *The Communist States in Disarray, 1965–71* (Minneapolis, 1972); J. E. S. Hayward and R. N. Berki, *State and Society in Contemporary Europe* (1979); R. Bahro, *Alternatives in Eastern Europe* (1977, trans. 1978, NLB); Hewett, *Foreign Trade Prices in CMEA* (Cambridge, 1974); M. Kaser, *Comecon* (2nd edition, 1967); M. Kaser (ed.), *Economic Development in Eastern Europe* (1968); M. Kaser and J. G. Zielinski, *Planning in Eastern Europe* (1970); M. Lavigne, *Le programme du COMECON et l'integration socialiste* (Paris, 1973); M. Lavigne, *The Socialist Economies of Soviet Union and Europe* (trans. 1974); NATO Colloquium, *Progress and Prospects* (COMECON) (Brussels, 1977); A. Nove and D. M. Nutti (eds.), *Soviet Economies* (1972); R. Szqwlowski, *The System of the International Organisations of the Communist Countries* (Leyden, 1976).

7. The USSR since Stalin

F. C. Barghoorn, *Politics in the USSR* (Boston, 1972); A. Brown, *Political Culture and Change in Communist States* (1977); A. Brown and M. Kaser, *The Soviet Union since the Fall of Khrushchev* (2nd edition, 1978); J. Dunsten, *Paths to Excellence – the Soviet Education System* (1978); N. Grant, *Soviet Education* (1972); M. Kaser and J. G. Zielinski, *Planning in Eastern Europe* (1970); N. Khrushchev, *Khrushchev Remembers* (2 vols, 1974); D. Lane, *Politics and Society in the USSR* (1970); D. Lane, *The Socialist Industrial State: towards a political sociology of Soviet Socialism* (1976); M. McAuley, *Politics and the Soviet Union* (1977); A. Nove, *The Soviet Economic System* (1978); A. Nove, *Stalinism and After* (1976); NATO Colloquium, *Regional Development in the USSR* (1979); H. Seton Watson, *The New Imperialism* (1974).

8. Cold war to Détente

C. Bell, *The Diplomacy of Détente: The Kissinger Era* (1977); H. Brandon, *The Retreat of American Power* (1973); H. Kissinger, *American Foreign Policy* (1974); H. Kissinger, *The White House Years* (1979); P. Mooney and C. Brown, *Truman to Carter* (1979); R. M. Nixon, *The Memoirs of Richard Nixon* (1978); R. S. McNamara, *The Essence of Security* (1968); H. S. Parmet, *Eisenhower and the American Crusades* (New York, 1972); C. M. Roberts, *The Nuclear Years: The Arms Race and Arms Control, 1945–1970* (New York, 1970); J. Stockwell, *In Search of Enemies* (1978); A. R. Ulam, *Expansion and Coexistence* (1968); W. Woodruff, *America's Impact on the World* (1975).

9. Unity or Fragmentation?

Atlantic Treaty Association Seminar, *Does Euro-communism Exist?* (Lisbon, 1978); R. Bahro, *Alternatives in Eastern Europe* (trans. 1978); D. Bell, *Eurocommunism* (Fabian Research Series, No. 342, 1978); N. Brown, *The Future Global Challenge* (1977); S. Carrillo, *Eurocommunism and the State* (trans. 1977); Chalidge, *To Defend These Rights; Human Rights in the Soviet Union* (New York, 1974); F. Claudin, *Eurocommunism and Socialism* (Madrid, 1977, trans. 1978); Annie Kriegel, *Un autre communisme?* (Paris 1977); R. Heilbroner, *Enquiry into the Human Prospect*; H. Kahn and A. J. Wiener, *The Year 2000* (New York, 1967); W. R. Lee, *European Demography and Economic Growth* (1979); E. Mandel, *From Stalinism to Eurocommunism* (trans. 1978); Z. A. Medredev, *Twenty Years after Ivan Denisovich* (1973); N. McInnes, *The Communist Parties of Western Europe* (1975); P. Reddaway, *Uncensored Russia, the Human Rights Movement in the Soviet Union* (1972); Schumacher, *Small is Beautiful*; M. Stephens, *Linguistic Minorities in Western Europe* (1976); R. Tokes, *Dissent in the Soviet Union* (Baltimore, 1975); Wayland Kennet, *The Future of Europe* (Cambridge, 1976).

Index